This book is a must-read if...

- you like real-life stories;

- you are looking for inspiration;

- you want to be the best you can be;

- you have an interest in the military;

- you are interested in military heraldry;

- you are interested in adventure training;

- you are fascinated about war;

- you are interested in leadership and management;

- you are dealing with the loss of family and friends;

- you have an interest in the power of words.

What people are saying about George Greig...

Col (Retd) Graham Leach (Late R Signals)

January 1998. George was a key part of the Regimental Ops team planning for a busy year: RHQ and two squadrons were to deploy to Bosnia to support Divisional Headquarters, one squadron was to deploy to the Falkland Islands, and a squadron was to remain in Bulford to support training on Salisbury Plain throughout the year. George sat in my office. As I explained to him that he would not be going to Bosnia, he was crestfallen. But I needed a small Operation team in Bulford to coordinate the many activities of the training support squadron and the deployed squadrons, and I had no doubt that George was the right man to head this up. His disappointment was short-lived – he saw that there was an important job to be done and he grasped it. This was the mark of the man. Within a few days, Operations (Bulford) was up-and-running. George brought to the job his characteristic organisation skills, his attention to detail and his strong leadership style. I knew that George would 'cover my back' and he did not let me down.

Three years later. I was the Service Delivery Director of Global Crossing (UK) and I had recruited George to be one of my Project Managers. He was cutting his teeth running one of my larger delivery projects. He brought all the attributes of his military experience to the job and the customer was in awe of his ability to deliver whatever the challenge. But I had a problem – one of the key departments in the organisation was falling short and I had to make changes. So, I turned to George. Despite having no commercial experience and a dis-functional team, George was quickly on top of the job and turned the department around in a matter of weeks.

I have been privileged to work with George in both the military and civilian worlds. He has many skills and always sought to learn more. But above all, he is just a thoroughly nice chap.

Lt Col (Retd) Andy Forster (Late R Signals)

George Greig's candid and vivid account is a gem. It is a clear insight of the ups and downs of military life. Readers are taken on an emotional and amusing journey.

George is a product of the Yeoman of Signals Course, one of the many aspects of formal training of which the Royal Corps of Signals is justifiably proud. It equipped George with a breadth and depth of communications knowledge and it honed his many fine personal qualities of drive, determination and dedication to duty. George repaid, in spades, the tariff that was invested in him.

George was my Yeoman of Signals at 201 (22nd Armoured Brigade) Signal Squadron. When George arrived, he gave me sound advice and support that was above and beyond the normal call of duty. We had a mutual respect for each other that grew when we deployed to the Gulf on Operation GRANBY.

George performed brilliantly, just when I needed him to. The phrase 'Better than Outstanding' springs to mind.

Lt Col (Retd) Jonathan Sutton (Late R Signals)

Veterans always talk of their enjoyment, or not, of their postings and operational tours through the people who were there at that time. The people who shared the experience, the people who helped them, the people who they went running with or drank beer in the mess with. My time in Bulford was no different. It was memorable because of the people who were there.

George and I shared many a rib and bladder buster. How we often chuckled at the inflated egos and silliness of the Divisional HQ staff officers, particularly to pompous infantry or cavalry SO2s. We did quite a lot or jogging, but we called it running, up and down Kiwi Hill and generally chewing the fat about the difficulties with the Ptarmigan trunk system, the latest daft idea from the divisional staff or crazy plan from HQ LAND.

We laughed a lot. I will always remember my shock when the Regimental Carpenter, following what George and I thought were quite clear instructions, then made a large folding map board for the tactical operations room. It was to be stored inside an armoured vehicle and moved around regularly, but was built of the world's heaviest teak with dovetails joints and mitred corners and snooker table cloth. It was too heavy to lift and cost a fortune to make.

So back to the beginning, being in Bulford was one of the best postings. Working with George, who was probably the best of his generation was a magical, informative and memorable experience. A wonderfully, warm, funny and self-effacing man, husband to Sue and father to Mark.

Lt Col (Retd) Chris Wakerley MBE (Late R Signals)

I first met George when I took over as OC of 22nd Armoured Brigade Signal Squadron in Hohne. George was the Yeoman of Signals which was a pivotal role in any Royal Signals unit but especially in a Brigade Signal Squadron, where the team was small, and you were constantly on show.

George was an ebullient Scot. His enthusiasm was infectious and was matched by his drive and professionalism. We were a tight team and life at the squadron moved at a dizzying pace. Some of the reasons we were so busy were outside our control, but very often thanks to George (and a few dedicated others) we made it work.

George worked tirelessly for the squadron and for me. We very quickly came to trust each other, and we formed a close relationship that would last until this day.

I have known George for more than 30 years in the army and in industry. George is George. Ever passionate about what he is doing. Always on the detail. And always seeing the bright side of things. I am so pleased that we met, and that we have shared so many fun times together. I wish him all the best and await my invite to north of the border.

Maj (Retd) Ronny Allan (Late R Signals)

I'm absolutely delighted and honoured to provide this testimonial for George, someone for whom I have a great deal of respect and admiration. We first got to know each other in 1981 when we were serving in the 3rd Armoured Division HQ & Signal Regiment in Soest, then West Germany. As we were two ordinary lads from the north-east of Scotland, we immediately bonded and found many commonalities including work ethic, sense of duty, thirst for knowledge and experience, and most importantly, a sense of humour.

An ordinary lad, but George was an extraordinary soldier and someone who inspires and excels at everything he does. He is without a shadow of a doubt, the most professional soldier and communicator I met in my 30 years of service. If anyone was going to get it right, it would be George Greig.

We worked on several major exercises and other projects, and quickly discovered that a sense of humour was just as important given the challenging environment and sheer size of the task in hand. George certainly got me through some difficult periods by putting a smile on my face. As I departed for other tasks, I was proud to buy George a beer to celebrate his thoroughly well-deserved commission as an officer in the British Army, something I had known for some years would be a dead certainty. We kept in touch and have done to this day. Certa Cito, George!

**A huMAN story of endeavour
reaping life's rewards**

UNTAPPED
POTENTIAL

**Born in Scotland
Found in the Royal Signals**

GEORGE GREIG

First published in Great Britain in 2022
by Book Brilliance Publishing
265A Fir Tree Road, Epsom, Surrey, KT17 3LF
+44 (0)20 8641 5090
www.bookbrilliancepublishing.com
admin@bookbrilliancepublishing.com

A CIP catalogue record for this book is available at the British Library.

ISBN 978-1-913770-44-0

Typeset in Adobe Caslon Pro.

This book is a memoir. It reflects the author's present recollections of experiences over time. Identifying names and places have been changed, some events have been compressed, and some dialogue has been recreated.

DEDICATION

As I wrote this book, it brought back so many memories, most of them happy ones, but it also stirred a great sadness within me, remembering so many special friends that never made it through; that will never leave me. Knowing these guys enriched my life and I dedicate my story to their memory. They are:

Lance Corporal Steve Richmond, Royal Signals

Corporal Rab Burns, Royal Signals

Lieutenant Jim Barrie, Royal Signals

Staff Sergeant (Yeoman of Signals) Robbie Davies, Royal Signals

Corporal Del Wood, Royal Signals

Sergeant Mick Newman, Royal Signals

Staff Sergeant Kev Froggett, Royal Signals

Warrant Officer Class 2 (Squadron Sergeant Major) Pete Griffin, Royal Signals

Warrant Officer Class 2 (Regimental Quartermaster Sergeant) Steve Simpson, Royal Signals

"They say the good die young;
the above list is proof of that saying.
At the going down of the sun and in the morning,
I will remember them."

Certa Cito

WARNING!

This book contains military humour and is deliberately written to reflect the era in which it is written. As a consequence, some of the language is also reflective of the times and is used to achieve context; such language is not intended to be offensive, but rather to highlight the general ignorance of the times.

CONTENTS

LEXICON

My Units – abbreviated and in full

AAC Harrogate	Army Apprentice College Harrogate
249 Sig Sqn (AMF(L))	249th Signal Squadron (Allied Command Europe Mobile Force (Land))
3 Armd Div HQ & Sig Regt	3rd Armoured Division Headquarters & Signal Regiment
RSS	Royal School of Signals
7 Sig Regt	7th Signal Regiment
14 Sig Regt (EW)	14th Signal Regiment (Electronic Warfare)
1 Armd Div HQ & Sig Regt	1st Armoured Division Headquarters & Signal Regiment
201 (22 Armd Bde) HQ & Sig Sqn	201 (22nd Armoured Brigade) Headquarters & Signal Squadron
HQ 11 (ARRC) Sig Bde	Headquarters 11th (Allied Rapid Reaction Corps) Signal Brigade
3 (UK) Div HQ & Sig Regt	3rd (United Kingdom) Division Headquarters & Signal Regiment
HQ DCSA	Headquarters Defence Communication Services Agency

Other Key Army Units – abbreviated and in full

HQ UKLF	Headquarters UK Land Forces
HQ BAOR	Headquarters British Army on the Rhine
HQ 1 (BR) Corps	Headquarters 1st (British) Corps
BATUS	British Army Training Unit Suffield
JCUFI	Joint Communications Unit Falkland Islands

Soldier Ranks – abbreviated and in full

Sig	Signaller
LCpl	Lance Corporal
Cpl	Corporal
Sgt	Sergeant
SSgt	Staff Sergeant
WO2	Warrant Officer Class 2
WO1	Warrant Officer Class 1

Soldier Appointments – abbreviated and in full (with rank shown in brackets)

FofS	Foreman of Signals (can be SSgt, WO2 or WO1)
YofS	Yeoman of Signals (can be SSgt, WO2 or WO1)
SQMS	Squadron Quarter Master Sergeant (SSgt)

RQMS	Regimental Quarter Master Sergeant (WO2)
SSM	Squadron Sergeant Major (WO2)
RSM	Regimental Sergeant Major (WO1)

Officer Ranks – abbreviated and in full

2nd Lt	2nd Lieutenant
Lt	Lieutenant
Capt	Captain
Maj	Major
Lt Col	Lieutenant Colonel
Col	Colonel
Brig	Brigadier
Maj Gen	Major General
Lt Gen	Lieutenant General
Gen	General
FM	Field Marshall *(Reserved for special circumstances)

General Abbreviations and Acronyms (including some "informal" ones)

AAC	Army Air Corps
APC	Armoured Personnel Carrier
ARAB	Arrogant Regular Army Bastard
Armd	Armoured
A/T	Apprentice / Tradesman
Bn	Battalion
BCR	Battlefield Casualty Replacement

BG	Battlegroup
CO	Commanding Officer (usually Regiment)
Comd	Command or Commander
CSM	Company Sergeant Major
Def EW Team	Defensive Electronic Warfare Team
Div	Division
ENDEX	End of Exercise
Gp Capt	RAF rank equivalent to a Colonel in the Army
IFV	Infantry Fighting Vehicle
JCSC	Junior Command & Staff Course
JDSC	Junior Division Staff College
JNCO	Junior Non-Commissioned Officer
NAAFI	Navy Army & Air Force Institute
NCO	Non-Commissioned Officer
OC	Officer Commanding (usually Squadron)
PB11	Posting Branch 11 (Royal Signals)
RD	Regimental Duty
Reg C	Regular Commission
Reg C (LE)	Regular Commission (Late Entry)
Regt	Regiment
RTg	Radio Telegraphist
RV	Rendezvous
SNCO	Senior Non-Commissioned Officer
SSC (LE)	Short Service Commission (Late Entry)
Sqn	Squadron
STAB	Stupid Territorial Army Bastard

TA	Territorial Army
TOT	Technical Officer Telecommunications
Tp	Troop
Tfc Offr	Traffic Officer
2IC	Second in Command

Squaddie "Isms"

Basher	Shelter
Blanket Stacker	Logistics person
Bocky	Bockwurst (smoked German sausage)
Bollocking	Tongue-lashing akin to Fergie's "hairdryer" (but worse)
Bratty	Bratwurst (German sausage)
Brew	Tea or coffee
Chunky	Pioneer Corps
Dicked	Selected on a non-voluntary basis
Dobby	Wash
Grunt	Infantryman
Gungy	Unclean
Herbert	Idiot
Jankers	Restriction of privileges
Liney	Lineman
Pad	Married person
Pit	Bed space
Plank	Artilleryman
Plonker	Idiot
Recce	Reconnaissance
Rodney/Rupert	Officer (normally Junior Officers)
Roger	I've got that

Rook/Rookie	Boy soldier recruit
Scaley or Scaleyback	R Signals
Slop Jockey	Army chef
Sprog	Recruit or newly qualified soldier
Squaddie Brat	Child from a military family
Teeth Arms	The Army's Combat Arms
Wooden Top	Guardsman

FOREWORD
by Lieutenant General (retired)
Sir John Kiszely KCB MC

I first met George Greig on the day I arrived in Hohne, West Germany, to command 22nd Armoured Brigade. He was Yeoman of Signals of the brigade's Signal Squadron. The Signal Squadron is absolutely key to the operational success of a brigade headquarters – it provides and manages all the communications – and the Yeoman is absolutely key to the operational success of the squadron; it's him or her who makes it all happen. So I was interested to meet him. I remember being struck by his obvious capability, his self-confidence and the twinkle in his eye which indicated a ready sense of humour, but above all, by his youthfulness. It was only later that I discovered that he was the youngest Yeoman of Signals in the British Army. I knew that the Royals Signals sent their best people, particularly squadron commanders and Yeomen of Signals, to armoured brigade headquarters, and it became apparent to me that I had been blessed with the best of the best. Whatever challenges were presented on the many demanding exercises in which we took part – for example, over-hasty moves of brigade headquarters in the middle of the night, ordered by the brigade commander – the Signal Squadron could be relied on to produce the goods. They and their leadership were simply outstanding. How lucky I was!

In subsequent years, it did not surprise me to learn that George Greig had been promoted to Warrant Officer Class 1 and then commissioned, and I was only sorry that having reached the rank of Captain, he had left the army. In my opinion, he would have reached the highest rank then available for an officer commissioned 'from the ranks': that of Lieutenant Colonel. It did not surprise me in the least that his subsequent business career was a huge success.

This book follows his career in the army, from the age of 16 when he joined the Army Apprentices College, of which he became the Junior Regimental Sergeant Major, to the moment, 27 years later, that he reluctantly decided to leave. The story, told with great frankness, relates the good times and the less good times, the ups and downs, the sad events as well as the happy ones; but the characteristic sense of humour is never far below the surface – indeed, seldom below it at all! It is also an account that graphically illustrates what it was like to serve in the British Army at the time.

PREFACE
Awa Te Jine e Army

Doric is the dialect spoken in the north-east corner of Scotland, predominantly in the Banff and Buchan region (around Banff, Fraserburgh and Peterhead); in all honesty, it might as well be a foreign language given the fact that nobody beyond that region within the British Isles can understand a word of it! Having spent all my life in the small village of New Pitsligo, known in Doric as "Cyaak", I didn't realise just how much that small fact would matter over the coming years. (I will come back to that at a later stage.)

At 16 years of age and pretty much a total waste of space, here I was waiting for the bus to go and join the army. This was all because I was severely pissed off that my first job, as an Apprentice Stonemason, had seen me doing everything from labouring to scaffolding and unsupervised building; in fact, anything other than training under a qualified tradesman. I figured this probably wasn't a great career choice and didn't want to hang around for the first of my "projects" to collapse on somebody's head. In future years, I would return regularly on leave and whenever I passed one of my "creations", I actually winced but was secretly proud that it hadn't fallen over yet…

JUNIOR ARMY ACCEPTANCE CERTIFICATE

This is to certify that

GEORGE THOMAS GREIG

of 3 CHURCH CRESCENT, NEW PITSLIGO, ABERDEENSHIRE

has been accepted by the Army for training as

AN APPRENTICE TELEGRAPHIST ROYAL SIGNALS

at the ARMY APPRENTICE COLLEGE, HARROGATE, YORKSHIRE

and has won a guaranteed vacancy for the WINTER 1975 *term*

which starts on 9TH SEPTEMBER 1975

subject to maintaining satisfactory medical and character standards.

Officer Commanding Army Youth Selection Centre

Accepted as an Army Apprentice

PERSONAL WELFARE

Pay

An Apprentice while at the College receives pay at the rate of £1.94 to £3.46 per day dependent on his age.

Daily food and quartering charges are deducted at source. They are as follows:-

Food 51p.   Accommodation 22p

When the Apprentice is on leave, the food charge is NOT levied.

In order to provide an Apprentice with pocket money during his leave periods, his weekly issue is limited to £2 per week for the first term. There are of course occasions when a boy requires more than the £2 (eg purchase of a birthday present etc) and he then draws on his credits. An Apprentice thus has plenty of pocket money saved up for his first leave at the end of the First Term.

The Army is keen to encourage soldiers to save and a National Savings Bank account can easily be opened. It would be appreciated if you would recommend regular saving to your boy. Additionally, voluntary allotments may be made to individuals (Next of Kin/Guardians, blood relatives only) Banks, Building Societies.

Termly cash stoppages are levied on all Apprentices for such items as haircuts, sports subscriptions/Hobbies and Cinema (2nd Term onwards) amounting in all to no more than £1.50 per month.

Extra pay is given to Apprentice NCOs as follows:-

LCPL 21p per week. CPL 28 p per week. SGT 42p per week.
WO2 49p per week. WO1 70 p per week.

Army policy is moving towards monthly payments through Banks and all soldiers are therefore being encouraged to open Bank Accounts. This is a convenience for the soldier and also reduces administrative costs.

-3-

It wasn't for the money!

This is from a poem entitled *Anither Hairst Deen* which I have written in both Doric and English for comparison. Enjoy!

Doric

The corn crap noo turnin ripe
Green heids hae aa bit gone
The binder stanin ready iled
Blade sharpit an canvass on
New blade fitted tae the scythe
nae yet straikit wi the broad
Gin neist morning be half dacent like
Roon the lay park redd a road

Weel noo the hairst is aa bi'han
we'll hae the meal an ale
Tae dance an hooch the nicht awa
suppin ale stracht fae a pail
Syne heid for hame , some bleezin fou
Aneath the hinmost hairst meen
Shakin hans wig gweed auld friens
Haen seen Anither Hairst Deen

English

The corn crop now turning ripe
Green heads have all but gone
The bailer standing ready oiled
blade sharpened and canvass on
New blade fitted to the scythe
not yet stricken with the broad
Come next morning it will be half decent
round the prepared field lead a road.

Well now the harvest is all by hand
we'll have the meal and ale
To dance and drink the night away
supping ale straight from a pail
Then head for home, some steaming drunk
beneath the harvest moon
Shaking hands with good old friends
Having seen Another Harvest Done.

This is one of the reasons that I am so very proud to be British; our small island is completely unique and the blends of dialect can change every 30 to 50 miles, not to mention our individual national languages. Britain really is Great and we must be proud of our heritage and protect it at every turn:

Is toigh leam Alba, tìr m'Athar. Bidh mo chridhe an-còmhnaidh am laighe ann am beanntan Ghleann Comhann, ach tha mi Breatannach cuideachd agus moiteil às. Is mise Seòras à Alba

Leaders are made more often than they are born.
You all have leadership in you.
Develop it by thought training and by practice.

Field Marshal Sir Bill Slim, *1949*

Leadership is that mixture of example, persuasion and
compulsion which makes men do what you want them to do.
If I were asked to define leadership, I should say it is the
'Projection of Personality'. It is the most intensely personal
thing in the world because it is just plain you.

Field Marshal Sir Bill Slim,
Courage and other Broadcasts, 1957

The day the soldiers stop bringing you their problems is the day
you stopped leading them. They have either lost confidence that
you can help them or concluded that you do not care.
Either case is a failure of leadership.

General Colin Powell

POSTING 1
Civvy to Squaddie – AAC Harrogate (Harrogate, North Yorkshire)

Leaving Home

As usual, my dad wasn't around to see me off on my great adventure; he had four kids and money to earn to keep them fed and clothed. I didn't think anything of it though; my dad was and always will be my hero and I both understood and accepted the priorities. He probably expected me to be back in a few weeks anyway. I hadn't given him any reason to expect any better, that's for sure.

My mum was with me, of course, having put absolutely everything into preparing me and spending nearly every penny she had (and probably a few she didn't have) to make sure I had everything I needed to survive this life-changing experience. My mum was a feisty little 'Mackem', born and bred in Sunderland and as tough as old boots; she needed to be, having married my dad when he was serving in the RAF in Yorkshire. It must have been a hell of an experience to end up living in this little village in the middle of nowhere, where everybody spoke in a completely unintelligible dialect (not to mention their hatred of everything English!). I have met a lot of great leaders and managers in my life but just in case I forget to mention it later in the book, my mum taught me more than all of them put together; she was class. That said, I didn't want my hard-earned reputation as a local "bad boy" to suffer if I was spotted being seen off by my mum, so I quickly gave her a peck on the cheek, promised to phone on arrival and set her off up the brae (hill) towards home.

It was a beautiful sunny day in late August and despite what they say south of the border, it does occasionally get above freezing in the Scottish Highlands. I was eventually joined at the bus stop by one of my dad's drinking buddies, a very strange-looking chap with glasses so thick his eyes appeared to be the size of a five-pence piece. Mind you, he was usually so drunk that he had learned to conduct his life using an inbuilt radar so probably wasn't particularly hampered by his poor eyesight.

In typical Doric fashion, he asked me, "Far ye gyan, min?" (Where are you going, man?)

"Am awa te jine e army," (I'm away to join the army) I replied excitedly, pausing for the anticipated praise.

"Ach weil," (Oh well) came the response, and he didn't say another word either before the bus arrived or during the long, slow 36-mile journey into Aberdeen. Doric men are not given to wasting words.

Luckily the main bus station in Aberdeen was, in those days, directly opposite the railway station, so my struggle to drag two huge, heavy suitcases was less painful than it may otherwise have been. My travelling companion from the bus had a good chuckle as he saw me set off between the sites dragging twice my own body weight behind me. Ba heid (twat), I thought to myself.

The wait for my train wasn't too long and I eagerly stuffed my suitcases into the rack and grabbed a seat for my journey south to the Army Apprentice College (AAC) Harrogate, where I was to undertake a two-year apprenticeship as a Radio Telegraphist (RTg) in the Royal Corps of Signals.

This sounded good to me but then again, at this point I didn't quite realise that being a Jock who spoke fairly crap English, and had absolutely no military background or knowledge, placed me firmly in the bracket of "little Scottish bastard". This title would shortly be bestowed upon me by my caring, sharing instructors. The truth of it, of course, is that there was nothing personal in it, everybody was treated in exactly the same way; it's quite amazing the variety of "bastards" that they managed to define! I certainly never took any such comments to heart and have no doubt that this was the start of the character-building exercise that was to shape my early career, and to think of it, probably my entire life.

I noticed quite a number of guys of a similar age getting on the train on the way south. Having not had the common sense to have a haircut before leaving home (prior planning and preparation wasn't my strong point at that stage of my life), even I could work out that those whose hair had been cut using a petrol lawnmower were likely to be future colleagues. However, not knowing these lads, I thought it best to avoid the initial engagement and almost certain language issues at this stage. Little did I know the depth of the bonds I would form with some of them, nor indeed, the fact that a few would be dead and buried before they got a true shot at life.

The train duly arrived after what seemed like an eternity, and we were met at Harrogate Station by a very strange individual in military uniform who didn't seem to realise that we had first names. He called everybody by their last name and was shouting very loudly for us to get on the waiting trucks. He also seemed to have some form of Tourette's syndrome, often twitching uncontrollably and shouting expletives whenever anybody asked a question.

Luckily the journey out to Uniacke Barracks on Penny Pot Lane wasn't too long, but within a few minutes of arrival I think most of us probably wished it had been a few hours longer!

"Off the bus, you grotty shower of shite," shouted this very smart person whom I recognised, from the movies, was a Sergeant. He did seem a bit hyper though and he too quickly demonstrated symptoms of Tourette's, leaving me worried that there was some form of pervading illness within the barracks. I was also witness to an extremely bizarre exchange between the Sergeant and one of my new colleagues.

On innocently asking, "Where's the toilet, Sarge?" he was almost swallowed whole as the Sergeant bellowed menacingly, "if you ever call me Sarge again, I will massage my sausage right up your fucking passage!" The other guy looked at me, clearly shitting himself and wondering, as I was, if the Sergeant was some form of rampant gay.

We were quickly sorted into groups, each being led off to their new accommodation, apparently referred to as squadrons. To be honest, my lack of military knowledge kicked in at this point and I started to worry that I had somehow arrived at an RAF base, because as far as I knew they were the ones with squadrons!

We duly arrived at the squadron building having what can only be described as "minced" across this large open piece of tarmac, which I was later to discover was the Parade Square and revered as almost hallowed ground. I was aware that we probably weren't walking in the expected manner, as the little creepy guy with us spent the journey repeatedly screaming at us, questioning our parenthood, whether we had something concealed in our rectums, and other such bizarre queries.

As we approached the building, all of us became aware of a man-mountain standing very upright, wearing a cap with a peak that seemed to lie flat against his forehead, and carrying a large stick with what appeared to be bits of gold attached to it. This individual had started to join in with the creepy little guy, shouting in an alarmingly loud but fairly incomprehensible voice and in our general direction. It seemed to me that he was joining up a vast array of swear words, but neither I nor my new comrades could quite interpret what he was actually saying.

Rather embarrassingly, this giant of a man was Company Sergeant Major (CSM) Bill Jamieson, Scots Guards, a fellow Highlander who hailed from the small Aberdeenshire town of Turriff. I say embarrassingly, because even I could not work out what he was saying beyond the swear words and I inevitably felt that I had failed my first test in support of my new mates. I later came to terms with the fact that Bill had spent so many years "growling" words of command on drill parades, that he had actually lost the ability to speak any form of intelligible English (or Doric, for that matter)! He was, however, a true leader and despite his persistent complaints about having to continually wipe our arses, he was a natural in terms of his ability to turn unruly, untidy, ill-disciplined young wasters into smart, focused and committed soldiers. I was secretly very proud that Bill, a fellow Jock, was my Sergeant Major and I learned a lot from him in the years to come.

After Bill had "spoken" to us, welcoming us to the College (at least, that's what we all thought he was trying to say), we were ushered into the accommodation block and spread out along a seemingly endless corridor with rooms off one side and toilets/washrooms off the other. Outside each of the rooms stood a (generally) very smart young soldier with some form of rank on their arm; these guys, we were to learn, were the "room NCOs" – with groups of us being allocated to each of the rooms. The room NCOs appeared to be little older than we were but as they were to explain to us at a later point that evening, they were soldiers, whilst we were civvy scumbags who just might, if we paid attention to everything they said and did as we were told, follow in their footsteps.

After this and many other pearls of wisdom were shared with us, we were eventually told to unpack our kit into our lockers, make our beds and get into them as "it will be a long day tomorrow".

I didn't need to be told twice! In those days it took a long time for a train to reach Harrogate from Aberdeen and given the mind-boggling briefings we had been subjected to since our arrival in camp, I was truly knackered. Looking around at my new room-mates – Eck Hardy (Dundee), Jim

McKinnon (Glasgow), Flash Eeles (Eton or somewhere equally posh), Brian Burkill (Scunthorpe) and some Geordie guy (who left so quickly I can't even remember his name) – I reflected on what a strange day this had been and wondered what the fuck I had let myself in for.

Noticing that I hadn't yet dropped off, my new mentor and room NCO, A/T LCpl Ian Davies gently advised that I should "get to fucking sleep" or he would find me some shit jobs to do. How bizarre, he seems to have Tourette's as well, I thought, as I drifted off to sleep…

At 6 am, the door of our room burst open. "Hands off cocks, hands on socks," screamed the very smart sergeant that had met us off the truck on arrival the day before. He seemed to almost float across the room, in one door and out the other, repeating his wake-up call in each and every room along the corridor in an alarmingly loud voice.

As you might anticipate with a group of 16-year-old kids, we felt the request to place our hands elsewhere was probably a little premature at this ungodly hour of the day and the majority quickly turned over and tried to get back to sleep; big mistake!

The Sergeant's second entry was like a whirling dervish, the door crashed open, and beds were immediately tipped over with the incumbents sent sprawling across the floor.

"When I say shit, you shit, do you understand me?" screamed the Sergeant (Sgt). Whilst we were all trying to find the link between getting out of bed and bodily functions, he appeared to be experiencing some form of fit, eyes bulging and frothing at the mouth. "Do you understand me, you shower of shite?" he screamed once again. Before anybody could reply, he quickly informed us that the answer was "Yes, Sergeant!" and encouraged us to respond to that effect.

He then decided to ensure we had no doubt that this was the correct answer by encouraging us to repeat it three times in a very loud and committed manner.

Prior to departure, he also informed us that people that slept without pyjamas were dirty, perverted little creeps and that in future, anybody found sleeping in the buff would have his pace stick (the gold-tipped stick we had seen the day before) inserted into their rectum. This was clearly not an experience that any of us wished to endure, and to the Sergeant's credit, his warning appeared to have the desired effect the next morning, with everybody literally springing out of bed to his early morning call, "Hands off…".

We were soon to learn that this individual was a bit of a legend on camp, greatly feared by the Apprentices for his uncanny ability to see things seemingly out of the back of his head and his ability to deliver the most ferocious bollockings ever encountered. Although I knew absolutely nothing about military things at this very early stage of my career, something told me this guy was special; he was absolutely immaculate, with boots that appeared to be made of glass and creases that looked dangerously sharp, to the point that they would cut you if you ran your finger along them. His name was Sergeant Ron Hails, and he was to play a very significant part in providing me with the tools I needed to succeed in my chosen profession.

Day 2 started with a trip to the barber where we formed a very long queue. Sgt Hails decided that the "gaylords" with the long hair, of which sadly I was one, should wait until the end for their "appointments". The queue seemed to move surprisingly quickly and as we approached the window and were able to see what was happening, it became clear that the barber didn't have any aspiration to be a stylist. Generally speaking, he was taking five to six strokes across the head of the person whose hair he was cutting. Sgt Hails appeared to be enjoying this tremendously, continually shouting "To the wood, to the wood!" as the Sweeney Todd impersonator scalped his victims.

Inevitably the turn of the gaylords arrived, and it was obviously a group that had been singled out for special treatment and on whom "styling" could be practiced. Luckily for me, I was fairly well down the queue and following a number of new styles being applied, including a cross on one guy's head, a Max Wall cut and a Sottish bloke (who was later to become a very close mate) getting only one side of his head shaved, with the other side left at shoulder length, they seemed to have had enough fun; I was simply scalped like the majority of others. The guy with the one-sided cut was made to live with that for a whole day and as could be imagined, visiting the cookhouse for food in the interim period was a particularly humiliating experience for him; he literally ran to the barber shop when Sgt Hails mentioned a slot was available the next day!

Like any other college, the academic year was split into terms with periods of leave between each of them. The curriculum encompassed both trade and military training, with a strong element of general education to O-Level and A-Level standard and ran from Monday morning to Saturday lunchtime. They were long, hard days during which the instructors, either serving officers/soldiers or civilians, would push us non-stop, many seeming to thoroughly enjoy the pain they could inflict upon us. The truth, of course, is that they simply wanted us to be the best we could be but it's asking a lot of a 16-year-old to recognise that fact; we also preferred to take the "them and us" stance.

Recruit Troop

First term, or "Recruit Troop" as it was known, was especially hard, with seemingly endless inspections of our lockers, our rooms and not least ourselves, all before a full day's training and generally directly afterwards as well. I have too many memories of these occasions to recall them all but just let me recount a few.

The revered Sgt Hails had spent a significant amount of time showing us how to fold our uniform to a certain size so as to fit neatly into our individual bedside lockers. Having left us with our room NCOs to continue the lesson, he decided to conduct a personal inspection whereby he arrived with a metal tape measure to check we had understood his sizing. Unsurprisingly, none of us had fully understood the need for each item to be exactly 8 x11 inches. The penalty for failure was rather severe, with every item being extracted from the locker and thrown out of the window whilst the ranting Sergeant screamed obscenities.

We quickly realised that windows featured highly within his punishment regime, and I remember many an occasion where he would check how highly polished our "best boots" were, only to hear him declare "shite state" and throw them out of the open window. This is bad enough if you are on the ground floor but somewhat ruinous when they are launched from the third floor! For clarity, these boots were the ones that we had to prepare for parades and as such, had hour upon hour lavished on them applying the necessary spit and polish.

During our time as recruits, we were confined to camp, so there was no opportunity to let off any steam by going out after work or at weekends, not that we had any spare time or energy for that matter. However, the end of term brought our first leave period and the chance to return to the world of beer, girls and a lie-in, otherwise known as paradise! The fact that we were allowed the princely sum of £2 cash per week, whilst the remainder of our wages were placed in a savings account, made life during term time very hard; even in those days, buying shoe polish, soap, washing powder, and anything else you needed from a £2 per week income was pretty challenging. It did, however, mean that we all had some cash to spend on leave, or should have done. All of that said, I had suffered a huge drop in salary as a Stonemason's Apprentice on £40 per week, to a junior soldier on £13.44 a week! As you can imagine, this had quite a severe impact on my morale.

As mentioned, Recruit Tp was very hard with several brutal lessons being learned along the way. In fairness, we were just kids, many of whom had never spent a day away from home in their entire lives. Unsurprisingly, quite a few lads just couldn't come to terms with a regime that dragged you out of bed at 05.30 and then filled your day with a non-stop round of activities through until midnight.

Every morning started with a gruelling bit of physical training, come rain or shine, followed by a rushed round of ablutions, breakfast at breakneck speed, and a morning parade in which you were ridiculed for an over-sized beret, poorly pressed uniform, or having some form of imperfection in your personal hygiene. Most of us had never shaved before, so it wasn't that surprising to find some of them with a bit of shaving foam behind their ears; that led to some serious punishments, including being forced to run around the parade square whilst shouting "I'm a gungy bastard who doesn't know how to wash!" – a bit harsh, we all thought.

Those that just couldn't cope with it were allowed to leave but not without going through a process that was designed to retain their services and that left many of them seriously traumatised. For those that could adapt and who had the necessary resilience to get on with it, it became easier as the weeks and months passed; human nature is such that this type of pressure inevitably brings you closer to your colleagues, and you grow stronger individually and as a group. You quickly learn that there is no "I" in team.

As we climbed off the bus at Harrogate Station on our route home at the end of our first term, we were all in a happy-go-lucky mood, knowing that as soon as we escaped the gaze of our instructors, we could buy the world's supply of beer and let the party commence; happy days! It's amazing just how little it takes a 16-year-old who hasn't seen, let alone tasted a beer in 12 weeks, to get drunk.

Several of us settled into the long train journey north, downing a few beers as the train rattled along; I was woken from a beer-induced sleep by the train guard as we arrived in Edinburgh. My mate Wolfy was with me and as Edinburgh was his home city, he got off the train. I was meant to change trains and head for Aberdeen. As I scrambled to get my kit together, I stuck my hand into my jacket pocket to locate my wallet, only to find that some needy soul had decided this young squaddie was easy pickings; my wallet had been nicked whilst I slept!

Unfortunately, the effects of the alcohol hadn't worn off and whilst I staggered around complaining about my loss, I attracted the attention of a couple of Royal Military Policemen (RMP). Having listened to my tail of woe and assessed my general state as inebriated, they decided to provide some accommodation whilst I sobered up, after which they could sort me out with some cash and get me on my way. The accommodation in question was the cells in Edinburgh Castle, so my recovery didn't take quite so long as it might have, had it been a hotel! Anyway, it taught me a real lesson and was the one and only time I transgressed (or at least, got caught) throughout the remainder of my military career. I still chuckle every time I watch the Edinburgh Tattoo though and despite the beauty of the castle, I wouldn't recommend the accommodation provided to me that night!

Toughening Up

Leave passed very quickly and before I knew it, we were all back from our holiday and settling back into life in the college. In early February 1976, my Squadron 2IC, Captain Charlie Kemp, decided that as a fairly reserved recruit, I would benefit from a bit of toughening up to bring me out of my shell. Personally, I think he just missed the fact that I was still a bit overawed by the new world I had recently entered. Either way the Outward-Bound Course he decided to send me on sounded exciting and it would get me off camp for a few weeks which was welcome at that point. Armed with my Travel Warrant, I headed off by bus to pick up my train to Towyn in North Wales, where the course was based.

Trains back then were inevitably quite slow unless you were travelling between major towns and cities, so I knew that it would be a rather dull, lengthy trip to... *where was I going again?* The trip didn't disappoint, with a number of changes at odd sounding places and taking several hours to complete. On arrival, I was met by a couple of instructors, who guided a few of us from the train to a 4-ton truck, where they told us to get on-board.

Luckily, it was only a short trip to the camp, which was right on the beach, the relevance of which I didn't quite grasp at that point. The accommodation consisted of old wartime Nissen huts, but they were clean, dry, and warm which was all that mattered. The students were drawn from across the army, but most were obviously youngsters. Our initial welcome was delivered that evening by a chap I would now refer to as "eccentric", but back then, he just seemed barking mad! A full Colonel of some vintage, he informed us all that we were weaklings, but we needn't worry as he would rebuild us over the next three weeks. With that, we were ordered to bed.

The next morning started with an early parade, 05:30 to be precise; in standard PT kit of baggy blue shorts and a red or white PT vest, we were taken on a fast-paced run down to the beach. On arrival, the eccentric Col was waiting for us. He confirmed whether we could swim, assuring those who couldn't that they would be fine as we would not be going in above neck depth. This was fine for the six footers, not so much for those of us that were some way off that mark! Anyway, we were ordered into the sea, unsurprisingly a bit chilly in February in North Wales, where we did a few exercises, had to fully immerse ourselves, and then complete a three-mile run. I think we were all in shock as we sat in silence eating our breakfast. This became our early morning routine throughout the course.

We were taught basic survival theory, how to build rudimentary shelters and undertook some awesome practical adventurous training activities. I did potholing and rock climbing for the first time in the slate mines of Blaenau Ffestiniog (a place that could double for the surface of the moon!), map reading in local forests, and a range of other activities that I just loved. I did find potholing a bit disconcerting at first but that was down to the method of entry to the chosen "pot". Even my slight build required the instructor to stamp on my hard hat to send me shooting down a shaft onto a ledge below. Once inside, the cave just opened up and shining our torches showed an eerie but completely fascinating underground world; I was hooked. During this session, we crawled through caves so tight most of us got stuck and had to be pushed/pulled through, waded through partially flooded caves, abseiled between levels and had to free climb on our extraction; wow!

Our first effort at rock climbing was something I will never forget. With no previous experience, I thought the selected climb was way beyond our capabilities. I was teamed up with an Infantry soldier called Jimmy Kelly, a happy-go-lucky Glaswegian from the KOSB (King's Own Scottish Borderers). I think it was when I was upside down on an overhang that I realised I wasn't a natural, but the adrenaline rush is incredible. The instructors were outstanding but at 16 years old, you just assume that you will die.

As I managed to right myself and tried to claw my way up the rock face inch by inch, the worst happened – a body came hurtling past me to my left. There were no visible ropes, so I knew this was bad. To my complete horror, the body hit an outcrop and a limb detached. The thump as he hit the ground took me a long time to erase from my memory, and as you would expect, I became a human limpet instantly. This is where the instructors stepped up and gently coaxed and encouraged several of us to complete the climb, after which we were told the casualty was a local man who regularly undertook the climb. Apparently, he never used ropes and his footwear of choice were standard training shoes; simply unbelievable given the conditions.

I took a lesson from that totally avoidable tragedy that never left me; always wear the correct kit, maintain it scrupulously, always follow the rules, and never take unnecessary risks.

The rest of the course brought me a lot of enjoyment, fuelling a passion for adventure training that would last throughout my career, and drive a personal desire to become an instructor who could introduce colleagues to this hugely exciting, challenging world. I was so tired by the end of the course that the trip back to the college seemed to pass very quickly.

"Rookie" No More

No longer recruits, the terms rolled past with never a dull moment and although we were actually allowed out at weekends, there wasn't much time to do anything other than constantly prepare for the next instalment of training.

My early career was going well, and I was being promoted at regular intervals; boy soldiers could attain ranks to match their regular counterparts, from Private (referred to as Apprentice Tradesmen or A/T), to Warrant Officer Class 1, except for Staff Sergeant which was missed out. I didn't realise it at the time, but I had inherited a "smartness" of appearance from my parents and under tuition from various parties, I was able to turn this into a massive plus. My eye for detail, already strong, was honed to perfection by a combination of the ever-eagle-eyed Sergeant Hails and other instructors. It is with immense pride that I recall being the only boy soldier (as far as anybody of the permanent staff knew or could remember) to have won the "Best Turned Out" Apprentice on five consecutive inter-squadron drill competitions, which were held every term. The fact that I took to drill very easily and quickly learned to master the "drill voice" was also very helpful.

I have always been incredibly proud of the quality of R Signals soldiers from a military perspective. The standard of our training is second to none, and it starts from Day 1. For me, this was under the tuition of one of the Corps' most, if not **the** most accomplished, drill instructors, Sgt Ron Hails. Luckily for me, Ron was a Troop Sgt when I arrived in Bradley Squadron, one of five squadrons in the college, the others being Penny, Phillips, Scott and Rawson.

I knew immediately that he was something special; he was the smartest, loudest (in terms of his drill voice), best drill instructor and probably the best actor I had ever come across. He always played the hard, nasty bastard but it was an act; underneath the rough exterior, all he wanted was for the Apprentices to be the very best they could be. Between him and CSM Bill Jamieson, Scots Guards, we couldn't have had better mentors. Because I had absolutely no military background or prior knowledge, I put everything I had into whatever we were doing. Ron saw that and also respected it.

As we went through training, there were many things that made me chuckle about Ron, but never in a disrespectful way; he was definitely my role model. I will never forget the day he was slightly late and he was changing into his uniform in the office. He was rushing and as he rammed an arm into his perfectly ironed shirt, he ripped the arm straight off; it was so heavily starched, it just broke off. I must admit I have seldom laughed so hard in my life, although I did take cover in the toilets so he wouldn't hear me. Ron had a great sense of humour, and you could have a laugh with him, but the reality is that the other side of his personality was so scary that few took the risk. It is rumoured that when, many years later, he was the RSM (Regimental Sergeant Major) at 1 Div HQ & Sig Regt in Verden, West Germany, soldiers who worked in one barracks, which was separated by a road from another, would walk all the way round the second barracks, rather than use a shortcut that would take them directly past his office, adding around a mile to their walk.

As we gained experience, the restrictions on our social lives were relaxed still further and we were able to go out and about; in other words, go to the pub. Harrogate had some lovely old bars, but we had to be careful. With hairstyles that identified us as squaddies, we were easy targets for the local 'bad boys' who were always looking for an opportunity to start a fight. Inevitably, they were always in larger numbers and usually significantly older; the oldest lads in the college were only 19, albeit that did include some very hard guys. If you managed to avoid trouble in the pub all evening, the trip to the nightclub would almost always scupper that, with most such visits ending in a mass brawl at closing time. If the police didn't lift you, it was quite normal to get collared as you booked in on your return to camp; you couldn't win.

In order to avoid this type of situation, a gang of us decided to head for Leeds at the weekends. We didn't stand out in the same way and whilst fights did happen regularly in the city centre pubs, they didn't tend to include soldiers with such regularity. Eventually we discovered the Hofbräuhaus, in the Merrion Centre, where the beers were enormous and the atmosphere was brilliant, at least from a 18-year-old's perspective. That soon became our regular haunt and we had little or no trouble from the locals, which was a real bonus.

However, we did have a few challenges, such as trying to get through the guardroom without being nicked when we returned from Leeds; those large beers had a habit of turning us into rubber men who found it difficult to walk in a straight line. To be fair, the Apprentices on guard duty tried to turn a blind eye to the fact that several of us seemed to have one leg shorter than the other, but if the wrong permanent instructor was on duty, it often led to a night in the cells if your stagger through the booking-in process was too unconvincing.

The A/T RSM was the only boy who was allowed to stay out all night. I do remember one night when I was the A/T RSM. A large group of us returned back to camp and were systematically being pulled out of the line and locked up, so I decided to duck out and head back to town. I had forgotten a key point; I had no money left so couldn't afford a cab. Dismayed by my lack of cash, I knew I couldn't take the risk of getting jailed, so I had no option but to spend the night in a bus shelter; luckily it was July, so it wasn't too uncomfortable. I was able to stroll into camp at 6 am looking convincingly sober, so avoided a potentially early career disaster. Those were very happy days indeed.

Every few months, we would be deployed into the field, either on military training or to consolidate our classroom-based trade training. On one of these trade-related exercises, we were in Ripon Park, an absolutely beautiful area of North Yorkshire. The training had been extremely intense, and it was clearly an aim of the exercise to put us under real pressure, including subjecting us to sleep deprivation at a level we had never experienced before. In outline, we would spend all day on a specific skill, such as HF radio installation and operation. We would then pack up in the early evening and move tactically to a new location, where on arrival we would set up and share guard duties, allowing all the students to get some sleep. Raids on the locations by regular staff in the guise of "enemy" were common, disrupting any sleep that we were able to grab, whilst we also undertook "stand to" at first and last light. These stand to exercises were held at these times as they were considered to be a high risk of enemy attack as the sun was rising or falling.

With all these pressures being applied, I remember having trouble even keeping my eyes open on numerous occasions. On the final day of the exercise, my group were being tested on generators, including the dual fit, trailer-mounted 3.5 kVA. It seemed to last forever as we were taken through several lessons on various aspects, followed by each of us undergoing an individual assessment. Our instructor was a real stickler for detail and any mistakes or omissions were almost certainly punished by a failure result, so we had to remain focused or accept failure. That type of pressure mixed with a lack of sufficient sleep is a recipe for disaster, evidenced by the fact that during a lesson I genuinely fell asleep on my feet, only waking as I hit the very cold, hard ground. Luckily, the instructor had his head in the trailer, so he missed my collapse and the chuckling of my mates, otherwise I would probably have spent the next 15 minutes running around Ripon Park with my rifle above my head shouting, "I must not fall asleep on the job!" Yes, they thought that was a hilarious punishment.

Losing My Dad

Despite my dad being a relatively young man, he became ill during my time in Harrogate and eventually had to give up work due to a heart condition. He was the kind of bloke that simply didn't know anything other than hard graft and didn't know what to do with himself when he wasn't working. On the few occasions when I did see him, whilst on leave, it broke my heart to watch this tough north-eastern Scot hardly able to walk 100m up the hill if we went for a pint. Despite this very clear evidence of his condition, men like my dad always recovered from illness and got back to work, or so I thought.

A few weeks after having returned to Harrogate from that particular leave, I was awoken by a loud banging on my bunk door.

"RSM, are you awake?" came the booming voice of SSM (Squadron Sergeant Major) Dave Sixsmith, who was the Duty Warrant Officer.

"Yes, Sir," I replied as he thrust the door open.

"Sorry to tell you this," he said, "but your dad has died..." His words just ran around my head, and I thought I was dreaming. I was 18 years old, a boy soldier, and this was how a highly experienced Warrant Officer broke such news to a kid. I think it was how the message was delivered that

My dad was my hero

led to my initial period of denial and a very strong urge to break a brush over his head! In reality, the army system dealt with my loss with significantly greater compassion, and I was quickly dispatched on special compassionate leave to attend my dad's funeral and to spend time with my family.

What was already a long journey seemed infinitely longer this time, largely because I had convinced myself that it wasn't true and that I would arrive home to see my dad standing smiling at the kitchen window when I got there. In those days, there was only one bus per day from Aberdeen to New Pitsligo and I had missed it: so, with no other option, I set off on the 36-mile walk, hoping that I might get lucky and get a couple of lifts along the way.

I did get lucky and was picked up around six miles outside the city and got a lift all the way home. As I stood at the top of the garden, I could see there was nobody at the window and I think that was when my denial faded and I just knew my dad had gone; he was just 45 years old.

My dad was a popular bloke, and his funeral was well attended, which meant a lot to the family. My mum, who was only 42, was distraught and I guess the fact that my little sister, Gill, was still in primary school brought everything into very clear perspective; life would simply never be the same again. I have thought a lot about this period over the years, even having regular dreams where it hadn't happened and Dad was back home, fully recovered from his heart condition. If I had had the option of not waking up and staying in the bounds of that dream, I think I would happily have done so. I also became very aware that alongside Mum, my sister was the one who lost the most. I have two elder brothers and we were all making our way in the world; Gill, on the other hand, had to spend her formative years without her father.

I can remember the night she was born and to say my dad was excited would probably be the biggest understatement of my life; I have never seen anybody so deliriously happy and I guess with three boys, he had every right to be. She was the apple of his eye and remained so for the rest of his life. I sincerely hope she is aware of the truth of that statement. Personally, I took some comfort from the last time I had been able to visit my dad in hospital. I did so in full dress uniform, wearing leather (belt, cross strap and scabbard), complete with ceremonial sword; I wanted him to see that I was a junior RSM. He did, and was very proud.

Although I have two older brothers, they had both left home and I wasn't sure how much my mum would see of them which was a real worry with me being in the army. This worry was compounded by the fact that Gill was only nine at the time. As mentioned, she had been the absolute apple of his eye and it broke my heart to think he wouldn't see her grow up. I felt that pressure very heavily, to the point that I was considering leaving the army to come home to look after them, but my mum put paid to that straight away. She knew I had found something special and wouldn't even discuss it with me. She always put her kids first.

The remainder of that leave was spent trying to comfort my mum, but it was an impossible task, as she missed my dad so much. Now, after 40 years of marriage, I can understand her devastation completely and exactly why she never got over it for the rest of her life. Somehow, I knew this would be the case but of course, the day came when I had to return to Harrogate. This time I really didn't care who saw me give my mum a massive hug and kiss on the cheek as I got on the bus. How my life had changed in two very short years.

I was truly devastated by the loss of my dad. It had come only six weeks before I was due to command the Graduation Parade that would see me and my senior term colleagues graduate and leave the college for our first working units. I had to get that right in my dad's memory and despite the daunting prospect, I could feel him willing me on.

Graduation Parade

When I returned from compassionate leave following Dad's funeral, I was welcomed back by the new College RSM, an Irish Guardsman. He had replaced RSM Harry Forrest, Scots Guards, whom I hadn't known was leaving. The new guy was very pleasant towards me but had decided that the format of our Graduation Parade would change to mirror the Queen's Birthday Parade. That was a very scary prospect for an 18-year-old boy soldier, but I immediately decided this would be for my dad and that I could do it, no matter how hard. Little did I realise the complexity of the new parade, nor how important Ron Hails' input would be.

When I got back to Bradley Squadron, having been briefed by the new RSM, Ron was standing at the main entrance.

"Everything OK, RSM?" he asked me.

"Yes, Sgt," I said but probably didn't sound too convincing.

"A 5 am start from now on," he said "in the Indoor Arena. See you in the morning in full parade rig."

Five o'clock in the morning is an early start for anyone, but when you are wearing full No 2 Dress, Sam Browne (leather belt and cross strap) and sword, carrying a pace stick, it is quite a shock to the system.

On arrival at the indoor arena, Ron was waiting and explained his plan for foot and sword drill practice for the next six weeks, with a run-through of the full parade in terms of words of command every single day: this was on top of a full rehearsal three to four times a week on the drill square with all the troops present.

By the time the formal parade came round, my drill was polished to perfection and Ron informed me that his only concern was that I might lose my voice due to all the practice! Unfortunately, this was a risk that you couldn't remove, only mitigate, and I did that by gargling with TCP every morning and evening until graduation day arrived.

I'll never forget that beautiful late summer day in September 1977. Here I was, a rag arse from the Scottish Highlands, about to take command of my Graduation Day Parade. Whilst this may seem a small matter to some, I can assure you that the thought of taking charge of a parade of approximately 1,500 Apprentice Tradesmen, with a Major General as the inspecting officer, was a daunting prospect. What if I forgot my words of command, or those on parade couldn't hear me? My stomach was doing backflips. The fact that the format of the parade had been changed just six weeks earlier, largely because the "real RSM", an Irish Guardsman, wanted to make his mark on the college, certainly didn't help my confidence.

I had never seen or heard of the Queen's Birthday Parade, so having to learn every individual word of command in six weeks was a huge challenge. The first act of the parade sees the six squadrons (five full squadrons plus the "Senior Squadron", comprising those that would graduate) march on, each commanded by an Apprentice Tradesman Squadron Sergeant Major.

Once they were on the square and halted, it was over to me. I was at the top of the parade square and at the head of the College Band with the Pipes and Drums immediately behind me. I was actually shitting myself and not quite sure my voice would work as I prepared to step the band off. At that moment, I felt a sense of calm come over me and I realised this was my chance to make my dad proud.

"Pipes and Drums ready, by the front, quick march!" and the next thing I remember is asking the Inspecting General for permission to march the Senior Squadron off parade, having graduated; luckily, everything had gone perfectly, no loss of memory or squeaky voice syndrome to reduce me to a laughing stock.

The loveliest thing of all is that my mum, Uncle Geordie (standing in for my dad) and my little sister had been watching the parade throughout; when we were eventually allowed to go and join our families, my mum asked where I had been standing on the parade. That burst my balloon, given I had been the guy commanding the parade, standing in the centre, delivering all the words of command! It just served to reinforce why I loved my mum so much; she was such an easy-going, humble person who really wouldn't have cared where I had been, as long as I was OK.

Uncle Geordie, on the other hand, had seen and heard enough, so he was very keen to reacquaint himself with the NAAFI bar, something he hadn't been near since his National Service days! He was a little put out when I informed him that we had to attend a prize-giving session in the cinema before we could get to the bar. "Howay then," was his retort, "the sooner we do that, the sooner I can get a beer." I loved this big, shy 'Mackem' and I will never forget his kindness in being there for me; he was the next best thing to my dad.

Having received the Commandant's Prize for Conduct, Discipline & Example and watched the other prizes being presented, we were eventually able to hit the bar and Geordie sank a few ales. I tried to keep up but after the first three, I simply gave up - he was a beer monster!

The adrenalin that builds up when you take command of such a spectacle is astounding and I had felt 10 feet tall, not the five-foot-eight-inch, eleven-stone short-arse as was reality. It was like some kind of drug, as though I was floating on air; most significantly, the pride I felt in leading my Senior Squadron colleagues off parade having graduated and become "real" soldiers, is indescribable to this day. These guys had taught me what camaraderie was; they were quite simply the best group of people I had ever met, and they were my friends; how lucky am I, I thought to myself.

Squaddie humour made an appearance as I marched the guys off. As the A/T RSM, I was the senior apprentice in the college, and as such, you enjoy almost god-like status. However, I was an RTg (Radio Telegraphist) and therefore, on graduation, I became a private soldier, or Sig as is the rank in the R Signals. However, Apprentice Technicians, irrespective of their A/T rank, graduate as L/Cpls which made them instantly senior to me. All I can say is that particular manoeuvre is a great leveller! As you can imagine and quite rightly, some of my technician friends made their instant promotion very clear to me.

I set off home on leave with a very warm glow, proud of my personal achievements during my two years in training, but also starting to realise what a special group of guys I had served with, many of whom I may never see again; it was a big Corps in those days. With the benefit of hindsight, I can say that whether each of us stayed for three years or forty-plus years, the bond has never broken amongst this "band of brothers". Even now, some 45 years on, many of us remain in touch via social media, in some instances, we may never have physically met since the day of our Graduation Parade. This type of relationship is unique and is something I am proud to have been part of throughout my adult life.

AAC Harrogate Graduation –
Me, Mum & sister Gill

A/T RSM Board, AAC Harrogate – My name is
on the right-hand side, seventh from the top

POSTING 2
249 Sig Squadron (AMF(L)) –
First Regular Army Unit
(Old Sarum, Salisbury, Wiltshire)

When The Sprogs Come Marching In

Following a long, warm summer break, I was full of trepidation as I got on the train at Aberdeen for the long journey south to Salisbury in Wiltshire; a fully qualified soldier, destined for his first unit in the regular army. It was a well-known fact that the "Boy RSM" was likely to get a good shoeing on arrival at his first working unit, if only to let him know that he wasn't the "Head Boy" anymore. Never one to ignore a good tip, I was considering my options as to how I could put this off as the miles rolled past.

As I joined the Salisbury train in London, I was very pleased to meet up with a few other ex-Apprentices heading for the same unit and started to relax as we chatted about the adventures that lay ahead of us. After all, this was a highly prized posting, with the squadron being part of the Allied

Command Europe Mobile Force Land (AMF(L)) and therefore, regularly sent to warm climes such as Turkey and Sardinia, and to Norway on ski training and arctic exercises every year; cushy or what!

We caught a taxi from Salisbury to Old Sarum, an old RAF camp only a mile from the city that had been taken over by the army some years before. Unloading our suitcases, we reported our arrival to the guardroom where we were expected and the JNCO on guard duty assured us that as 'Sprogs', we would be made very welcome! He then called somebody to greet us and take us to our assigned accommodation.

Some 15 minutes later, the guardroom door opened and in came probably the campest person any of us had ever met. "Oh lovely, fresh meat!" he shouted, "I'm Chalky, follow me!" I'm pretty sure each one of us was secretly hoping that we would not be sharing accommodation with our new friend and that he wasn't the leader of some gay group within the squadron to whom he would seek to introduce us in the future.

On arrival at the block, Chalky showed us in and in my case, as he pushed the main door open, there was something obstructing it. He pushed it open far enough to get through and when we stepped inside, we noticed a huge pile of rubbish behind it. As we began to move the rubbish out of the way, we heard groans coming from the pile and a guy stood up, swore a few times, and staggered off.

"Oh, that's where Taff has been all evening," said Chalky, who then continued to show us to our pits. Apparently, Taff, or to give him his real name, Cornelius, was one of the squadron's most accomplished drinkers who had a propensity for disappearing when inebriated.

The accommodation was basic in the extreme; large dormitories that had been split into individual areas with the use of three-quarter high stud walls, with the rooms running off a central corridor. Doors had clearly been deemed an unnecessary luxury, having been replaced by a single, hairy GS (General Service) blanket; they weren't big on privacy! However, it was your own space (ish) and better than an open dormitory.

As an old airfield, the working area/garages were actually vast old aircraft hangers, so quite spacious. So big in fact, that a full troop could get all its equipment (including vehicles, trailers and so forth) into a single garage, which was great, particularly in the rain or winter in general. There were also small individual rooms within each hanger that were used as offices for the SNCOs, stores and the like.

On our first morning parade, my fellow Sprogs and I were quite taken aback to learn that rather than standard working dress, everybody seemed to have decided on a varying range of uniform, something that would have been unthinkable in the training environment at Harrogate. Naively, I decided to ask one of the Junior NCOs what we were expected to wear to work. His answer, "Nobody gives a flying fuck, Sprog," wasn't quite what I had anticipated but I decided not to pursue my line of questioning, as he appeared rather upset that I had raised it. It didn't really matter in any case; as Sprogs, we didn't own any American Jump boots, Italian jerseys or German fatigues, so our choice was simple: either regular British Army uniform or naked (and with Chalky in my troop…)!

Inevitably, the identity of the former boy RSM came up and to be brutally honest, I owe Dave Smith (a fellow Sprog) an apology to this day. One of the biggest blokes I had ever seen wandered menacingly towards me and asked, "Are you the fucking boy RSM prick?"

Which didn't take me long to answer. "No," I assured him.

"I knew it was that posh wanker Smith!" he shouted and before I could say anything, he barged past me in pursuit of poor old Dave. I never did find out exactly what the outcome of that situation was, but it was rumoured to have included removal of trousers and pouring of engine oil into underwear. Anyway, I owe Dave a beer and sincerely hope to deliver it at some point (albeit 45 years late).

As certified Sprogs, we were obviously unaware of certain key traditions, such as Market Day which occurred in Salisbury every Wednesday. The first Wednesday of the month arrived and having not been briefed on any tradition, we worked the morning as usual but on our return from lunch, found the garages completely empty apart from the Sprog contingent. Having been told no different, we decided the best way forward was to get on with work until the other guys arrived, which they did around 3.30 pm on the back of a 4-ton truck, most of them completely legless!

"Welcome to the real world, Sprogs!" they shouted as they got/fell off the vehicle. "Don't you know its Market Day?" they bellowed, as if that was somehow going to explain the mass absence and subsequent return of the squadron in a completely inebriated state.

As we were to learn, Market Day for squadron personnel was celebrated on the first Wednesday of each month, where every able member of the unit knocked-off work and went to the market in the afternoon. For absolute clarity, when I say 'market', I mean the Market Inn on the edge of Salisbury Market Square, where they then drank themselves into oblivion, before most of them got the 4-tonner back to barracks. Wednesday afternoon is normally dedicated to sports in the British Army and whilst in training, that was baked into the programme. Clearly, it referred to a different kind of sport on Market Day in this unit – "Oh, Happy Days!"

Initially, I was quite surprised at how the Junior Officers were treated by the soldiers. It was very different from my experience at Harrogate, but I guess that's because I didn't understand seniority or respect at that point. Anyway, the first time I saw the "Rodney (young officer) initiation", I literally couldn't believe my eyes. One of the more senior Signalmen, Titch Fallowfield, appeared to own this specific activity and had perfected it to an alarming point. Titch usually had a finely-tuned Cortina or something similar and his party piece was to use his car to pick up newly arriving Young Officers from the guardroom to take them to their respective troop offices. He would pick the individual up and head towards the big aircraft hangars. Increasing speed, he would drive towards the huge steel doors, open the driver;s door and climb onto the roof whilst the panicking officer inevitably yanked on the handbrake, usually stopping just feet from the door. Whilst the soldiers all fell about laughing, Titch jumped back in his car and roared off; the officer tended to stagger around in shock!

The army has an unjustified reputation as a hot bed of bullying and whilst it does exist, it's all part of the test, particularly when you first arrive in a working unit; 249 was no exception. The main culprits were a couple of Cpls, or "full screws" as the rank was referred to. The individuals in question were Taff and Skully, a pair of vertically challenged NCOs who thought it was great fun and their absolute right to mess the youngsters around. "Go and get me a left-handed screwdriver, a tin of tartan paint," – all the usual nonsense. But what they seemed to forget was the fact that we had all spent two years at the AAC, where all the tricks had been played on us by the regular staff instructors. Sadly, for the two short-arses, this meant that we had heard it all before and their tasks were seen through straight away, which infuriated them both, leading to even more tedious and pathetic attempts to get one up on us.

Another unfortunate but common view of army personnel is that they are all a bit thick. Without courting too much controversy, this is particularly short-sighted given the many hugely capable technical trades and professions within the services. However, every now and again I did wonder how some individuals made it through the rigorous selection process. In those days, we weren't particularly well paid, and it was fairly common for some folk to be on their uppers towards the end of the month. As we all know, there are bad apples in every barrel, but the worst offence in the army is to steal from colleagues.

One of the married guys was in a bad place, and under pressure he swiped a cheque book from the accommodation block. He then travelled into the Lloyds Bank in Salisbury with the intention of cashing a cheque. In what can only be described as a flawed plan, he approached the cashier and handed over the cheque to be cashed. Now this was common practice at the time, but the flaw in his plan was the fact that the cheque had a name on it that didn't match the name tag on his uniform jersey; oh, oh, caught!

"Chilling" in Norway and the Arctic Circle

It soon began to trouble me that this elite unit was actually a "shower of shite", dressing as they wanted, sports day being nothing more than a giant piss-up and little, if any, discipline; what had we got ourselves into? The saving grace was the fact that the lads were all great characters and they stuck together like glue. I don't think I have laughed so much in my life as I did in the two years with the squadron in Old Sarum.

Our trips to Norway were incredible and despite their general lack of interest in anything other than beer in the UK, these boys were something else in the field. They were outstanding skiers, and for those that have ever come into contact with NATO planks (solid wood, extremely heavy skies with awful, inflexible metal bindings), you may start to imagine just how skilful you needed to be to move with a 45 lb rucksack and a rifle on your back, the worst ski footwear ever designed and multiple layers of army clothing on. It wasn't just moving, however. Much of the time we were on a mountain in the middle of nowhere, hurtling at breakneck speed down a slope shouting "Banzai!" before the inevitable wipe out where, if you were lucky, you would get away with a 10-minute struggle to get your head out of the snow, or regularly, a trip to hospital!

This type of training was an annual event but every second year we would then travel north, well into the Arctic Circle in order to participate in multinational exercises with our allies. Normally between -10°C to -25°C in the south, this was a whole new ballgame, with temperatures often as low as -40°C. Again, to see the survival skills my colleagues had built up was awesome and helped my attention span when it came to building shelters and learning other survival techniques.

The main objective of our trip to the north was the joint exercise whereby the squadron provided three-man detachments to the various nationalities. These detachments were known as "Key 1 – 6" and I was part of Key 3 with my Detachment Commander, Cpl Kev Froggett and LCpl Bob Martin; amazingly, both came from the small Derbyshire town of Belper, but it didn't seem to bring them particularly close as individuals. Key 3 was attached to the Italian battalion known as "the Alpini" who were superb hosts and provided a bottle of red wine in each of their daily ration packs, a fact that drew considerable jealousy from the other detachments. I did wonder about priorities sometime, as the US detachment had the benefit of a McDonald's burger bar trailer and endless Coca-Cola on tap and given the "quality" of the Alpini wine, I for one would have happily traded with them! Talking of trading, my fellow Sprogs and I were to learn how this was done "British Army style" on this trip, and boy, was it an education!

I have often wondered if Derek Trotter from *Only Fools and Horses* did any time in the army, if only because everybody seemed to have a touch of Del Boy in them. Our allies, of course, were completely unprepared for the application of every dirty trick in the book whilst "trading" with the Brits. To explain how these transactions tended to pan out, I will share one of my favourite stories from a Norway trip.

It was standard practice for all nationalities to rendezvous in a large area of open space, each country being allocated a specific piece of ground. In every instance, the troops would soon start to intermingle, with envious eyes being cast over each other's better pieces of equipment. We Brits especially liked the opportunity to barter with our US allies, not because they automatically had the best kit, but rather because they were generally the most gullible people on earth!

On this particular trip, we found ourselves in the usual rendezvous (RV) set-up, when Taff and Vic decided it was time to say hello to the Yanks and of course, to engage in a bit of trading with them. I thought it was a bit strange when they set off with only one item for exchange between them, a Heavy Duty (HD) jersey. Although such jerseys were much coveted by the US soldiers, given their quality and heat-retaining characteristics (which are highly valued at -40°C), taking only one seemed a bit suspicious; I therefore decided to go along and watch the fun.

Approaching a long line of US Gama Goat lorries, all of which had a driver sitting inside trying to keep warm, I noticed that Taff and Vic had spaced out, with one on either side of the lorries; clearly, this was a tactic being deployed. Taff, on the driver's side of the vehicles, then started knocking on the windows and engaging with the drivers, generally through a small gap as it was far too cold to open it any further. Whilst I couldn't hear the discussion over the howling wind, it was clear that bartering was underway and quickly concluded with Taff handing the HD through the window and accepting a wad of notes in exchange. He then quickly wandered off, returning only a few moments later and this time knocking furiously on the cab door.

Watching keenly as the scene unfolded, I noticed that as the shocked driver opened the door and jumped down to talk to Taff, big Vic opened the door on the other side very gently and swiped the HD jersey, before closing it and making off. Taff finished the discussion with the driver and following a firm handshake, he headed off down the line at a sprightly pace. I decided to move so that I could continue to observe their antics. A few minutes later, I noticed Vic knocking on the window of a truck some distance down the line, this time on the other side of the truck. I then witnessed the whole sequence play out all over again, this time with Taff undertaking the stooge role. They sold that jersey about 20 times over the next few days, much to the annoyance of our allies!

A year after I joined the squadron in Old Sarum, a few more guys arrived from Harrogate, including Jonathan Craven (JC), Ian Philo (Flo), Dave Catchpole (Snatch) and Jimmy Johnstone (JJ). Having completed a year in the squadron, I was clearly vastly experienced, or so I and others of my vintage thought, but that's an army thing, which makes me chuckle when I think about it. Anyway, it was great to have some new guys in the squadron, as it took the pressure of those that arrived with me and suddenly, we weren't the Sprogs!

Truthfully, these new lads were a great bunch and settled in very quickly and easily; the biggest compliment I can pay them is 44 years later I consider each of them to be lifetime pals. JC ended up on my crew and I soon discovered his love for everything Tetley. During the week he drank more brews, as we referred to them, than the rest of the Tp put together; all Tetley's tea, of course. Weekends were reserved for the other type of Tetley's, where he tried, and often succeeded, to drink his own body weight in their beer. JC has always been a true Yorkshireman...

The remainder of the new group were spread across the other detachments and each of them proved themselves, some in quite difficult circumstances. Whilst bullying wasn't a major problem, as I have said, it did happen and as most people know and accept the best way to deal with it is to face up to it head on. In one instance, as a result of constant acts of humiliation, Dave had to make that particularly tough decision, otherwise it was clear that it would continue unabated. Although he was easy-going by nature, everybody has a breaking point and he had reached his. The bully got more than he had bargained for and happily, Dave had effectively removed himself from the firing line; job done!

I observed many ruses during my numerous trips to Norway and the jersey featured in many of them, but I guess the one that made me laugh the most and longest, involved our old sparring partners, the Bundeswehr, the German army. Germans are smart as many people will testify, and not at all like their American counterparts, so ripping them off required a much more robust plan.

Again, we were up in the Arctic Circle and having completed our exercise, it was time for the inevitable RV prior to heading our separate ways. This time, the UK contingent had been nominated to marshal the area, leading the other countries into their respective locations; a task that some of my colleagues seemed uncannily keen to undertake. Still a relatively young soldier at this point, I was allocated to work under a well-known "wide boy", directing the German vehicles into place. The activity went smoothly but I could see that Skully, the aforementioned wide boy, wasn't too impressed by the German soldiers' reluctance to trade. So, having seen all their vehicles into place, I wondered why we were heading full circle on our way back to the UK lines.

As we made our way past the last of the German vehicles, we could see that the group had simply left their wagon fully loaded less their tent, which they had quickly put up and got out of the semi-blizzard that was blowing – big mistake! Skully and a couple of the team crept up to the tent and seeing some metal stakes had been left lying around, they used existing tent door loops to push the pegs very quietly into the compacted snow. Fully aware that these would freeze solid in a short period of time, we quickly made our way back to our accommodation.

An hour or so later, Skully and a couple of lads went back to the German tent with a snow pulk (sledge) and loaded certain elements from the German wagon onto it, whilst the owners struggled to try and get out of their tent which, as expected, they were not able to do. Just to make their point, my colleagues booted the tent repeatedly whilst laughing uncontrollably and then, pulling their pulk behind them, headed off into the snowstorm.

Crewing a Green Goddess

The national fire strike of 1977 took me down a path I hadn't expected – that of an interim firefighter as part of a Green Goddess crew. The military had been stood-up to provide cover in place of the striking Fire Service and along with everybody else in the squadron, I had been trained, allocated to a crew, and assigned to a "fire engine" (of sorts).

My crew was led by SSgt Vic Shillingford, a guy with Caribbean roots who always had a big smile on his face and was a highly competent SNCO, as well as the previously mentioned Chalky White, the gayest guy on the planet, and a guy who was known as 'bungalow' for some reason! We also had Steve Wright and Brett Ford who, like me, were still relatively new.

I mentioned being trained but that, to be fair, is somewhat of an overstatement; we had been bussed down to the Naval Docks in Portsmouth where we undertook a very aptly named "crash course" in firefighting under the guidance of the regular Navy instructors. I don't think their lesson plans took too long to prepare, as most of the course comprised starting some fires inside metal containers, ensuring they were red hot and full of smoke, before chucking us inside telling us to put the fire out. Given we didn't have any breathing apparatus, we were not particularly successful and spent most of our time banging on the door, begging to be let out. Anyway, we all miraculously passed the course and were duly dispatched to the front line. My crew was stationed in Warrington and when we did our first practice call-out, goodness knows what the locals must have thought; six guys in camouflage gear wearing the old WWII tin hats, hanging on for dear life as we nearly toppled the Green Goddess on every corner. That was just the start! Some of our antics, whilst well intentioned, couldn't have been bettered if they had been filmed in Hollywood as a silent movie.

Our first "shout" was to a fire on a barge in the local canal, so we quickly grabbed our gear (let's face it, we didn't have much to grab), and set off at speed for the scene. On arrival, we decided to draw water from the canal, so we were able to get "water on" with impressive speed and attack the burning barge with gusto. Unfortunately, our plan failed to recognise the need to turn the water off once the fire had been extinguished and we continued to douse the embers. Well, we certainly put it out, as the weight of the water sank the barge! The local press couldn't believe their luck. They could maintain their support for the strike whilst reporting on our incompetence, all whilst giving their readership the best laugh they'd had in years; talk about a great story!

We did manage to repair our reputation over the coming days and weeks, but I will never forget the first truly dangerous shout we attended. We were called out early one morning to a house fire and on arrival we were told that there were people trapped inside, including children. As we rolled out and attached the hoses, we could see the house was well alight and heard screams from the property. It was at this point that our lack of key equipment really hit home; we had no breathing apparatus, no fireproof clothing or indeed, anything of genuine benefit. Still, the truth is, it just didn't matter – there were people trapped in the house and we were going to get them out alive.

I did worry when I was assigned as number one on the hose, specifically as Chalky was number two. Anyway, my ten-and-a-half stone somehow kept control of the hose as we made our way inside the fume-filled house, Chalky pressing hard against my back! We reached the parents on the stairs, who pointed to a bedroom door and confirmed that their two daughters were inside. Not really having a clue what to do, Chalky and I just ran at the door and rammed it open, immediately noticing the two little girls cowering in the far corner of the bedroom. Luckily, there were no flames in the room, just a lot of smoke, so having shouted "Water off!" we grabbed the kids and ran quickly out of the house, picking up the parents on the way out.

The kids were fine, although they did have relatively minor respiratory problems, but it was certainly one of the scariest things I have ever had to do. On reflection, I really don't know how I would have lived with myself if we hadn't got them out.

I've always respected our Fire Service and it is only when you consider they do these things on a regular basis that you recognise the amazing service they provide to us all. The people of Warrington were fantastic to us during our time in the town; on our periods off, they wouldn't let us buy a beer, food, cinema tickets or anything really, everything was free. For a young lad, that felt very special indeed. Anyway, before we knew it, we were on our way south back to Wiltshire.

As with most things in life, the quality of a military unit is hugely dependent on its leadership and management. As I grew in experience, it became very clear that an exceptionally weak OC and an SSM with limited respect or empathy for anybody, was a dangerous mix. The only plus side was that both seemed content to keep their heads down and let the individual troops get on with things. Sad as it is, this was the main reason for the lack of discipline, abuse of uniform and general mess the unit was in, but little did we know change was afoot!

Transition to Glory

Things seemed to happen almost by osmosis, as a new OC, Major Danny Fisher arrived, closely followed by a new SSM, Steve (Snake) Marshall. Overnight the squadron changed forever and very soon thereafter, we were on the move, from Old Sarum to Bulford Camp, still in Wiltshire but also within a multi-unit Garrison type environment.

I'll never forget the day that Danny Fisher had us on parade on Ward Barracks just after we arrived in Bulford. "This unit has a unique role," he said, "and with that role comes responsibility to represent our country to the very best of our ability. As I look around the people in front of me, I see a lot of flashing neon lights and they say, 'I'm a wanker', 'I don't give a shit', or 'I'm lazy'. You know who you are, so don't get comfortable here, you're not staying."

Within a year, 40% of the squadron personnel had moved on, the majority of them had actually asked for a posting because they realised he was right! If this was to be the elite unit he had described, a large number of the guys just didn't fancy it.

Danny's promise quickly took shape, with the levels of turnout, attitude, fitness, and self-pride rocketing as the weeks and months moved on.

Steve Marshall was an absolute standout SSM; immaculate, fit and a simply excellent role model, so youngsters like me had a real soldier to look up to and be mentored by.

My Troop SSgt, Ricky Garrod, was overly relaxed but a genuinely lovely guy. If he hadn't been coming to the end of his career, I am certain that Danny would have "moved him on" but he realised that Rick was good for morale, so he let him see out his time with us as he restructured the unit.

Despite the hatchet man job that Danny did on the squadron, everybody that served under him of any note would readily acknowledge that he built the unit from the ground up and in his own image. On the latter fact, this was even to the point of introducing the wearing of a green towelling neck scarf as a formal part of our working dress uniform; rumour had it that this had family connotations, as the scarves were made by his brother's company… To be honest, I didn't care as their only purpose from my point of view was to ensure we stood out from other units, and it certainly achieved that; I have long suspected that is exactly what the boss was seeking to achieve from the outset.

The fitness regime was incredibly ferocious, but the harder it became, the more the guys rose to the challenge. We did an hour of PT before lunch Monday to Thursday with Danny's "special treat" every Friday afternoon. The latter was always something extra demanding, such as jumping on the back of a fleet of 4-ton lorries that would whisk us off to the western end of the Kennet & Avon Canal where we would be dropped off and made to tab (run) back to Bulford Camp, some 30 miles. It was tough, and we always whinged about it, but secretly all enjoyed it. If nothing else, it prepared us for our inevitable attempt to drink Salisbury dry when we went out that evening.

The PT and fitness training bug really took hold, and the basic levels of fitness and competitiveness went through the roof. As a direct consequence, the squadron started to win almost every competition it entered, and not just in sport but activities such as shooting, vehicle maintenance and several other obscure things. These successes really put the squadron on the map which helped the whole rebuilding drive, with people joining 249 from the recognised specialist units, such as the Para and SAS Signal Squadrons, by choice, as opposed to pressure.

One such individual was Frank McAleer who arrived from 264 (SAS) Sig Sqn. A Cpl at the time, Frank was already a bit of a legend in the Corps. A monster Glaswegian, he wasn't the sort of guy you wanted to cross, unless you were equally as bonkers as he was, and there were some! To this day, R Signals folk tell stories about Frank, but the reality is most of them are embellished and not a true reflection of the man and his antics; if they knew what I knew and had witnessed, they would be very scared. Frank had joined us as a result of an assisted departure from the SAS squadron; this doesn't often happen but Frank was a one-off and may have dealt out his special punishment to the wrong person... When he first arrived, he wasn't in a good place; although he had somehow managed to hang on to his rank, he was drinking way too much. Most of us probably fell into that category, but we weren't all as intimidating as him and as most people realise, it can be a real pain to be the big guy that every drunk wally wants to fight.

Known affectionately as "Ug the Bug", Frank was the source of some great memories during our time together in 249. I am not going to try and capture them all; there are just too many.

Those that stand out though, include the time where the whole squadron was on parade ready to undertake a PT session on a Monday morning. The SSM was calling the roll and when he got to Cpl McAleer, there was an awkward silence; nobody said a word although everybody knew big Frank had been completely wasted the night before. Steve 'Snake' Marshall called the name out another couple of times, again to complete silence.

As we stood there, we could all hear a scraping, squeaky noise that could only be one of the old accommodation windows behind us being forced open. "Sir," came a loud response and we could all see the SSM's frozen expression of horror before he went apoplectic, screaming at two of the SNCOs on parade to "get him down here!".

We all looked behind us to see a large, hairy arse hanging out of a second-floor window.

"Ah, that's where Frank is!" commented George "Spartacus" Williamson, a close pal and drinking partner of Frank's. On joining the rest of us and once Snake Marshall had regained the power of speech, a still heavily inebriated Frank was left in no doubt that his entire future was dependent on his ability to complete this PT session, which he duly did and I for one will never understand how he did it. I did understand what Steve Marshall was doing though; the only other option he had was to discipline Frank, and that would probably have led to him being posted out. Steve Marshall knew a good soldier!

Pre-HARDFALL Training

Our annual trips to Norway were known as Ex HARDFALL and as you would expect, we undertook significant preparation for these deployments. This preparation known, unsurprisingly, as Pre-HARDFALL was, in itself, quite testing.

The training kicked off each year with the issue of our ski march boots around October. I suppose the one benefit of the boots being issued early was that it enabled us to break them in, the thought of doing that in the snow is not a good one; rather wet feet in UK than blistered, freezing feet in the Arctic. Initially, it simply consisted of wearing these boots to work and to undertake PT in, but the real training was conducted on the open, barren, but rocky environment of Dartmoor.

The annual trip down to Okehampton was a relatively slow, boring drive undertaken in convoy from Bulford along the infamous A303. Anybody who has travelled to Devon or Cornwall on holiday will know where I am coming from. Back in the late seventies and early eighties, there was very little along the route in terms of services, so that made the journey even more tedious. There was one reasonable stop which was big enough to take a lot of vehicles, and to be honest it probably provided a decent uplift in profits each time we drove in; it's truly amazing just how much food and drink soldiers can consume in a short space of time.

One instance stands out in my mind relating to my mate Frank and his very strong Glaswegian accent. Having arrived at one of the few service areas one day, we strolled in and sat at a table, smiling nicely at a pretty young waitress.

"What can I get you?" she asked sweetly. I recited my order which she recorded before repeating the question to Frank.

"Soup a ra day," says the big man.

"Yes," she says, "it's a beautiful day, but what can I get you?"

Looking confused, Frank repeats, "Soup a ra day,", which resulted in a very strange stare from the waitress.

I was almost wetting myself laughing, so I put her out of her misery. "He wants soup of the day!" I said, almost choking.

"Oh, I thought he was saying 'super day'!" she retorted, bursting into laughter. That lovely young waitress will probably never realise how lucky she was to be a girl; Frank was not impressed.

Okehampton Camp was a dull, uninspiring group of pre-war Nissen huts, but it was warm and dry with beds, so we knew only too well that we should enjoy this luxury before we were deployed out onto the moor. In reality, Dartmoor was often more challenging than Norway itself at this particular time of year: cold, wet, and regularly covered in impenetrable fog. The normal routine would be a series of training activities and a lot of physical training on camp, culminating in a challenging, gruelling exercise to test our skills. The moor provides some really testing terrain and when you marry that with the often-terrible weather, it is certainly fit for purpose as a pre-training location. We usually weren't allowed off camp during the week but that didn't stop the lads enjoying a few beers; the NAAFI bar was cheap and bribing the bar staff to stay open beyond the allocated hours was straightforward.

Another major benefit of the on-camp training phase is that it was fully catered, with army chefs serving up half-decent food. One morning, following an extended evening session in the bar, Frank and I headed over to the cookhouse for a nice greasy breakfast, famed for their recovery powers. I had previously noticed that a rather rotund chef from another unit liked to bully some of the lads by knocking food off the serving utensils if he thought they were taking a bit too much. He must have been bored that morning and his bully radar let him down very badly.

As Frank put a few sausages on his plate, "Porky" decided he was being greedy and reaching across the hot plate, he knocked the food off the plate and followed up by rapping Frank's bare knuckle with a large metal spoon; "Two sausages only," he said, loudly.

Very bad move by Porky, he couldn't have picked a more dangerous victim, even if Frank hadn't been suffering a bit from the night before. What ensued was one of the funniest scenes I have ever witnessed. The stupid smile on the chef's face didn't help his case. Without blinking, Frank stretched across the hot plate, grabbed both the guy's wrists and rams his hands into the pot of beans. Holding the culprit firmly in his grip for a couple of minutes, during which he was screaming at the top of his voice, Frank explained that the next time he saw Porky bullying anybody, it would be his head in the beans. The chef certainly didn't show any appetite for argument, as he ran to the nearest sink to immerse his hands in cold water. It was a bit of tough love, but I have always hated bullies and anybody whose target selection is that bad deserves everything he gets. I didn't see that particular slop jockey again during the exercise.

As always, the final exercise was a demanding one covering lots of ground in awful weather, almost constant fog and rain. Being truthful those conditions were extremely well suited to making map reading very difficult which, in turn, was excellent practice for the inevitable white-out conditions we would encounter in Norway. It certainly ensured that our physical fitness was also well-honed prior to our eventual deployment.

Another Norway

Frank became one of my very best friends and provided some of the funniest moments in my life, several of which fall into to the bracket of "squaddie humour", which others may find bemusing.

On one Norway trip, we had finished training in the south and had the usual huge piss-up the night before we were due to travel north to the Arctic Circle for the multinational exercise. Let's just say it was a heavy night and most of us, including Frank, staggered back to our accommodation blocks and flopped into bed. None of us had considered that the morning would see us handing back our accommodation and of course, our individual bedding; this was always a testing time in 249, as a significant number of my colleagues had, shall we say, bladders the size of a thimble.

It was a slow start to our preparation in the morning, with all the usual suspects trying to manoeuvre their mattresses into the darkest area of their bed space or doubling them over somehow expecting only half the mattress to be checked when handed back. These guys were sworn members of the 'Yangtze crew', all of whom could be relied upon to wet the bed at every opportunity. Frank, whilst not a founder member, had previously been awarded several canoe badges, having tipped into the Yangtze on occasion. He had been sleeping in the bunk above me, so I will be forever grateful that he had an absorbent mattress, otherwise I would have had a shower of the wrong type.

I noticed that Frank had jumped out of bed and placed his mattress flush against a very hot radiator. Smiling to myself, I thought, "Oh well, that's another canoe badge for Ug." The Squadron Quartermaster Sergeant (SQMS), Vic Shillingford, eventually made his way to our block and clearly a bit traumatised by his findings in the other blocks, he announced with his Caribbean twang that, "Anybody who piss the bed will be charged £100 to pay for a replacement." To say there were a few worried faces is an understatement.

Inevitably, Vic banked a few quid on his way through the block and when he got to Frank, he asked, "Why de mattress is resting against de radiator, man?"

Quick as a flash, Frank replied, "I was boiling the kettle for a brew, and it accidentally boiled over."

"Turn de mattress around," which Frank duly did. Vic then queried why he had been drinking yellow water and why he had a stain that looked like a map of Europe on his mattress.

Never one to give up easily, Frank retorted, "But I had a yellow ice lolly on my bed and the boiling water melted it..."

Vic, a genuinely fair man, simply replied, "If you can show me the wrapper, I will pay the £100 fine myself," at which point Frank accepted defeat.

Madcap Memories

I knew that I was very lucky to have been allocated to Key 3 as my first detachment. I couldn't have asked for a better Detachment Commander than Kev Froggett – he was experienced, highly capable and a natural mentor. Bob Martin was a bit more formal, but a good tradesman, nonetheless.

As mentioned, for the first 18 months, we were attached to the Alpini Bn, the Italian army's specialist mountain infantry. We had a lot of fun with them and to be honest, getting a half bottle of red wine, chocolate milk and excellent cheeses in your daily ration pack is quite a good motivator. The Italians never bothered us and were just happy to have communications available to them, particularly when we were stuck way up north in Norway, miles inside the Arctic Circle; they may have been mountain troops, but they weren't particularly keen on the cold.

As Kev and Bob moved on and I managed to get promoted, I eventually became Key 3 Detachment Commander but by that time we were supporting the US Bn and usually attached to "Hard Rock Charlie Coy". I learnt a lot during that part of my career; sadly, most of it was around racism and how disgustingly evident and institutionally embedded it is in the US military. I felt very uncomfortable around it but given the whole of Hard Rock Charlie company was black, the only time it raised its head was when white US troops were around. My crew were white, yet completely at ease with and accepted by everybody in the company. I coined a phrase from Robert Burns during my time with them, "A man's a man for a' that," which I have always taken as meaning, a man's colour, creed or beliefs do not affect his position in society; we are all the same, and I have stood by that throughout my life

On yet another annual pilgrimage to Norway, we were still in the south and taking part in survival training, which was always fantastic fun from my perspective. One of my best mates George Williamson and I – both qualified Nordic ski instructors – had led our groups to an area of dense pine forest in which we were overnighting. On arrival, it was snowing heavily, so we took our groups through the improvised shelter-building exercise fairly quickly and set them to work on constructing their bashers for the night. As always, there was a mixture of good, creative and downright awful examples, but it was clear the guys were extremely tired, so we let them get their heads down. We had been briefed that we were to RV later that evening with the other instructors at a location about a kilometre away, so we decided to get some kip ourselves before setting off.

It was still snowing heavily when we got out of our sleeping bags, so it didn't take long to get dressed and ready. George and I were both experienced skiers, so we weren't worried as we set off for the RV. As we skied along, it was a dark night which is fairly unusual in that region, but it was overcast so the amount of starlight normally available was greatly reduced. We must have travelled about 400-500m when I heard George shout, "Avalanche!" just as the ground slipped out from under my feet. I knew we were at the top of whatever had given way and it was a slab as opposed to powder, so we should be OK. It should still have been terrifying, but it's difficult to be scared when all you can hear is your mate screaming and laughing his head off as you slide down the mountain. After around 500m, we came to a halt, and I heard George shouting my name and saw his torchlight. We had to traverse back up the hill, but we arrived at the RV only 15 minutes late, so it was panic over.

Young officers joined the squadron on a regular basis, most of them doing a two-year tour and moving on; their posting cycle was designed to maximise their accumulated experience. Many of the soldiers, on the other hand, extended their tours from three years to as many as five or six years, such was the spirit of comradery in the unit. On one of the young officer changeovers, a guy called 2nd Lt Jim Barry arrived and took over as Troop Commander of Main Tp. There was something special about this bloke – he listened, which Sandhurst graduates aren't renowned for! He was curious, which you need in a youngster, but he actively sought answers from the experts whoever they were, paid attention to the answers, and learned how to get things done; the guys respected him for that. Of course, they didn't want him to know he had won their respect, so he was christened "Barry Bowfer" just to keep his feet firmly on the ground; after all, he was a sprog! Jim and I got on famously and by the end of my tour, we had built up a great bond. Mutual respect (and a couple of beers!) led us to agree that when he commanded his Regiment, I would be his RSM and that became a focal point in my career at that stage.

Mind you, my naivety did lead to him getting a huge bollocking from the OC at one point. As an ex-boy-RSM, I always took great pride in my turnout and that never changed throughout my career, but as a relatively young Cpl at this point, I decided that Jim was, to put it mildly, a bag of shite tied in the middle, so I decided it was time to smarten him up a bit.

"Sir, you are a bit of mess," I told him one day in the Tp office. "You need to sort yourself out."

"What do you suggest, Cpl Greig?" he asked.

"Bring in a spare set of working dress tomorrow," I said, "… and leave it to me, I'll get this sorted."

He brought the kit in the next day, handed it over and left me to it. Off I went to my tailor in Salisbury and explained what I wanted him to do with the kit. "Just do the usual sewn-in creases for the trousers and jersey sleeves," I said, "and taper the shirt and trousers; he's the same build as me."

Off I went, thinking what a favour I had done Jim and how pleased the boss would be that he had smartened up so much. Big mistake! The day after I gave Jim his kit back, he turned up looking like my twin and although I was very proud that I had turned a scruffy Rupert into an immaculate soldier, the OC didn't see it that way. What I had forgotten in my haste to help a bloke I really liked to make an impression, was that Jim wasn't a soldier, he was an officer and as such, wasn't expected to dress like an enlisted man. Soundly bollocked for his misguided attempt to smarten himself up, Jim quickly headed back to the mess and got changed, returning to the troop office looking like a typically dishevelled young officer. Interestingly, the OC never gave me a dressing down for my part in "Rupert Gate" and I am quite sure he understood my intention and forgave my naivety. A useful lesson for me and Jim.

Lads' Trip to Wales

My mate Taff had decided that he would invite a few of us down to his home in Llanelli for the christening of his son Gareth so Guy Benson, Frank McAleer, George Williamson and Wolfy, aka Gus Webster, and myself gratefully accepted.

On the Friday, all five of us packed my old bull-nosed Jag with kit, crammed ourselves in and set off for South Wales. It was like something out of the Cliff Richard film *Summer Holiday*, with five wallies setting off for the seaside. Anyway, despite the inevitable messing around, we eventually arrived in Llanelli at Taff's house. We quickly said hello and had a beer, after which Taff showed us to our B&B a couple of miles away. Frank seemed particularly annoyed by the fact that we weren't staying at Taff's house, but he could never have accommodated all of us.

We were allocated our rooms and decided we would get showered, changed and head back to join Taff. On arrival, Taff led us to his local pub which bizarrely was a terraced house four doors down from his own place. It felt strange to be sitting having a pint in somebody's front room, but it is supposedly quite common in that part of the world.

After a few pints in the strange "front room" pub, we decided to head off to Llanelli Rugby Club as there was some live music going on. When we arrived at the club it was absolutely full, and we had to push our way to the bar to get a drink. The atmosphere was great, and the next few hours flew past, but suddenly the crowd seemed to instantly disappear.

"Where has everybody gone?" we asked.

"They have gone upstairs for the bingo," the barmaid informed us.

By this time, we had all had quite a few beers and Frank was clearly feeling a bit restless, so he headed for the door; wondering where he was going, we all followed on. Up the stairs he went, with the rest of us right behind him. As he swung open some double doors, we saw loads of people seated and heard the bingo caller announce, "2 and 8!" but before he could say the number, Frank screamed out, "35! You boring arseholes, the bar's still open!" The silence was deafening, and I thought we were about to be beaten to death. Grabbing Frank and pulling him back through the doors, I prayed that nobody would follow and thankfully, they didn't, the game kicked back in. Leading Frank down the stairs, we headed back to the bar; I think we all needed a drink.

Back in the bar, we noticed a short tubby bloke standing by himself and decided to keep him company. Taff seemed to know him and for some reason he looked familiar to me, but I had never been to Llanelli in my life before. As we introduced ourselves, I realised I did know him. It was Max Boyce, the Welsh comedian; apparently this was one of his haunts. The next hour and a half were a feast of laughter.

Max was even funnier in the flesh than on TV and he just kept telling stories that were exceptionally funny. By the time the bingo crowd returned, it appeared as if they had mellowed and accepted Frank's intervention as a prank. Relieved, we kept on having a laugh with Max, who seemed to have no end to his supply of crazy anecdotes; he also seemed to be enjoying our company.

Everything seemed to be going well when I noticed Frank at the bar, staring directly at two man-mountains and then, unbelievably, drawing his finger across his throat! That's it, I thought, we are about to be murdered, killed in Llanelli of all places. As I looked over towards the two monsters, I saw one of them stand up and head directly towards Frank. Here we go, I thought, but amazingly, the guy put his arm around Frank's shoulder and they both start laughing together. A few minutes later, the other huge guy joined them at the bar and all three were having a drink together. To this day, Frank has never told me what it was about, but I was just glad to be in one piece at the time.

The rest of the evening passed without anymore "concerns", but that was probably because none of us retained the power of speech. On arrival back at Fawlty Towers, we all staggered back to our rooms and got our heads down. I did remember a little commotion in the early hours but was too wasted to care and fell back asleep quickly. I discovered the cause of the noise the next morning when I opened the window to get some fresh air, as George's clothes had somehow ended up in the middle of an enormous puddle, apparently the result of an argument as to who had which bed. I will let you guess who his room-mate was…

After enjoying a superb full Welsh breakfast, we decided to head off for a couple of beers before lunch. In reality this was just a top-up, as none of us were anywhere near sober following the night before. Having supped a few pints and grabbed a light lunch, we headed back to our digs, got changed and set off for Taff's house. I don't know what Taff must have thought as the two taxis arrived outside his house and we spilled out; probably, "Why on earth did I invite this lot?!" We had a quick cup of tea and headed off for the christening. The event was quite short and went very well, after which we again headed back to Taff's to celebrate and for a bite to eat.

We were all having a great time when we noticed Taff had disappeared and as we looked around, Frank too was nowhere to be seen. Sitting around swinging the lamp is something all servicemen love, but as we did so with Taff's family in front of the fire, we began to hear some very strange noises. I think most of us realised as we tried to drown the noise out by talking louder, that somebody was being beaten up.

After a few minutes, Frank reappeared and without a blink started to engage in the conversation.

"What was that strange noise?" asked one of Taff's family.

"Oh, nothing," replied Frank. "I was just talking to Taff when he fell off the bed. I've sorted it so he's asleep now."

Very unconvincing, I thought, and looking at the other guys, I knew they agreed. So, we quickly drank up and decided it was time to head back to the B&B; it had been a long day.

The next day, we packed our things up and for some daft reason, headed down to Taff's to say thanks and then head home. Taff had clearly fallen on to a fist the night before, but either didn't remember or just chose not to say anything; he claimed he had hit a piece of furniture as he fell, but I don't think any of the lads bought it. Having said our goodbyes, we all jumped into the Jag and headed home to Bulford Camp.

On quizzing Frank in the car, he admitted he had to sort Taff out, as the B&B had been an unexpected cost and he felt Taff should have forewarned him. I think it was a bit harsh, but given squaddie humour, we all laughed our heads off.

In the army, it is common practice to have specialist personnel, such as cooks, mechanics and logistics staff, attached to units to fill key roles. In 249, we had some real characters in such posts, but the one that sticks in my mind most is a Scottish chef. Mac, as we christened him, almost predictably liked a beer, but usually in very large quantities which often resulted in him being found completely comatose in a range of bizarre locations. Sober, he was a great guy, but as he drank, he became ever increasingly crazy, becoming quite dangerous along the way. His normal resting place on Saturdays, when not on shift, was the gutter at the top edge of Salisbury Market Square, just outside what was then the City Arms (now the Ox Row). Because we all liked Mac, we used to take it in turns to swing past the pub and recover him on a Saturday afternoon, either driving him back to Bulford or putting him on the bus where the bus driver would allow it.

However, Mac had a troubled relationship with Steve Marshall, the SSM, and this often led to very disruptive but inevitably funny encounters. On one particular deployment to Norway, the local kids were often found hanging around the camp; nobody was too bothered as they were well behaved, but little did we realise why they were so interested in being there. We found out in rather embarrassing fashion during a visit by a senior officer from UK.

The OC and SSM greeted the visitor on his arrival by helicopter and as they made their way to the squadron HQ, Steve Marshall decided to impress our guest by demonstrating how friendly the local kids were. On passing a group of the kids, Steve wished them all a hearty "Good morning, children," to be met by a resounding "Fuck off, asshole bandit!" in very clear English. As you can imagine, Steve was absolutely mortified, not to say somewhat embarrassed by the response. I guess he must have found out later that Mac had been running some very 'rudimentary' English lessons, but I think Mac escaped punishment as Steve couldn't gather any concrete evidence.

Another legendary escapade saw Mac achieving the relatively impossible; he managed to melt the ice cream for pudding, remarkable at -30°C. During his preparation for dinner, Mac had been secretly imbibing, or as he saw it, testing the quality of the local beer which was to be sold in the squadron bar. Consequently, his culinary timings were somewhat impacted. He had removed the ice cream carton from the freezer and placed it on the worktop, to ensure it was sufficiently soft to serve. But having placed it alongside a fully lit field gas cooker and left it for 20 minutes, even the outside temperatures of -30°C couldn't prevent the inevitable!

My Love Affair with Haukeliseter

I first visited Haukeliseter Fjellstue when we were on exercise, using it as a base location. It is a mountain hotel relatively close to the town of Hovden on the edge of the Hardangervidda, a mountain plateau in south central Norway. It is set in a truly beautiful place, just below the plateau, and has been run by the same family for decades. One of the staff is a chap called Carlos, a Portuguese ex-sailor with a well-travelled history; he had even lived in Dudley in the West Midlands! I mention this not because of any knowledge or love of Dudley, but rather the fact that it had allowed Carlos to develop outstanding English which was very helpful.

The snow can be so heavy there that I have seen the hotel and outbuildings completely covered beyond their roofs, which meant that on many occasions, Carlos and Morten (the current owner) had to dig themselves out. If they were off-site for any reason, they also had to dig themselves in! Often, the approach roads are so blocked that you are required to travel between tunnels, following a snowplough as they clear the road in front, only for the roads to block again behind you immediately. Since that time, I have had the opportunity to set up and run adventure training skiing expeditions on the Hardangervidda twice, once whilst serving in 201 Sig Sqn and again when I was with 11 Sig Bde. These were very challenging but rewarding times; knowing Morten certainly helped me to keep my costs down in a country famed for its very expensive cost of living. I will tell these stories individually and in chronological order as my memoir unfolds.

Luckily, we didn't suffer too many injuries on our trips to Norway, a few breakages over the years but nothing life-threatening. On a personal note, the scariest thing that happened to me, was when we were deployed to Ness Fortress up in the Arctic. It was a particularly harsh winter with extreme snow conditions, and I hadn't been wearing my snow glasses as regularly as I should have been. I finished a shift and went to bed feeling tired but with no other issues, then unfortunately I woke up unable to see, which is a frightening experience. I felt it was probably snow blindness, but it still hadn't worn off a couple of hours later so my fellow crewman summoned help on the radio. As our location was very remote, the HQ arranged for a local mountain rescue team to call in; luckily for me, they confirmed temporary snow blindness and said it would clear up in a few hours, which it did. They also told me in a very polite Norwegian way not to be so daft again and wear my goggles every time I went outside. I took their advice!

Military Training in Catterick

The first post-Harrogate military training we had to undertake was the Royal Signals Detachment Commander's Course (RSDCC) held at 11 Sig Regt in Catterick, North Yorkshire. The course was for JNCOs, and they were required to achieve a pass before they could hold the substantive rank of Cpl, so it was hugely important for those that sought to build a career in the Corps. I had never liked Catterick, but the course was essential and whenever we got a free weekend, I jumped in my car and headed off to visit family in Sunderland, 44 miles up the A1.

Talking about cars, I travelled up to Catterick in my yellow Ford Capri, which had been custom sprayed and had a huge

JPS (John Player Special cigarettes) logo on the power bulge on the bonnet. My mate, Paul Norrie, one the Lineys in the squadron, was travelling with me. As we were winging our way up the M18 in the fast lane, we heard a loud blast and I lost all power; luckily, the motorway was quiet and Paul was able to jump out and push me onto the hard shoulder, but the engine had gone. Trust me, pushing a car from the fast lane onto the hard shoulder is a bit frightening; ask Paul!

Our arrival at Helles Barracks, the home of 11 Sig Regt, drew a few strange looks and some laughter but that's life, we got there in time for the course: bonus! The course was intense but also very enjoyable, with lots of drill which, given my antics with Ron Hails in the indoor arena in Harrogate, was a very strong activity for me. That cut me some useful slack with the drill instructor, who was probably second only to Ron in his ability and quality in that space, although I chose not to mention this to him. Failing this course is a real career stopper and while I was always very confident that I would pass, anybody can get injured and if serious enough they may be returned to their unit. So, you guessed it, during a drill session I drove my right heel down so hard, I felt huge pain sear through my foot; I knew it was serious, but I chose to avoid reporting it otherwise I would have been sent home. The next day was a Friday, so as soon as we finished work I set off for Sunderland Royal Infirmary with a mate. I had an X-ray which revealed a break, so I knew that I couldn't say anything back in Catterick. The medics gave me some thick foam insoles and strong painkillers, so it was just a case of whether I could hack the pain during drill and walk properly if I was to stay on the course. If the instructors found out, it was probably game over.

Luckily for me, we were moving on to the final exercise at Warcop ranges, where your performance on command tasks is assessed over the week, and then your scores for in-barracks and exercise work is combined to provide a final score. Warcop is usually a horrible, cold, wet place at the time of year I attended the course, and it didn't disappoint. The ground was absolutely sodden and that potentially saved my neck; albeit my heel hurt, I was walking and running over soft heathland which took a lot of the impact away.

I made it through the exercise and the last real challenge was the drill teaching practices which were to be held on our return to camp. There were other tests but not of any real physical challenge, so I felt I could make it. I knew my experience in drill could help me blag my way through, because I had long perfected the drill voice, my personal drill was good, albeit I would need to be very careful when driving my foot in, and I knew the teaching practices inside out.

The day came and having put a few more studs into the sole of my boots, I didn't need to worry about the sound on impact with the ground; the challenge was to try not to show the pain I felt whilst going through the actions. I made it and got an exceptional review from the Drill Instructor. Two days later, I was on a train to Scotland and my home village where my girlfriend Susan was having her 21st birthday party in the family pub run by two of her aunts. By the time I arrived back in Salisbury, my heel was well on the way to a full recovery, but I often thought about what might have been and the impact it could have had on my career.

Military training courses brought a lot of benefits and not just the obvious lessons in soldiering. Over the years, many people have asked me why servicemen are often so comfortable with the delivery of presentations and public speaking in general. The simple truth is rooted in courses such as the aforementioned one, where it was common practice to be given an obscure item, such as a pencil, with no warning and then be told to deliver a 15-minute presentation on it to a class a couple of minutes later. For many, this would be their idea of purgatory, but for those who have undertaken such an exercise, weaving a story that might discuss the source of the wood used in the pencil, how it was planted, grown, farmed, cut down, and then transported to a factory in which it would be used to produce pencils... easily eats up 15 minutes; it also grows courage and confidence in addressing an audience. Simple things can have a life-long benefit.

RSSDC 1979 –
I am fourth from the right, rear rank

Old Habits Die Hard

Whilst the squadron went from strength to strength as a highly professional, super fit and immensely capable military unit, some things never changed. The legendary partying was still an important part of our end of exercise routine and kept the 'Yangtze Club' alive and well.

On our way back from an exercise in southern Germany, we had planned a blowout at an overnight stop in Belgium and were all looking forward to it on the long drive north towards the channel ports. Unfortunately, the autobahns were very busy, and we didn't make it to the Belgian camp till 10 pm, to be met by the disastrous news that the bar was just closing; this clearly pleased the senior personnel who, quite rightly, were thinking of the drive in the morning. However, where there is a will, there is a way; one of the guys had quickly contacted the bar staff and offered a suitable bribe to keep the bar open. Grabbing a bed in the accommodation, kit was rapidly dropped off and a swift entry made to a dimly lit drinking hole.

It was quite a funny scenario where we all agreed that we must keep the noise down or risk being rumbled and ordered to bed. As you will probably have guessed, the quiet period lasted around an hour which is a miracle when you consider that we hadn't touched a drink for around a month. The gradual increase in volume, fired mainly by the singing of "Get 'em down, you Zulu warrior!" eventually reached the required decibel level to wake anybody within five miles of the site and very shortly thereafter the duty Sgt arrived and evicted everybody. If my memory serves me correctly, the unfortunate Sgt was Pete Clarke and to be blunt, it isn't the type of task I would wish on my worst enemy.

I doubt very much that anyone could remember how they got back from the bar that night, but the problem was always going to be the morning after. I have always had a strong constitution and a remarkable ability to recover quickly from a night on the tiles, but many do not!

Following the early morning call from the duty Sgt, I got up without putting the main light on and headed off for a shower. On my return to the shared room, I remembered two of the empty beds had belonged to Taff and Skully, who had clearly gone for a shower, shave or whatever. Then it dawned on me; those guys were the founder members of the 'Yangtze Club' and were very unlikely to have made it through the night without having swamped their beds.

Panicking, I quickly checked my mattress to see if it had been switched, which was one of their tricks; luckily, it hadn't. Skully, who was first back to the room, literally tore Taff's sheets off and at lightning speed, he swapped his mattress for Taff's, laughing like a maniac as he did so. Taff returned just as the SQMS was starting the accommodation handover which, of course, included a bedding check, so he had to hurriedly pull his kit on and tidy his bed up before it was our turn. I wondered why Taff was looking so concerned as the SQMS bloke checked his bed, declaring it "pissed wet" but it was Skully's smug little face that made me chuckle as the SQMS checked his bed which, to Skully's complete surprise, was also dripping wet. I guess the moral of the story is don't swap a pissed mattress with somebody who spends more time using his as a latrine than you do. Poetic justice really, and £100 each for their trouble!

Class 1 Tradesman

In my trade, Radio Telegraphist, we left Harrogate as Class 3 tradesmen and although upgrade to Class 2 was an in-unit exam, it could take several years before you were afforded an opportunity to attain Class 1 status. This course, termed your A1, was run at the R Signals training establishment, 8 Sig Regiment, in Catterick, North Yorkshire, which as I have mentioned, was one of my least favourite locations on the planet. It did have a number of pubs and a nightclub, but these places are not quite the same when the vast majority of revellers are the same folk you see at work day in, day out, with the remainder largely being squaddies from other units in the garrison. It inevitably led to some pretty ferocious evenings, as the various units tried to outdrink and outfight each other, but there wasn't a lot of enjoyment or relaxation to be had.

Luckily, I had a fantastic group of guys on my course, so we managed to stick together, have a laugh and occasionally go out together to significantly more enjoyable locations. As my mum's side of the family came from Sunderland, I used to grab a couple of the guys and head off up there most weekends. We tended to visit my Auntie Georgina on Farringdon estate, although I did have family on most of the estates in the town, so did have some options. Georgina had been married to my mum's brother Geordie, although they were separated and heading for a divorce. Her new bloke Ronnie was a bit of a character and although Geordie was undoubtedly my favourite uncle, I got on well with Ronnie. My cousins from Geordie and Georgina's marriage were also the closest relatives I had beyond my immediate family in Scotland.

There was little doubt that "Uncle" Ronnie thought all his Christmases had come at once during my A1; he was out of work and seemed very happy to be so, but that meant beer tokens were in very short supply. So, as you can imagine, three or four young squaddies turning up for a weekend of debauchery was a dream come true – he just tagged along! To be fair, we usually ended up carrying him home from whatever pub or club we ended up in; quite often this was the local working men's club where the beer was so cheap, it was almost free. Once we had thrown him into bed, the next phase was usually to spend most of the night consuming vast quantities of our carry-out, making things up to Georgina and preventing her from beating the hell out of Ronnie. She was a great sport and always took fantastic care of us during our stay.

I have so many crazy memories of that time, but one that will always stay with me relates to my car. I had a terrible black Cortina Mk3 with a dodgy engine and on one of our journeys up to the north-east, the engine gave up the ghost and I had to have it recovered to Sunderland. It was a lovely bright day when we arrived, and my cousin Gary and a couple of his mates were sitting in the garden having a great laugh as we arrived on the back of a recovery truck. They quickly offered us some cold beer and we simply got stuck in.

The subject of my car's engine did crop up, of course, and one of Gary's mates chipped in with a "Dinit worry, man, a've got a spare one in me garage." With that statement, he finished his beer and headed off, returning about 10 minutes later with two of his brothers carrying a Ford Cortina 1600 engine. After agreeing a price of "five pund," he then proceeded to open my bonnet, undo the appropriate bolts and disconnect a few things, then with help from his brothers and me, lifted the old engine out and put it on the pavement. He quickly got us to lift the other engine into place and commenced to fit it, after which he quickly did a bit of strobe testing and tuning the "new" engine. Amazingly, within an hour and a half of arriving on the back of an AA truck, my car had an engine swap, was tuned up and ticking over perfectly; I couldn't help but wonder how on earth he had achieved that. Talking of wondering how the engine change had been possible, I decided not to spend too much time thinking about where the engine had come from.

Having returned from one of our R&R trips, I was asked to phone Sgt John "Salty Dog" Salter back in Bulford. Salty was the chief Liney, so I really had no idea what he could be after; maybe he was the Duty SNCO and needed to pass a message on. Having located a phone that I got authority to use, I spoke to him and he had some very bad news that he wanted to share. One of my mates, L/Cpl Stevie Richmond, had died whilst taking part in a tug of war competition on Wednesday Sports afternoon. Steve was a great lad, and everyone was absolutely devastated; he was only in his mid-late twenties, married but mercifully, with no children. Salty Dog knew that I would want to attend Steve's funeral and that given he was from Sunderland, it wasn't too far (little did he know of our regular trips to the town). Promising to let me know the details when they were available, he wished me all the best and apologised for having to give me the bad news. I will always appreciate that call and I could tell just how upset Salty was, he had just lost one of his own team.

The following week, having cleared the Friday off to attend the funeral, I set off for Sunderland. I didn't know the estate that Steve had lived on, but on arrival I went to Georgina's as usual, knowing there would be a bed for me. My cousin Gary drove me to the church where I met up with a group of the lads who had travelled up from Salisbury to attend the funeral. We were all dressed in our No 2 Dress, which is a ceremonial uniform and were looking exceptionally smart; Steve's parents had decided that the coffin would be carried by family as opposed to colleagues, but I know they were so pleased that we were in uniform for the ceremony. As you would imagine, there was a wake which was very well attended and as Steve's mates we decided to see him off in style (as we saw it).

Despite consuming copious quantities of alcohol, none of us got particularly drunk, perhaps a result of high adrenalin levels or just wanting to celebrate our mate's life without embarrassing his family or ourselves. However, the local guys didn't behave in a similar way and made it clear that if we hadn't disappeared by a set time, they would not be happy. So, using better judgement, we said our goodbyes and left quietly. I jumped into a cab and headed back to Farringdon, whilst the other lads set off for their B&Bs.

My A1 finished a couple of weeks later and I headed off back to Salisbury in my rather unreliable Cortina; at this stage, it had developed a problem which would not allow me to go over 60 mph, so it was quite a long trip. As I always did, I planned to sell the car on or scrap it, dependent on its condition when I arrived back in my unit. I had only been back a week, and hadn't decided on the car's future, when one of the lads offered me £500 for it; sold! Happy days!

Mountain Leader

Although still relatively young, I had qualified as an instructor in all three skiing disciplines, albeit Nordic ski touring was most definitely my favourite. This didn't go unnoticed within the squadron, and I was given the opportunity to attend a winter Mountain Leadership course at the British Outward-Bound Centre (BOBC) just north of Kristiansand, near Evje in Norway, which really appealed to me, so I quickly said yes. I had to travel to BOBC before the squadron deployed on the annual exercise in Norway, and it was agreed that I would travel to join the squadron by train via Oslo after I completed the course.

Evje was just as beautiful as all the other Norwegian towns and villages I had visited, and it was exciting to be joining an All Arms course with students drawn from across the army. Competition across the army is always fierce and that helps drive you on when the going gets tough, and I had absolutely no doubt that this course would deliver plenty of challenges. There was no rank used on the course, the only stipulation in that space was that students referred to the instructors as staff. I had no problem with that, as my instructor was SSgt Phil Watkins who was an awesome character and like quite a few of the staff, he was a Physical Training Instructor (PTI). He had been one of our boxing instructors in Harrogate, so I had no desire to upset him!

The course content was remarkably varied, with weather patterns, survival techniques, shelter construction, clothing, improvised stretcher construction, and much more. It was also quite a social course with time found for games' evenings where the student teams competed against each other and the instructors. This was great for morale which, of course, is a very strong component of any leadership training. I wasn't quite so keen on the singing and acting activities, which we referred to as "smokers", probably because I can't sing.

We were certainly extremely well-prepared before the practical exercise came around, something I was very much looking forward to. As we set off with large, full backpacks on our very well-prepared skis, all I could think of was how much better they were than the NATO planks I was used to with my unit. Navigation is never easy in arctic conditions, but the reality of compass usage remains the same; trust your compass.

On Day 1 of the expedition, we were heading to a DNT (Tourist Board) hut which many may think would be very easy – wrong! Particularly when the hut is completely covered in snow. Phil Watkins asked me how close we were to the hut as I was leading in late afternoon.

"It's over there, staff," I gesticulated, hoping beyond hope that I wasn't kidding myself.

"I can't see it," he said, smiling broadly. We covered another 100m and I brought the group to a halt, tasking three team members to join me in digging to find the hut whilst the others got a brew going. I was cock-a-hoop when one of the team struck the roof after about 10 minutes; Phil didn't say much, but I am sure he was pleased.

We continued to dig down to the hut and eventually cleared the doorway. The equipment inside the hut was amazing with beds, bedding, canned food and a supply of wood for the fire under a shelf in a small side room. Most impressive of all was the honesty box in which those using the facilities deposited their payment before leaving; it was stuffed with cash and I must admit, I considered whether it might be a little lighter if we were back home. I think understanding that these huts save lives made a very significant difference, although I never once doubted the honesty of the Norwegian people or their visitors.

The next day, we took a detour past some pretty impressive waterfalls, and on arrival we were invited to have a brew before we undertook a bit of snow and ice climbing. Whilst climbing wasn't one of my preferred activities, I had never experienced this variant of it and wondered just how different this would be from standard rock climbing. The answer is very different, although I wholly admit the height and gradient of the climb was much less than I had previously experienced in rock climbing. I found the crampons worked well and the ice axe or "brake", dependent on how you see things, gave me a lot of extra confidence. I thoroughly enjoyed the experience and decided it was something I would happily repeat in the future.

That evening we arrived at a second DNT hut which was somewhat easier to locate, as it was only sitting in four to five feet of snow and you could see its roof from some distance away. We enjoyed another very comfortable night, albeit collecting the snow for melting to produce water was a bit more challenging as you had to go out in the howling wind to do so.

Day 3 was expected to be significantly harder as we knew we were sleeping in a snow hole that night. I had built and slept in lots of snow holes/snow caves, so I was quite relaxed, but aware that the type of construction could make a huge difference. However, the weather decided to put us under the cosh, and we spent most of the time in a complete white-out; to be honest, I don't think even Phil Watkins really knew exactly where we were, the visibility was just so bad! I never asked Phil, but I suspect he called it when we reached a good snow holing area, a good slope with no overhanging cornice. Unfortunately, the instruction was to build a team cave, whereas I had hoped we would go for two to three-person snow holes which was my preference, the main reason being if one collapses, those in separate holes can quickly dig their colleagues out. Luckily, we didn't have any collapses and the weather had vastly improved overnight, so we grabbed a quick breakfast, broke camp, and set off on our way.

The next two days went fairly quickly, and we were back in Evje before we knew it. I think I am right in saying everybody thoroughly enjoyed the expedition, learned much more than they had expected, and were secretly quite sad that the course was all but over. That night we held an end of course party which was great fun, and the following morning we each had a final interview in which we were given our grades. I was ecstatic to pass the course and happily set off to join my squadron further north.

As I mentioned, I was travelling from Kristiansand to Oslo by train and then on to the squadron location. As there was only one train to Alesund per day, I was required to overnight in Oslo and I had been booked into the Permanalen Club, which I was looking forward to.

As I settled into my seat on a very clean, well-presented train, I was looking forward to joining up with my mates and to be putting some of my new skills to use. The end of course function the night before had added to the tiredness that had accumulated during the expedition so, unsurprisingly it didn't take long before I drifted off to sleep.

I was jolted back to my senses as loud gasps filled the carriage. I thought I was dreaming as I looked out of the window to see monsters on skis chasing somebody down a steep slope at breakneck speed. One of my fellow passengers spotted my mouth hanging open and put me out of my misery.

"They are characters from *Star Wars*!" she told me. "They are filming here at the moment!" That was good to know as I had feared I had lost the plot!

The rest of the journey passed without further incident and as we pulled into Oslo's main station, I could hardly believe my eyes; we were on time to the minute, something Brits are just not used to. I jumped in a taxi and headed off to the hotel which wasn't too far away, although the fare was an unpleasant surprise; at least I could claim it back, I thought.

On arrival, I was quite impressed by the building, so I quickly parted with a wad of cash, grabbed my kit and got checked in. The room was very comfortable and after a welcome shower I headed downstairs for something to eat. The food in Norway isn't particularly exciting but there was a steak on the menu, so that made my decision easy. After dinner, I popped into the bar for a beer, but at 80 Krone (c£8) per beer, I drank it slowly; remember this was 1979 so the price was excessive.

Up early the next morning, I was getting on the train at 9 am and again we pulled out of the station at 9.15 am exactly, heading north-west to Alesund which was another long haul. I was met at my final destination by one of the squadron drivers who took me to the camp we were using during our training period. It was good to be back with the guys. The squadron training went exceptionally well, and I was delighted to be playing an evermore prominent part on the instructional side.

Commissioning Revisited

One day back in Bulford, the SSM, Steve Marshall, sent for me and hoping I wasn't in trouble, I headed over to his office in the headquarters.

"Come in, Cpl Greig," he shouted as he saw me from the mirror, strategically placed above his door, as part of his monitoring system. I marched into his office, not knowing what lay ahead of me.

"Close the door," he said in a very calm voice. Now I was worried! He may have been a little guy, but I had no doubt he could handle himself and the usual reason for closing a door in such situations was to lamp the miscreant for some wrongdoing.

"Do you want to be an officer?" he asked.

Bemused by the question, I replied "Yes, Sir, once I have reached Warrant Officer Class 1."

"I meant, do you want to attend the Regular Commission Board (RCB) in your current rank and if successful, go to Sandhurst as an Officer Cadet?"

Whilst I wasn't sure why the SSM had raised the question, I informed him that such an offer had been made to me in Harrogate when I achieved the rank of A/T RSM just before my Graduation Parade, and I had said no as my ambition was to be promoted through the ranks.

Steve was undoubtedly pleased by my answer and went on to tell me about a plan the OC, Danny Fisher, had to get me commissioned as quickly as possible, and that he wanted me to be brought in for a chat the following day. The funny bit is that Steve then made me promise never to refer to the conversation again; this was a guy who was as loyal to his boss as any SSM could ever be and he was taking this chance, because he felt that the move would not be right for me. I knew at the time that he was right, particularly as I had been through the thought process a few years earlier and had quickly come to the same conclusion. As anybody who has been a WO1 will tell you, there is something very special about the rank, and to be commissioned from that position, as far as I was concerned, was proof that you were the best of the best.

Danny Fisher was one of the finest officers I ever served with and when he spoke, I tended to listen. During my interview the next day, I explained the previous situation at Harrogate but as far as he was concerned, it was just a case of timing and whilst I hadn't been ready first time around, he felt that I was now. I think there was an element of keeping the peace from my perspective, but I decided that in line with the boss' request, I would attend the pre-RCB and give it my best shot. From there he said that he would respect any future decision that I made.

The actual course, held at Catterick Garrison, was without a doubt the worst experience of my military career to that point. I was the only serving soldier on a course of 16 people, the majority of whom were decent folk and were there to give their best. Having been assured that we were all in the same position, I was then referred to by my rank by all the instructors whilst they used the first names of

94

the other students. I was also very disappointed when I was not invited to an introduction to the officers' mess. I put everything I had into the course and will always be proud that I was recommended to progress to RCB. Professionally though, my treatment had hurt, and this reinforced my view that the route to commission for me was progress through the ranks.

When I got back to 249, the SSM had left a sticky note on my bunk door asking me to go and see him as soon as I arrived. Again, behind a closed door, he made it clear to me that the OC was pleased by what feedback he had already received and was anticipating a complete change of heart on my part with me embracing the RCB stage. Steve himself was cock-a-hoop that I was even more determined not to follow this path, but both of us realised that the next discussion with Danny would be a very tricky one and that it could potentially be career-limiting for me.

"Just to give you some added confidence," he added, "I spoke to Ron Hails a couple of days ago and he agrees with our stance." He didn't need to say anything else; between them, these two guys had driven my career and made me the soldier I was, if indeed I was any good. "Same rules on the discussion, George," he said, but there was never any chance I would let him down.

The next morning, the SSM marched me into the OC's office and then left the room so that I could talk openly to the boss. After a very upbeat introduction by Danny, I thought it best to cut to the chase and simply stated my position as unchanged and my intention to be commissioned as a WO1. I didn't think it appropriate to burden him about the rank versus name issue, nor my omission from the mess invite. I had absolutely no doubt that if I had done, he would have investigated and rectified it for the future, but it wasn't for me, so I buried it. The best thing of all, is that it made no difference to my relationship with the OC, and he continued to be a big influence on my career until I left the unit. He even gave me approval to get married when I requested it; yes, that was a prerequisite in those days!

I have mentioned the quality of the SSM, Steve Marshall, and recognised how much he did for me as a young NCO making my way through military life, something I will never forget. Together with Ron Hails, these guys were my heroes and I think the connection was simply based on a common denominator: all three of us were army barmy. Steve liked to walk around the barracks, talking to people he saw, whether they were soldiers or families.

He did make a grave error one day on his walk about though; one of the lads, christened "Fag Ash Lil" by his colleagues, as he was never without a roll up in his mouth, was walking to work with his wife and child. As they got closer, Steve shouted, "Morning, Fag Ash!" in a jaunty voice.

Sadly, this was his first encounter with this rather feisty wife who decided that she didn't like the nickname. "Fuck off, you little snake!" she shouted at the top of her rather loud voice. "His name's Tony!"

I think that was the first and only time I ever saw Steve Marshall looking sheepish, turning quickly on his heel, and legging it out of sight. I'm not sure what Fag Ash thought, but I would imagine he had a bollocking in the bank for later.

As an RTg, security featured very highly in my role with a need to handle lots of information of varying security classifications. In addition, a significant amount of HF, VHF and SHF radio traffic required encryption, so gaining a crypto qualification was another sensible move.

Despite another trip to Catterick, I was delighted to be selected to attend a course; it added another string to my bow and in your early career it is so important to keep developing your skill set, adding flexibility to your employability. The course isn't exactly a barrel of laughs and to be blunt, it was extremely turgid at times, but it is a very worthwhile undertaking that teaches a skill that is essential in meeting the Corps', and indeed, the army's needs. Some of those that attend the course realise that they are suited to it as a speciality, to the point that they spend the rest of their careers in the role. That was not something that I would ever have considered, but I must give a shout out to several of those that did. These guys inevitably worked hard for me in future years, and I owe several of them a real debt of gratitude. Crypto isn't an area in which mistakes are forgiven, so having a team that can be relied upon in that space is an absolute blessing. Personally, I had had my fill by the end of the course and headed back to Bulford before the need for a frontal lobotomy overtook me.

We never missed an opportunity for a knees-up, so when Wally Callow's birthday came round without the usual fanfare one year, we hastily arranged a trip to Southampton. It was a fresh afternoon as we all piled into the minibus taking us to Southampton for the party. There was Wally (obviously), Guy Benson, Frank, Geordie Simpson, myself and a few others, and I had no doubt that the evening would be a great laugh, with a few pints thrown in. The driver dropped us off in the city centre and we poured into the first bar we spotted, being as selective as ever; mind you, our selection criteria was never too exacting. We proceeded to tour the pubs and clubs having a great laugh along the way, but eventually we noticed that we had lost Frank and Guy, a dangerous combination when they had consumed a lot of alcohol. Showing predictable concern, we thought they would catch us up and got stuck back into our party. The hours passed and unfortunately Frank and Guy didn't reappear, so we had a quick sweep of the local area, decided they had met some girls and jumped in our minibus. As we headed back to Bulford, those that could stay awake lamented on how lucky our missing colleagues had been, telling each other how much we envied them.

Meanwhile, back in 'party city', Frank and Guy, realising that they had missed the bus home, were searching for some overnight accommodation. Sadly, they were somewhat limited, having no money left between them. Ever the optimists, they decided to swing past Southampton Central railway station to see if they could strike some kind of deal to get a train back to Salisbury, not realising that the last train had left over an hour before. There was one bonus though: the tramp who had offered them a quick swig of his beer didn't mind when they borrowed his carry-out and ran off.

The lads had an idea and decided to head into one of the city's tower blocks. They headed to the top floor; perhaps they were remembering that heat rises! On arriving at the top of the block, they decided to just stay there, so Frank lay down on a doorstep and put the doormat over (a very small part of) himself for the night. They must have made a bit too much noise because the owner came to the door, at which point Frank asked, "Any chance of a brew?" The request was met by a very robust slamming of the door, rather unsurprisingly. They managed to make it back to camp the next day having caught a train, under what circumstances we will never know, but bet your bottom dollar we took the mickey for many months to follow!

Turkish Sunshine

I think Turkey was my last exercise with 249 and I had volunteered to go with a small advance and recce party with Lt Jim Barry, my Tp Comd, and a young Sig called Mark. We flew into Istanbul, unloaded our Land Rover and trailer, and headed over the Bosphorus into Asian Turkey. After several hours of a boring drive, we arrived at our destination, the town of Çorlu, where we were to spend the next two weeks in a hotel on the edge of town. I was absolutely delighted with the accommodation, as I had fully expected to be in a sweltering tent. Whilst the hotel probably wouldn't have secured too many stars by British standards, it had large fans, superb staff and comfortable beds; happy days! Mark and I quickly set up our long-range HF radio link, stretching our horizontal dipole antenna from the wall of our hotel to what appeared to be the only telegraph pole anywhere in sight.

As the first few days passed, the staff at the hotel just got friendlier and because I love my tea, it became a bit of a competition between the waiters to see who could fill my empty cup the quickest, hence my ongoing love of Turkish tea (no milk, one sugar).

On Day 4, Lt Jim Barry and I drove out into the desert to meet with a couple of Turkish Liaison Officers (LOs) who were to join us on some site recces. At lunchtime, we stopped alongside a tree line to take some shade and grab something to eat. We sat under the trees – me, Jim, two Turkish officers and their driver, a Private soldier, albeit he sat a little distance away from the rest of us. After we had eaten our respective ration packs, one of the Turkish officers asked if we would like some karpuz (watermelon); unsurprisingly in 40°C+, we all said yes. The officer shouted something in Turkish and the driver jumped up, went to his truck, and came back with an enormous karpuz and an equally large machete. He deftly chopped it up and handed large pieces to each of us. I'm not usually a fan of watermelon but given the heat, I quickly devoured it after which I went behind a tree for a pee.

When I got back, the same officer asked whether I had been offered some more karpuz to which I replied no but before I could explain that I had gone to the toilet, he angrily lashed out with a riding crop, striking the Turkish driver across the face. It must have been agony and left a bright red wield across his face; to say I was mortified would be a massive understatement. I wanted to punch the Turkish Rupert in the mouth, which I think Jim Barry had some sympathy with.

"What on earth did you do that for?" I shouted at the Turkish officer with the crop.

"He should have offered you some more karpuz, you are a guest!" he replied.

"And you should have listened to my answer fully before hitting him!" I said.

The other Turk stepped forward and in a very plummy voice stated that it didn't matter anyway, as the guy was just a 'conscript' and that was how they expected to be treated. I'm very rarely lost for words but on that occasion, I decided the best move for me was to retreat to the wagon and calm down; I've never been a fan of conscription but found it very hard to accept that it facilitated beating another human being with a stick.

I was quite sad when it was time to leave Çorlu to join the rest of the squadron as they arrived in Turkey. The hotel staff had been outstanding and looked after us as though we were VIPs during our time with them; courtesy and kindness is hugely important to the Turkish people and of course, it has helped them immensely as they grew the tourist business in their country. I would advise anybody travelling to Turkey to spend a little time away from the resorts to see the real Turkey. At the end of a three-week exercise, we made our way back to Istanbul and had the pleasure of setting up our administrative site on the edge of the beautiful Bosphorus, where we cleaned everything up in preparation for travelling home. This was a little slower than the outbound journey as we were travelling by Landing Ship Logistic (LSL), a flat-bottomed Royal Navy Auxiliary ship. Thankfully, it was largely through the Mediterranean and not the Skagerrak straits, as it would have been if we were travelling to or from Norway. A flat-bottomed boat in those conditions is a whole different story.

Many more memorable trips ensued, visiting countries such as Denmark, Greece and Sardinia; there are stories attached to every trip but what I take from all of them is the sense of togetherness, fun and adventure that I enjoyed as part of this remarkable group of rogues. We were known as the

RFA Sir Galahad (LSL).
Me in the Radio Room.

249 Sig Sqn Football Team 1979.
Me 3rd fm R, back. My great friend Guy Benson, 1st L, back.
Dodgy poses…

*Me during a ski race
in Norway.*

*On Parade in Norway;
The Arctic Warriors of 249 Sig Sqn.*

"Arctic Warriors", a handle we were immensely proud of, and we protected our reputation for fitness, toughness, and snow and ice 'mountain men' fiercely. Having been on the most remarkable journey from obscurity to legendary status with these guys, I knew I had been part of something very special. I also knew, even then, that the friendships I had built and the bond between us would last a lifetime. Your first unit is always special but as my time there came to an end, I was completely focused on my upcoming marriage to a girl I had been madly in love with for years and who would become my soulmate for the rest of my life.

I left 249 Sig Sqn as a Cpl, having been promoted twice, achieved Class 1 as a tradesman, having been crypto trained, and as a qualified ski instructor and mountain leader: what a tour! The levels of camaraderie in this unit were quite outstanding; borne out by the fact that we remain a tightly knit band of brothers some 40 years later.

The Girl for Me: Marrying the Love of my Life

Susan and I first met when she came to visit her grandmother who lived in the same village as I did. She had been brought up in Arbroath near Dundee, but her parents were both born and bred in New Pitsligo; if it hadn't been for the fact that her dad was a professional football player, the likelihood is that she too would have grown up in the village.

Susan's dad, Jim, or 'Bonzo' as he was known locally, was a bit of a legend in the village as he was the only professional footballer we had ever produced; that was despite having a lot of good amateurs. The difference of course, between those that make it and those that don't, is self-discipline and commitment; the only thing most of these guys were committed to was being in the bar as often and for as long as was possible (it's a bit of a thing with us Highlanders)!

Jim was a bit of a home bird, even to the point of travelling back to the village after games on a regular basis. I remember meeting him as he walked back from the pub one evening when he had played against Celtic earlier that day; I must have been around 10 years old at the time. He didn't look so happy, so I asked him, "What's up, Jimmy? You look a bit upset," thinking how cool it was to be talking to a professional footballer.

"It's about time I retired," he said.

"Oh, why's that?" I asked.

"Well, I got the run-around from a little kid this afternoon, he stuck me in his back pocket, and I couldn't get near him, or I would have booted him over the stand." Jim was an exceptionally tough centre-half, so not many players did that to him.

"Who was that?" I asked, thinking it must have been bad for him to consider retiring. "A wee boy called Kenny Dalglish," he replied. Enough said...

Susan and I were both around 14 when we met and I fell in love with her immediately. Despite some of the nonsense I used to get involved in, I was a decent kid who lacked self-confidence and I was completely besotted with this gorgeous lass. We went out together for some time but given we lived a long way apart, and my behaviour in terms of underage drinking, fighting and generally being a jerk, all led to us splitting up.

I was genuinely devastated but had my supposed reputation to think about so just got on with it. I thought about Susan almost every day but having joined the army 18 months later, I suddenly had very little time to focus on anything other than becoming a professional military communicator, and I guess Susan was getting on with her life. I was her grandmother's favourite though, so that was always in my favour!

Luckily, we did get those precious periods of leave and I used to take every opportunity to head home to the Highlands to recharge my batteries. By this stage, I had worked very hard to prove my commitment to my Corps, Royal Signals, and had decided that the army was my future. As mentioned previously, I was "army barmy"; my experience at the AAC had literally changed my life and taught me the basic rules by which you can become the best you can be.

At around 20 years old, I was on leave and enjoying a few beers in one of the local pubs. I was busily chatting to the barmaid when I got a tap on the shoulder. Turning round, I was delighted to see it was Susan, looking fantastic as always. She was out with an aunt who had clearly led her astray, so I was very pleased when she suggested we have a drink together. She told me a story about Christmas 1976 where I had been unable to get home and had taken my holiday with extended family in Sunderland. That year, she had visited my parents on New Year's Eve and had sat on my dad's knee and told him we were going to get married someday. Given I lost my dad shortly after that and he wasn't around when we did get married, it helped me overcome my sadness that he knew Susan's "plan".

We married on 1st August 1981 on what was undoubtedly the happiest day of my life. I was in No 1 Dress, as was my best man, Frank McAleer, and we walked the 200m from my house to the church. It was a beautiful summer's day, and I was delighted and relieved to see the wedding car come round the corner as Frank and I stood at the church door I wasn't worried that Susan may not turn up, but there was always a chance that her dad, Jimmy, may have changed his mind!

He had given me a straightforward pep talk two days before which went something like, "Take care of her or I will break your back," and I had no doubt that he meant every word of it. After all, she was the apple of his eye and in truth, I was extremely proud that he trusted me, despite my reputation.

The wedding was attended by several of my closest army mates who stayed for a day either side of the wedding itself; God only knows where they slept, but they all had a great time, and it meant the world to me that they had travelled so far to attend. I realised at that point just how special these guys were and what real friendship felt like.

Susan and I had a fantastic time and although we stayed in the UK for our honeymoon, we knew at that point that our first posting as a married couple would be to Soest in West Germany, where I would be joining the 3rd Armoured Division Headquarters & Signal Regiment, which formed part of the British Army on the Rhine (BAOR). Whilst we were excited, I guess both of us felt a little bit of trepidation, it was a foreign country and a long way from home. We didn't dwell on it though and enjoyed the rest of our holiday before I set off alone to join my new unit, settle in and prepare for Susan's arrival once we had been

Me and Sue on our wedding day –
1ˢᵗ August 1981.

allocated a married quarter. It was fantastic to be married to a girl that was everything I ever wanted and much more, so heading off to Germany by myself was a huge pull on the heartstrings, but the thought of setting up our first home together kept me going.

When I got married, my mum asked me to thank her as well as any others that I addressed in my wedding speech. I thought that she was kidding, but I didn't take the time to reflect on how hard her life had been since my dad had died. I spent most of my time hundreds of miles away and although my mum and little sister were always in my mind, I just wasn't fully aware of their daily hardships. My mum had always been there for me, no matter what her situation was; she was a great sounding board and always took the time to listen. When I have reflected on her request, particularly since she died in 2003, I have deeply regretted my oversight because I owed her so much. Like many sons in that position, I just assumed that she knew how grateful I was and how much I loved her.

My advice to anybody finding themselves in this type of position is never assume; do or say something. I have previously mentioned that my mum was a diminutive, little Mackem, but let me address my previous mistake: she was the strongest, bravest, and most influential person I have ever met, and a wonderful mother. Thank you for everything you did for me, Mum, I love you.

POSTING 3
3 Armd Div HQ & Sig Regiment (Soest, West Germany)

The Long Drive

I drove my new Venetian Red Ford Capri 2.0 S all the way south to Dover to catch my ferry to the continent; the truth is, I had never owned anything so beautiful, or new, in my life to that point and it felt good. The drive to Dover was long but the trip on the other side put things in perspective from a distance viewpoint, driving through France, Holland, Belgium and Germany to get there.

On arrival at St Sebastian Barracks, some 15 miles outside Soest, I reported to the guardroom, booked in and was escorted to my temporary accommodation; it was pretty crap but given it was a two-to-three-man room, it could have been a lot worse. As I sorted my bed space out, I couldn't help but notice a guy in another bed who seemed to be dead, making no movement or noise since I had opened the door. He must just be a bit unsociable, I thought to myself, so I just carried on making myself comfortable, deciding an early night was probably a good idea; it had been a strenuous journey.

I was up and dressed early the next morning and noticed that another guy had joined us in the room; either I had been very tired, or he had crept in extremely carefully. Having introduced ourselves and exchanged pleasantries, I thought I should enquire as to whether the other guy, who had still not stirred in his bed, might actually be dead!

"Oh, don't worry about him," said Kev, my new-found room-mate, "that's Sponge Head, he does this all the time. He'll be OK."

With that, I set off to work with Kev showing me the way to "the prison" which was where the field squadrons worked. It had been a Canadian Prisoner of War camp at the end of WWII and had kept the name. The sites were separated by about 500m, but it was an easy walk in the sunshine.

Having informed Kev that I had been posted to Oscar Troop, 3 Squadron, he showed me to the troop office where I was introduced to the Troop Sgt, a newly promoted guy called Ronny Allan who was to become one of the best friends I have made in my life.

The Troop Commander, Captain Clive Cox, who was a relatively quiet chap, probably thought he would impress me with his authority, because as Ronny and I left the office, he shouted, "Mine's NATO standard, Sgt Allan," indicating tea, white with two sugars.

"Amazing!" replied Ronny. "So is mine and Cpl Greig's is white with one; we will be in the stores!"

Ten minutes later, Clive arrived with the two brews, and I was really pleased to learn that nothing had changed between units; the SNCOs still ran the show at troop level!

This was my first armoured unit and very different from 249. It was very much back to the reality of military life where getting caught wearing another nation's uniform would most likely see you end up on jankers (extra duties), if not a short, sharp spell in the nick. Of course, a regiment is around four times the size of an independent squadron (such as 249), with lots of Sgt Majs lurking around every corner and, even more terrifyingly, an RSM wandering around looking for 'victims'. Luckily for me, my previous Sgt Maj from 249 had been promoted to RSM and was posted to the Regiment a few short weeks after I arrived, so I had at least one friend in high places, albeit he was a monster and scared the shit out of absolutely everybody just by glancing in their general direction…

Getting back to my room at the end of Day 1, I was greeted by a grunt from Sponge Head, who was quietly supping from a clear plastic bottle. When I went for a beer with Kev that evening, I decided to ask him about our room-mate. To my absolute horror, he informed me that Sponge Head was an alcoholic who had just returned from Nettley (near Portsmouth) which was where the services sent their drink-dependent personnel to recover. Sponge Head had relapsed on the ferry on the way back and driven across a chunk of Europe completely leathered. He had come straight back to the unit but was still on leave, hence his failure to get up for work that morning.

"What do you think he was drinking this afternoon?" I asked. "I'm sure it was spirits of some sort."

"Yeah, you're right," said Kev, "it was White Spirit; he doesn't give a shit."

Having found out that Sponge Head's real name was Chris, I decided that we had a duty of care to the guy and needed to get him some help quickly. When the Duty SNCO came into the mess, I recognised him as a guy called (seriously) Bob Hope whom I had met in the morning and discovered he was from a town very close to my village in the Highlands. We had hit it off straight away. I pulled Bob to one side and explained what was going on; Bob knew Chris (aka Sponge Head) as they were both in the same squadron, so he thanked me and assured me he would get it sorted before the guy drank himself to death.

When we got back to the room a couple of hours later, Sponge Head had gone, and Bob had left me a note saying he had taken him to the Medical Research Station (MRS). He would be detained there until they could arrange his return to Nettley. I was pleased the guy would get another chance to get sober and hopefully save his career and more importantly, his life. Heavy drinking had been pretty common in the UK but in Germany it was an epidemic.

Settling In

I had my squadron commander's arrival interview the next day and had been pretty well briefed by Ronny Allan, on what to expect.

I knocked on the SSM's office door to report my presence for interview and heard a gruff "Come in." Being an experienced NCO by this time, I knew the invitation actually meant get your arse in here and do so in good order, as this guy's first impression really mattered, more than his bosses in truth. SSM Andy Hickling was an awesome figure of a man, captain of the Corps rugby team, six foot three and nineteen stones; not somebody you wanted to get on the wrong side of. He was clearly happy with my turnout and drill as I marched into his office.

"Welcome to 3 Squadron!" he bellowed. "The new RSM talks very highly of you, so you'd better not let me down, young man."

"No, Sir!" I replied, wondering whether his concern was for me or the fact that the new RSM might allocate blame to him if I crashed and burned. Andy was a very career-minded person, and I am sure he didn't want to fall out with the new senior soldier!

The OC's interview went off quite smoothly and to be honest, my main point of conversation was to remind the OC that I had just got married and was very keen to get my wife out to Germany to join me, which he assured me was a priority.

The pace of life in BAOR was hectic to say the least, with almost continuous exercises from April through November, and that didn't include some R Signals-only preparatory exercises, such as Ex Flying Falcon. Whilst I rang Susan whenever possible, I was on exercise a lot of the time which made communication really challenging. I had been given the role of General's driver/operator which was a coveted job for a guy in my rank; it obviously wasn't a good move to put somebody in there who cocked it up, as that could have very serious repercussions for the Signal Regiment Commanding Officer, never mind the guy in the job. I knew the importance and benefits aligned to this role and gave it everything I had.

Finding a Home

The General Officer Commanding (GOC) was Maj Gen Norman Arthur, a nice guy who was always very grateful for whatever I did, but on the other hand, the aide-de-camp (ADC) and I did not see eye to eye. Perhaps he felt I was stealing his thunder? Whichever way you look at it, his fears were ridiculous; he was a Captain whilst I was a JNCO.

The relentless exercise schedule continued, and I went to check my progress on the housing list at every opportunity, but I never seemed to be making any tangible progress. The families officer, Captain Wood, was a commissioned WO1, so he pretty much cut to the chase when I challenged this and told me that the wait could be three to six months in a worst-case scenario. I was deeply upset by this and for probably the first time in my career, I felt that I was being totally messed around.

Luckily, the Captain's office was down the corridor from the RSM's, and Steve Marshall had taken up his role a month previously. As I approached his office, Steve (who still had a mirror above his door) shouted, "Cpl Greig, my office!" and I marched directly in.

"Is everything OK?" he asked.

"No, Sir, I have just been told that I won't get my wife out here for another three to six months!"

"There's a huge shortfall in married quarters, as you know," he said, "but I thought you would be happy to pursue other options, knowing you."

"I'm not aware of any other options, Sir," I replied, "but I am more than happy to get stuck into anything that can move this forward."

He mentioned there was a system that allows you individually to locate a property for hire on the German market and if it met key criteria, such as distance from the unit, within a defined cost and so forth, he would ensure it was approved for hire and we could move in. I was over the moon, but a bit pissed off that the families officer had chosen not to make me aware of the system. I thanked the RSM and marched out of his office in a completely different frame of mind. I have never been the type of bloke to resort to threats and I will be forever grateful to Steve Marshall for calling me in that day; if he hadn't, my next move would have been to hand my notice in and leave the army! Whilst very little ever troubled me personally, impacting my family is something I simply would not accept, even at that early stage.

Now that I had an opportunity to fix the problem by myself, I set about visiting as many local properties for rent as I could identify. Pretty quickly, I came across a beautiful two-bedroom flat about 5 km from camp, just east of the Möhnesee in the Körbecke valley. My German at that point was virtually non-existent, so I took one of the guys from my squadron, who was fluent, as my interpreter.

The owner was a lovely guy who was easy to deal with and we brokered a deal between us, so all that remained was for me to document the details and submit my application to the families office, which I did first thing the next morning. The families officer was very impressed and having quickly looked through my application, he told me that he would be in touch shortly to confirm the decision and next steps.

I was getting a bit nervous after a few days, so I decided to check where we were. The families officer was on leave when I called in so I had to deal with his deputy, an old and bold WO2. He seemed a bit shifty when I asked about my application and then he proceeded to tell me that it had been refused based on being too far from camp at 8 km. I had checked the distance in line with the appropriate regulations, so I knew he was waffling; I just didn't know why, I was absolutely fuming.

"You will have to wait till Captain Wood gets back," he said. "You can then raise a query."

"The RSM asked me to keep him in the picture, so I will let him know what's happened," I replied, and I knew something wasn't right immediately, as the blood literally drained from his face.

The RSM wasn't in his office as I passed, so rather than wait, I jumped in my car and drove down to the flat. "Yep, 5 km!" I thought to myself as I pulled into the courtyard of the building, noting that the flat door was open. As I watched, a woman was moving stuff between her car, which had British Forces Germany (BFG) number plates, and the flat; it was clear that she was moving in. Fuming, I drove straight back to camp and went to see the Families WO2.

"What's the score?" I asked him, "I have just seen somebody moving into the hiring I found and applied for and which you told me this morning was too far out!"

Looking sheepish, the guy started to waffle about the 8 km again, so I asked to see my application and when he presented it, the '5' had been crossed out and an '8' inserted.

"Officers are allowed to be further from camp," he blurted out, but I knew I had him then; the hiring had clearly been allocated to an officer as priority over me, a Cpl. I didn't bother hanging around with this Herbert, I just turned on my heel and headed off in disgust. The RSM was at his desk this time, so I was able to recite the whole sad story to him. I'd known him long enough to see that he was very angry, so when he told me to leave it with him, I quickly made myself scarce.

A few days passed and I was considering telling Susan that we had a major problem when I got a call saying that the RSM wanted to see me. I covered the ground between the prison and the headquarters quickly as it's never good to keep the RSM waiting.

"I've got to the bottom of this, Cpl Greig," he informed me. "It was down to a simple error where the Families WO misinterpreted the rules when allocating the property." I noticed a faint smile on his face and knew that he was being diplomatic and trying to move things on with minimum fuss. I lost interest in any case as the RSM explained his solution, which was I had been allocated a hiring on the south bank of the Möhnesee and could move in around three weeks' time.

As you would imagine, I was absolutely delighted and couldn't wait to let Susan know! At that stage, we had been married three months and spent just two weeks together which is very far from ideal, to say the least. With things now sorted on the housing front, I did wonder why the RSM had let the Families WO off so lightly, given he had simply ditched my application in favour of an officer, but as a couple of friends pointed out, the guy had been Duty

WO every other night for the last few days! I couldn't resist the desire to see the house, so I jumped in my car after work and drove over the Körbecke ridge, across the bridge to the south bank (Am Südufer) and along until I spotted the sign, "10A-E Am Südufer".

I was totally speechless; it was like something out of a movie! The house lay up a stunning block paved driveway with an immaculately manicured, steep lawn on the right-hand side. It was around 30m from the lake and 100m from a footbridge that led to the outskirts of Körbecke village. With its numerous balconies, large drive and multiple garages at the rear, I initially thought I must have misread the sign and was about to go and check when a guy drove up to the house and jumped out of his car.

"Hi, I'm Dave Stansfield," he said. "You must be the new guy?"

"Yes," I said, "but for a minute, I thought I had come to the wrong address!"

"Everybody who comes here feels like that and to be honest, you and I are very lucky to live here, as everybody else is officer rank or equivalent!"

Ah, poetic justice, I thought. That said, we were both in uniform and I was aware that Dave was an SSgt, much more senior than me. I think the way Dave had introduced himself, using his first name, helped me relax, if we were to be neighbours then I really didn't fancy living next to some overly rank-conscious pain in the neck. Dave asked me in for a coffee and to meet his wife, Carol, which I also appreciated, as it kept me away from camp for a little while longer.

On first sight of the house, I had been blown away but following an hour with Dave and Carol, I was in a state of sheer amazement. They explained that the house had initially been intended for the General who commanded our division, but the first one to fill the role had deemed it too small. Instead, it was divided into five separate apartments, supposedly for officers up to the rank of Captain or equivalent civilian grade. At that time, there were four officers and Dave as a SNCO, so they commented that I had clearly got a great supporter somewhere to be allocated one of these apartments. I didn't recite the story because that would have been disloyal to the RSM, but inside I had a huge grin on my face. Dave and Carol further explained that we had a bar/restaurant on one side of the house and a fast food takeaway on the other, all the south bank was forested with all sorts of walks and picnic areas, and the BAOR Yacht Club was around three miles further along the bank. I couldn't wait to tell Susan and stupidly stopped to ring her on the way home to share the news. She was obviously relieved, excited, and extremely happy that we had been allocated such a beautiful property, but I should have waited until our move-in date had been formally confirmed, as these things had a habit of changing!

Before I knew it, we were on exercise yet again and I was very conscious that the deployment was just short of three weeks, so it would end just before our move-in date. I didn't tend to get a lot of sleep on exercise; the General seemed to need about three hours a night which meant we were constantly on the go. The boss was a great guy and would regularly ask me how my wife was and how things were going on the move-in front. I would tell him what I could but quite honestly, that wasn't a lot, considering we were on exercise and contact with the families office was sparse.

About midway through the exercise, I got an opportunity to ring Susan only to find that she had received a letter stating that our move-in was to be delayed for a further two to four weeks. She had no experience of military life and was both upset and disappointed. I was somewhat more irritated, as nothing had been communicated to me whatsoever.

The next morning, I decided to let my OC know what had happened and check why I hadn't been told. Unfortunately, we were just in the process of changing over on OC and he and his replacement had headed out early to visit some of dispersed detachments. Sgt Ronny Allan was at the Radio Control (RADCON) when I got there, and he suggested I come back later to see the OC in person. However, the Second in Command (2IC) said he would like a word with me after he had done a quick job, asking me to hang around until he got back. I chatted with Ronny who told me that the 2IC was perhaps not as reliable as might be expected.

On his return, he invited me to join him in the cookhouse for a brew and a chat, which I did. I briefed him on the situation and whilst he seemed badly informed, he assured me that this was nothing more than a glitch which he would personally resolve and update on as quickly as possible. He told me that there was no need to trouble the OC as he was on the case and would brief him accordingly when he got back. Given the positivity, I wondered if Ronny had misjudged the guy and headed back to work in a much better frame of mind.

A couple of days went by and I hadn't heard from the 2IC, so the worry beads were starting to reappear. That evening, I picked the General up to take him on a visit to one of the battalions, the Black Watch.

As he got into the wagon, he asked, "How are things progressing on your wife coming out and your move?"

Before I could respond, his ADC quickly replied, "Cpl Greig will be briefed in the morning, Sir. His Squadron 2IC and I discussed it and he will catch up with Cpl Greig in the morning."

Maybe he wasn't that bad after all, I thought, as I headed out of the headquarters towards the Black Watch location.

Despite a late night and the usual lack of downtime, I decided to go and see the 2IC as soon as I got up to hear what he had to tell me. When I tracked him down, he was looking very sheepish which set the alarm bells ringing immediately. As I pressed him, he informed me that he had suggested that I be released from the exercise early and replaced by another driver/operator, which would allow me to return to camp, fix a date for move-in and go back to the UK to collect my wife. However, to his surprise, the General had refused point blank when the option had been explained to him. At that point, I knew he was lying and wanted to throttle him, Ronny's view had obviously been accurate.

When I went to collect the General half an hour later, the ADC jumped in the wagon and in a panicked voice told me that 2IC hadn't spoken to the General at all but had confirmed that I would be available for the remainder of the exercise. The ADC had therefore relayed this directly to the General; the reason for their combined flapping was because the ADC knew the first thing the General would ask me was for an update on my situation. If I had delivered the story as told to me, there would have been a couple of Captains in very deep water. Having no choice but to get on with things, I completed the exercise and on return to barracks, was delighted to find that my move-in had suddenly been brought forward to the following week. 'Kipper', as we called the 2IC, was quick to point out that he had managed to resolve things in my favour, but I was in no doubt it was an arse-covering call from the ADC to the families officer that probably did the trick.

Worth the Wait

I arrived back in the UK a week later and met up with Susan and her parents in London, where we spent a lovely few days sightseeing before flying to Germany. I will never forget Susan's face as we arrived at our new home on the Möhnesee. She was as excited as I had been and couldn't believe the quality of the building or its spellbinding beauty. I was so pleased she liked it, as this was to be not only our first home together, but also where our son Mark would be born and spend his early years.

It really was an idyllic location, and we spent many happy days walking in the forest, visiting some extremely beautiful little towns and villages in the local area, or just strolling across the footbridge to Körbecke for coffee and cakes or ice cream. Our main shopping trips were to the NAAFI in nearby Soest, where most of the married quarters were located, but we always made the effort to also visit the German supermarkets which, in truth, were far ahead of anything in the UK at the time, never mind the NAAFI. The visits to Soest quickly made both of us realise that the delay in getting a house may well have been a blessing in disguise, given the relatively shabby state of the married quarters.

Sue showed her true strength during our time in 3 Div; it was her first time living abroad, we were way out in the sticks, and the non-stop cycle of exercises meant she just had to get on with things. With the nearest doctor miles away, no understanding of German and being a young, first-time mum, this was a tough gig. She never complained once, and I should probably have told her more often just how proud I was of her; I was busy, but she did the hard work. The fact that she was happy and loved the country as much as I did, meant everything to me and allowed me to pursue my career with a very clear focus.

As mentioned, our beautiful new home had a traditional German bar/restaurant on one side and a Schnellimbiss (fast food) stall on the other, so we were impressed. I decided it would be useful to pop into the bar occasionally to make some local friends and pick up some language tips. The very first time I went in, I used my best German to order a beer. In fact, it was my only German, so the barman's follow-up questions fell on deaf ears! However, they seemed to like the fact that I was showing interest in learning and were extremely friendly.

One particular guy, who I later learned was called Bruno and was the local Forstmeister (Forestry Master), seemed to enjoy pointing to all sorts of things and giving me the German word; the only drawback was that he wouldn't give up until I could repeat the word with perfect pronunciation. His approach was to provide hugely helpful as my German vocabulary and ability improved dramatically over time. Indeed, because I enjoyed trying to engage local tradesmen, he would help me prepare my approach. For instance, he would teach me the words before I went to a garage for new tyres. Inevitably this would impress the garage owner/

staff and I would get a slightly better price than other squaddies. Mind you, most squaddies just bowled into local businesses almost demanding the staff spoke English; whilst most of the staff did, it really wound them up, and they generally ignored the customer concerned, disgusted by their arrogance.

Things were going well at work and again, I had been lucky in that my colleagues were a fantastic group of guys. It got even better with the arrival of Dai Jones, who had been a good friend at Harrogate, albeit he had been a little older than me and in a higher term. Dai was just one of life's good guys, always there for his mates, great fun and fiercely loyal; he was a council house kid like me and very proud of it. His third child, Michael was born just before him and his wife Kathy arrived in Soest, so with three boys I think he was in a great place in his life and we often talked about where our careers would take us. He was very committed to becoming a Yeoman of Signals, whilst I remained focused on a more straightforward approach, seeing my future as an RSM in due course. Dai quickly became not just my best mate but my most trusted confidante and our deep friendship would see a lot of twists and turns along life's highway over the years to come.

My Transition – Preparing to Become a Yeoman

We knew there was to be a new SSM taking over from Andy Hickling, and that handover saw the arrival of SSM Dave "Pucking" Scott. Talk about chalk and cheese! To try and nullify the fact that Dave couldn't string two words together without swearing, he had decided that he would simply use a replacement theory, believing nobody could get upset if he used "puck or pucking", irrelevant of how loudly he screamed the words out. This, in fact, was a badly flawed theory and led to some of the worst mickey-taking I can recall in my entire life; everybody had a Dave Scott impression!

Not long thereafter, we also changed OC, with the new guy Major Chris Donaghy arriving. This guy was pure gold from a soldier's perspective; totally bonkers, loved a beer and with a great sense of humour. Couple that to the fact that he genuinely cared for his blokes, which they knew, and his abilities became almost secondary, which was probably a very good thing. The OC and SSM together were a bit weak, but both were decent guys and the lads would do anything for them. Ronny and I decided to christen the OC "Dinger" because he was fat and bell-shaped, but we were both fiercely loyal to him and enjoyed some of the best laughs of our lives with him.

Talking of Ronny, I had moved jobs a couple of times, initially to command the G3 Ops armoured vehicle in the headquarters and then to RADCON, as the senior Cpl Operator working alongside Ronny and the Squadron Yeoman, a very young guy called Mick. On exercise, I did shifts with Mick, whilst Ronny and another Cpl did the alternative slot. I never got the chance to tell Mick this, but he was the guy who changed the course of my career, and I will never forget that or the debt of gratitude I undoubtedly owe him. Until that point in my service, I had never worked up close with any Yeoman; they were the guys that planned and delivered communications and then took a load of heavy shit if anything went wrong. Working with Mick and observing his role, his responsibilities and how he was regarded and treated, even by very senior officers, was a massive eye-opener for me. Mick was a newly qualified Yeoman which carries the rank of SSgt and was on his first post-course operational tour. He had an incredible intellect, the ability to think and act almost simultaneously, and, it appeared to me, the absolute trust and respect of every officer up to and including the General himself. Nothing happened on the communications front without his engagement and agreement; his buy-in was more valued around the bird table (battle planning map) than any other signaller, even that of our CO.

Over the months working with Mick, I would silently marvel as he walked into RADCON following a few short hours in bed, correcting things on our map and communications board as he went. He had enormous energy and in truth, taught me what being a communicator was all about. Being very clever and knowing the RSM had been mentoring me for a few years, he played his approach extremely well, more for my benefit than his own, I think. He would replay his part in operational management, pre-deployment planning and preparation, involvement on bird-table briefings, even as an SSgt, highlighting the complete lack of any involvement from the regimental duty guys at almost all levels.

As he pointed out, those guys would be called upon to do some challenging work, such as setting up and tearing down the field headquarters, sorting out refuelling, and ensuring the officers were looked after from an admin perspective. His question, of course, was always the same: you don't need to be a professional communicator to do these tasks. I found myself agreeing with his points more and more, eventually deciding that if I was going to make my career in the Royal Signals, then I wanted to be the best I could be; and that was as a Yeoman.

We did a lot of military training in 3 Div and to be fair, it was usually of a pretty high standard, diverse and challenging. My favourite place to do such training was the Belgian army-controlled Vogelsang, or Ordensburg Vogelsang to give it its full name, a former Nazi estate placed at the military training area in the Eiffel National Park in North-Rhine Westphalia. It had everything from excellent shooting ranges, lakes for boatmanship, and miles of roads and heath to yomp along. It did have a bit of a creepy feel to it but that just heightened the training mindset. We even managed to take some of our APCs with us and test them in their amphibious role; trust me, it takes a bit of courage to drive an ageing 34-ton armoured vehicle into a lake! That said, it also gives a lot of confidence if it does float; the two knots per hour isn't very impressive but when the water is around 2-3°C, staying dry is more than enough.

In those days, becoming a Yeoman was a long, hard route. There was no "study time" – you were expected to do your job and manage your personal time for study. To be honest, that felt right to me, as generally speaking, the slackers would give up or be found out. The route incorporated a range of exams, including Pre-Yeoman Qualification (PYQ), Pre-Yeoman selection, Yeoman selection and the nine-to-ten-month residential course itself. In total, the fastest it could be done was around two years but if any element was failed along the way, you had another two chances at each point, so it could be a very long road indeed, and few if any ever completed that extended route. Anyway, I was only 22 years old at this point, so I decided to crack on with my job and do absolutely everything I could to achieve the two-year completion.

War Takes its Toll

As a young family living in a foreign country, we felt truly blessed. We had a beautiful home, a good social life and some great friends. I enjoyed my work and have so many memories from this period. As I was serving in BAOR at the time, my colleagues and I were spared any involvement in the Falklands campaign; as you can imagine, that's not what most of us wanted though. As professional soldiers, most of us were keen to get involved and found it very hard to watch the ships sail from UK ports, headed for the South Atlantic on an operation to take back UK sovereign territory from the Argentines. I was fixated as the conflict unfolded with significant media coverage, even in Germany.

War always takes its toll. Even when you aren't deployed, you will probably have friends that are and indeed, that was the case for me. I lost a great friend from my time at the Army Apprentice College, Cpl Rab Burns, who died in a helicopter crash whilst they were cross-decking prior to an operation. Rab was serving with 264 (SAS) Sig Sqn in support of 22 SAS Regt at the time. He was an excellent soldier and the finest piper of his age I had ever met; a true Scot in every sense, with a name to back it up. He was 22 years old and died two weeks before my son, Mark, was born.

Mark is now 39 years old and the apple of my eye. His birthday also ensures that I constantly remember my old friend, Rab Burns, who was just a boy at the time of his death.

Sadly, Rab wasn't the only close friend I lost. Lt Jim Barry, with whom I had built such a close professional affinity whilst at 249 Sig Sqn, was killed at the Battle for Goose

Green. He had been seconded to 2 Para just prior to the conflict and travelled south as part of Colonel H Jones' battalion. Jim lost his life during a lull in the battle where he had been told to go forward to take the surrender as a white flag had been raised on an enemy flank. Sadly, the enemy were very disjointed and as Jim plus two soldiers went forward, they were engaged by an enemy machine gun from the other flank. To this day, I can remember watching TV coverage as his body and those of his comrades were wrapped in waterproof ground sheets and carried away from the battlefield. Knowing Jim was gone and that our agreement that I would be his RSM would never be honoured, made me even more committed to becoming a Yeoman and I don't think he would have minded.

Lt Jim Barry, R Signals. KIA during the war to liberate The Falkland Islands. An outstanding friend and officer.

My great friend Cpl Rab Burns, R Signals. The finest Piper I have ever known.

Knowing the importance and impact of things being immaculately clean, I decided to pursue this line with my detachment at that point, G3 Ops. This was always the key detachment in any armoured HQ, where the big hitters worked, so providing them with a superb working environment and great communications was always a sure-fire winner. My crew, Sigs Del Wood, "Lloydy" and I worked very hard to get the vehicle right, with all the mod cons we could construct, so we were very well thought of and looked after by our staff. I doubt they had ever seen a vehicle like ours, from a condition perspective, before or after, and it was used for all the various demonstrations and presentations. Again, this did my career no harm whatsoever.

Seldom have I suffered the mindless tedium and boredom to the level that was inevitably associated with Site Guard. The sites in question were those where nuclear weapons, largely US, were stored and maintained, and which had to be guarded from the threat of terrorist attack or organised crime gangs. The BAOR units were cycled through on a roster and of course, 3 Div HQ and Sig Regt had to do their share. Luckily, I only got caught for two of these tasks but at two weeks per deployment, they were a real nightmare.

The site in Sennelager may as well have been on the surface of the moon! Once you arrived, unloaded, and took over the accommodation, you were immediately into the two-hour stag (duty) pattern for the next fortnight. The stag was undertaken in one of the towers located in each of the corners of the site, with a requirement to climb the ladder with all your kit, including weapon, and entering the room at the top to take over from a colleague.

Inevitably the off-going person would be in a zombie-like state, rushing to handover the live ammunition and get out of the torture chamber.

131

To this day, I remain surprised that more rounds weren't loosed off, particularly towards the end of the second week, by which time the mind-numbing boredom had reduced most folk to gibbering wrecks: the fact that we survived is undoubtedly testament to British patience. On both of my stints, we had cases of negligent discharge, with the guilty parties being heftily fined on return to barracks. Personally, I don't think either case had any sinister link, rather soldiers falling asleep with a finger on the trigger and squeezing one off. By the time the replacement unit arrived to take over the duty, most of us would have happily paid them to do so from our own pockets.

One of the funniest lads I came across during my time in Soest was a bloke called Les Donno; Les was a Cpl like me and was a real comedian. He was genuinely very funny, popular, and just great for morale; we were in the same Tp and often worked together on exercise. Like most of us, Les liked to let off steam in the corporals' mess and I remember his wife ringing me one night to ask if I had seen him, as he hadn't returned from a mess do.

"No," I said "but if he turns up here, I will send him home." I didn't hear anything further about his disappearance until I arrived at work the next morning, when everybody was looking for him.

After my usual cup of tea in the Tp office, I wandered back to the cells where our detachment kit was stored (after all, it was an old prison), and as I passed Les' cell, I heard some moaning. I pushed the door open and lifted an old camouflage net, to find Les half-asleep and still as drunk as a skunk from the night before. God only knows how he explained that to his missus.

Les and I went through the YofS qualification and selection process together, but unfortunately, he didn't make it, which was a real shame. Underneath all his clowning around, he was a good tradesman, who really enjoyed instructing and mentoring youngsters, and I think he would have made a good Yeoman.

The Morrison Cup was an annual sports event held across the 1 (BR) Corps area of BAOR. It was a very prestigious meeting, and the competition was fierce between the various units. The host unit was normally 7 Sig Regt in Herford and to be fair, they usually did a superb job. At that stage, I was a pretty good middle-distance runner, favouring the 3,000m steeplechase and usually getting dicked for at least one other event (800 or 1,500m in most cases).

I will never forget the 1982 competition where I bumped into my own RSM, Steve Marshall, with his close mate RSM Ron Hails: yes, the same guy from my time in Harrogate. These two had taught me everything and both had decided they would mentor me through to the point at which I would follow in their footsteps and become an RSM in the Corps. So, as I announced that I was training and planning to become a Yeoman of Signals, they screamed in unison, "A fucking Yeoman?!" I guessed that they weren't particularly impressed, something they quickly confirmed.

The funny thing about their attitude was the fact that I knew both had been on the potential Yeoman roster and had failed at key stages. To be honest, their stance just strengthened my resolve to succeed and secretly I think both were very proud of my achievement when I qualified, although neither would ever admit it in public. From my perspective, I was just very proud to have been taught so much by two of the best soldiers I had ever met.

The tour passed quickly, and I must have spent a good chunk of it laughing. On one of the last exercises where our HQ was used in a static control environment, set up just up the road from HQ 1 (BR) Corps in Bielefeld, I saw one of the funniest "sketches" of my life.

The OC, Major Chris Donaghy, had left site the night before to visit his brother where he was a guest of honour at their inter-squadron boxing competition. After-event parties are always interesting on such nights, and I am fairly sure that Chris didn't let us down. However, on his arrival back the next morning, with his brother in tow, he was clearly still the worse for wear. On questioning the OC's driver, they had apparently stopped in some random village on the way back because the boss and his brother had decided to climb the spire of a rather lovely looking church, which they duly did. This would be difficult in any case but it's a whole new challenge when you are three sheets to the wind! Quite how they managed to avoid arrest and incarceration, I will never know.

Having somehow made it back to site, the boss decided to show his brother around his empire: en route he spotted a mate of mine, Cpl Davie Dodds, a very jovial Mackem who had been running the on-site café for the guys.

"Cpl Dodds!" shouted Dinger, "Sort out an egg banjo (egg sandwich) and a brew for my brother and me please!"

"OK," says Davie, looking miffed to be treated like the local punkah-wallah and heading off to the café tent to prepare!

Dinger and his hangers-on eventually made it round to the café and Davie had timed their arrival perfectly. He guided them to their table and quickly followed up by delivering a couple of egg banjos. Standing there with quite a smug look on his face, he nearly fell over laughing as a still-drunk Dinger bit into his banjo and the yolk exploded all over his face. It was so funny, even the SSM had to get out of the tent quickly to recover some sort of composure. Unsurprisingly, this story fell into folklore.

Ex LIONHEART

I think my final exercise with the Regiment was Ex LIONHEART in 1984; this was, and I believe still is, the biggest deployment of British Forces since World War II. Over 130,000 British servicemen were involved and this mind-boggling figure simply could not be matched in today's military. I can remember watching a whole Regiment of armour (Challenger II tanks) tear across an open field at full throttle; what a sight to behold. Whilst we had to pay for the damage it did, it is the sort of sight and noise that can't be understood unless it is physically witnessed, so it had huge training value, particularly for the armoured crews themselves.

I was working in the RADCON on the exercise, with Ronny, Brummie Stewart, and Les Donno and, of course, the Yeoman, Mick. It was one of the most realistic and demanding exercises of my career; we moved every day and on occasion, twice a day. It was knackering stuff, where five hours' sleep was a real bonus, be it in an old barn, derelict house or even a disused pigsty and yes, we gladly slept in a pigsty if it was dry and warm!

In one location, I remember going to bed in a huge old barn with high rafters supporting the roof. I was sound asleep when I heard loud shouting and screaming. As I listened, I could hear *thump, thump, thump*, as if things were falling off the roof. As I unzipped my sleeping bag, I quickly realised what was happening: huge black rats were dropping off the rafters and landing directly on people's sleeping bags! Ronny and I got dressed, rolled up our bags and bolted out of there at breakneck speed. Funnily enough, we were really pleased to move during our shift and made sure that we avoided kipping under rafters for the rest of the exercise. That memory still makes my blood run cold...

LIONHEART was one of those huge scale exercises in which a level of fatalities was anticipated. In reality, the enormous cost to create and run the exercise made it necessary to absorb a set number of losses before a decision to cancel the exercise would be considered. With the sheer number of service personnel on the ground, there were a significant number of losses, all accidental and mainly through road traffic incidents.

I recall a fully crewed Armoured Personnel Carrier (APC) falling off a bridge over a motorway, and another rolling over into a body of water where the crew drowned before help arrived. This may seem very poor from a health and safety perspective, but you need to consider things in context, however tragic. The guys were driving heavy, dangerous vehicles, often at night in the dark and regularly with very little sleep over the previous days. In a war scenario, which we were simulating, all these things would be brought to bear on performance. Again, it delivered highly realistic training but at a heartbreaking cost. Towards the latter part of the exercise, I know we were getting close to pulling the plug because of the casualty rate, but the exercise did reach its conclusion.

Pace Yourself or Stress Will Bite You!

Arriving at work a couple of weeks after we got back from
LIONHEART, I overheard a couple of the squadron
SNCOs mention that our Yeoman, Mick, was "in the shit",
but didn't hear what for. I naturally assumed that as the
Crypto Custodian, it must be for a loss of secure equipment,
secure keys, or something of that sort. As a Potential
Yeoman, I was his Assistant Crypto Custodian, so I decided
to go and see him to offer any help he may require. When I
got to his office, it was empty but the SSM, Dave "Pucking"
Scott, saw me and asked me into his office. I think Dave
realised that I was in a position whereby I needed to know
what was going on, so he sat me down and recounted a
story that nearly knocked me off my seat.

The night before, Mick had been arrested by the German
civilian police in the act of stealing four alloy wheels off
a new BMW. This would have surprised me anyway, but
Mick had literally just taken delivery of his own brand-new
BMW Series 3 about a week before. Why would he nick
wheels off another car?

It took several months to fully unravel but the issue occurred
because of a breakdown that Mick suffered as a direct result
of the pressure he was under at work. His ferocious appetite
for work, which I personally witnessed on numerous
occasions, had driven him over the edge and he committed
this very silly crime. Whilst that would have probably been
enough to wreck his military career, the fact that he was a
Yeoman and security cleared to the highest level, without
which he could not fulfil his role, meant that his fate was
sealed; the Corps lost one of the brightest young stars
midway through his first tour in the appointment. I was

absolutely gutted but learned a huge amount about just how far a human being can push themselves before they "break"; that lesson proved to be invaluable. Mick was obviously devastated but never tried to hide. In my last chat with him, he simply said that he had been warned to slow down and ignored the advice; you do the crime, so you do the time. I have never heard of him from that moment to this, but I owe him a tremendous debt of gratitude.

Family Life in Paradise

Living in the Möhnesee valley was a real privilege. As many people will know, the Möhnesee Dam was one of those targeted by the famous "Dambusters" of 617 Squadron RAF who changed the direction of WWII by destroying this plus a range of others across Germany's Ruhrland.

Living on the south bank of the man-made lake was amazing. At 15 km long with a 40 km shoreline, much of which is sandy beaches, and surrounded by beautiful pine forest, it was a breathtaking environment. There are several lovely villages along the banks of the lake, with Körbecke closest to our house, despite being on the north bank! Our home was situated at the south end of a bridge which ran across from the village, so it was only a 15-minute walk from our property to the village centre; summers in Germany can be very hot, so the walk was a favourite of ours, particularly with Mark being so young and in his buggy.

The facilities in the village were excellent, with a butcher, baker and a small mini market, and handily for me, a good barber. German culture in relation to children is such that kids are usually given a free treat when they enter a shop with their parents; a slice of cold meat, a bread roll, or something similar. The local bread is particularly good and it was normally dry when it was given to the kids; 39 years later, Mark still prefers his bread without butter or margarine!

We would often spend time at the weekends in the small towns close to the reservoir, such as Arnsberg, Neheim and Husten, shopping and having something to eat. Whilst the food in Germany can be a little bland, their fast food is superb, and the various sauces and soups are inevitably outstanding. We also grew to love the continental breakfasts that were available in many of the supermarkets; frühstück (breakfast in German) was healthy, tasty and exceptional value, and when you consider it is normally served from 9.30 am onwards, it was really very civilised. The pubs, of course, were generally very pretty and quite uniquely trusting; you would order your drinks and they would be delivered, and a beer mat was used to record the number you consumed, a simple cross on the mat representing each beer. You settled the bill on departure and whilst I loved this custom, it did occasionally worry me when there were lots of soldiers involved, as I am sure you can imagine…

Living in the countryside was a great experience and there was always something to do in the local area. The BAOR Yacht Club was a few miles further along the south bank, where you could drop in for a drink or something to eat, have a sailing lesson or hire a windsurfing board. We also had the option to head down to the dam itself, which had a lovely restaurant, pub and several stalls selling gifts to the continuous stream of tourists. The walk across the dam wall was a lovely stroll with breathtaking views back over the lake and dramatic scenery from the wall further down the valley. It was very easy to see the damage that would ensue if the wall was breached, as it had been by the amazing bouncing bomb when it struck, back on the evening of 16th/17th May 1943. Talking of the bomb, the Germans had managed to recover one that had not exploded, which they had cut in half, placing one half on a plinth at either end of the wall, to demonstrate the sheer size of the munition; that really brought home the brilliance of the bomb's design. On one of our many visits, we stood Mark on top of one half of the bomb; the picture serves as a good measure of its size. With the many walks, beautiful villages, and sports facilities, it really was an idyllic place to live and work.

Having undertaken and passed all the components of the Yeoman's selection process, I was eventually given a start date back in the UK, where I was posted to the School of Signals, in Blandford, Dorset. It was a case of getting my family back to the UK and settled into a married quarter in Blandford, before setting off for Catterick in North Yorkshire to undertake my SSgt's course.

From a military training perspective, this was a very tough course and it would be held during winter, so I had no doubts it was going to be hard work. Luckily for me, I had a strong reputation as a good soldier on the Regimental Duty (RD) circuit, so a few of the instructors knew that I could get it done and wasn't hiding behind the Yeoman's course, something they tended to accuse all potential Yeomen of doing. In truth, this was largely because successful completion of the Yeoman's course carried immediate promotion to SSgt, which they greatly resented. This made me smile back then, but nowadays I recognise that they just didn't have a clue on what this was all about.

Our first tour in Germany started a love affair with the country that survives to this day. Back in the eighties, West

Germany, as it was then, felt like paradise on Earth; their standard of living was probably the best in Europe, if not the world. We benefited from this, enjoying luxuries that just weren't available back home in the UK at that time; huge entertainment parks were commonplace, the supermarkets stocked absolutely everything, and the proliferation of top-quality swimming pools, gymnasiums and sporting facilities was quite unbelievable. In contrast to the common view of Germany and German people held back home, fuelled by the two World Wars, we found most local people to be charming, helpful, and very accepting of the many thousands of foreigners living in their country. Most Germans, particularly those under 35, tended to speak very good English, having been taught the language at school; we found that trying to speak their language was hugely appreciated, so we always tried to do so. Unfortunately, a lot of our countrymen didn't share our view in this area and made little or no effort to learn German; unsurprisingly, this didn't endear them to the locals and in truth, it could be quite embarrassing if you got caught up in it.

Goodbye to Bruno

I recall a very large lorry standing on the driveway of 10A am Südufer with the guys loading our worldly goods into it; it was snowing quite heavily, and the evening was cold. Once we had finished the loading and the lads jumped into the wagon and set off, I told Sue that I was going to nip over to see Bruno and the other guys in the bar to say goodbye.

I arrived in the cosy, warm bar about five minutes later and there was Bruno in his usual seat.

"Are you all done and ready to go?" he asked me in German, and I proudly replied, also in German, that I was and that I wanted to thank him and his friends for helping me with the language, my various purchases and for being so kind to me and my family.

He stood straight up and said, "It has been a pleasure. You have done well on the language and bought your rounds," but he said it in fluent English! I had never heard Bruno speak English and had been convinced that he couldn't, so you could have knocked me over with a feather.

"Why didn't you speak any English to me before?" I asked.

Being Bruno, his answer was short and to the point. "You Brits are lazy bastards and you would never have learned any German if I had!" He just burst out laughing.

I obviously couldn't just walk away at that point, so I grabbed a seat whilst he explained his language skills. He had been a Prisoner of War during WWII and had been held in mid-Wales where they spent most of their time building dry-stone dykes. He had picked up English during his time there. I must admit, I did laugh when he told me and being frank, my respect for him grew even greater. He was right; if he had spoken English to me when we met, I would probably never have taken the opportunity to learn the language. His efforts had helped me save quite a few quid (sorry, Deutschmarks!), so it was all good. I stood up, grabbed his huge hand, and shook it as we both laughed together for the last time. What a character and what a friend.

I quickly headed back to the house, and we checked everything was packed, closed up and headed off for the ferry terminal, many hours away. The first posting of our married life was over, and it was time to move on to the next. Sue hated the ferry, of course, but I don't think that she wasn't too concerned by the long drive. Mark was just a baby, and he was always a great traveller; again, that made such a difference on what was a monster journey.

POSTING 4
Defining my Career Path
(11 Sig Regiment, Catterick,
N Yorks & School of Signals,
Blandford, Dorset)

Becoming a Yeoman of Signals

At least it wasn't snowing when we arrived in Blandford and drove up the hill to Blandford Camp – it was just dark, wet and cold; welcome home! I had visited Blandford several times over the years, not least during my recent Yeoman Selection Board, and whilst it was inevitably quite formal as home to the School of Signals, it was a lovely part of England. On the downside, the quality of soldier's married quarters in the UK tended to be tired and shabby at best; Blandford lived up to that statement, but with such a high throughput of courses, that was hardly a surprise. Whilst most service personnel take pride in their "homes", the constant turnover of occupants on 12 to 18-month courses impacted the standard of these quarters detrimentally.

We found our allocated quarter, 42 Gunville Down Road, at the bottom end of the camp, so taking a deep breath, we stepped inside. The disappointment on Susan's face was quite palpable, but I was prepared for that. We had just left a beautiful apartment on the banks of the Möhnesee, to move to what could only be described as a rather sad, worn, little two-up, two-down house in Dorset. This wasn't something that Sue could have been prepared for, given our initial years of married life had been spent in high spec house in Germany.

As always though, she got over the initial shock and by late afternoon, we were in Blandford Forum buying little bits and pieces for our new home. It was only for 13 months anyway if I made it through the course, so we accepted the need to grin and bear it option; the only other option would have been for me to leave my family in Germany and attend the course by myself and that thought simply never entered my head. We have always been a very close family and I just could not have lived in a different country for such a long period. It would have been different, of course, if it was an operational deployment, which we completely accepted.

Royal Signals Staff Sergeant's Course

After three weeks, it was time to head off to Catterick Garrison to undertake my Staff Sergeant's course at 11 Sig Regiment. Whilst this was a military leadership course, its importance could not be underestimated, as a pass was a prerequisite to attending the Yeoman's course. Failure spelt the end of the dream, whether you liked it or not.

In those days, there were always two courses running in tandem; in this instance, my course was composed of potential Yeomen whilst the other was comprised of guys on the Regimental Duty (RD) Roster i.e., lads that would stay within a non-technical role as they moved through their careers, providing the Corps with its SSMs and RSMs (for those that went all the way). As you can imagine, this made for a very healthy competitive challenge between the courses. I have always believed that this competition was great for the guys, the course, and the Corps. By most, it was perceived as just good banter and the majority recognised that we would have to work together and show mutual respect in the future, but not everyone! It was also made somewhat harder for my group, as the instructors were inevitably RD personnel, some of whom didn't appreciate my point on banter!

I must admit, I loved every minute of the course which was bloody hard. My time as a boy RSM really helped me, as drill was second nature to me and I was very good at it; additionally, I had the "smart" gene and always took care to ensure I used it to its maximum. Even the instructors accepted that my best boots and turnout couldn't be beaten, but they should have considered the fact that I had been taught how to achieve that by RD staff, and indeed, one of the best RD soldiers the Corps has ever seen. The course progressed well from an individual perspective and as a collective, we easily outstripped the competition, which I am pleased to say remained goodwilled throughout.

We did have a few incidents which made me laugh at the time, particularly one instance in the sergeants' mess. We had gone for dinner one evening and on completion, my best friend Dai and I retired to the TV room to relax for a while. When we entered the room, there were a few uncomfortable seats spread around, but one big comfortable looking armchair with nice cushions on it. There was also a packet of cigarettes and a lighter on one of the arms. Dai knew what this was about, keeping us students in our place, but it was a red rag to a bull. He picked up the items and put them down on one of the other seats, then jumped straight into the armchair.

Ten to fifteen minutes later, the door opened and in came a SSgt, the Senior Drill Instructor on the course. "Out!" he shouted and appeared particularly angry and unimpressed that neither Dai, his actual target, or I, moved. "Out of my seat, Sgt Jones!" he roared in a loud, bullying voice.

"Fuck off!" came the instant reply. "This isn't your chair, it's a chair in the TV room that is available to anybody if it's not being sat on!"

He may as well have kicked the SSgt in the balls; he became apoplectic, dribbling at the mouth and ranting on that students should know their place. Dai quickly reminded him that training had finished for the day and as a SNCO, he was in the mess with full rights and not to be bullied by him. The SSgt found this very difficult to accept and with his eyes bulging out of their sockets, he stormed off. In those days, there were no particular rules about staff or instructors bullying students but I think he thought better of reporting Dai on any trumped-up charge because he felt he had the power to address the issue through the course.

I made the point to Dai afterwards, but he just shrugged. Like me, he hated bullies and just wasn't going to have it from a passed-over SSgt with a poor attitude (in his view!). We had a good old chuckle and a bet on how long it would take the SSgt to get revenge as we walked back to our accommodation block. I knew though that Dai didn't give a damn, it would be worth it. Well, I won my bet. We had drill first thing and Dai was being marched off the square and on his way to jail after five minutes! He only stayed there for the rest of that lesson, so I have no doubt whatsoever that Dai felt it was worthwhile in every way (1-0 as they say)!

The SSgts course included a lot of drill and to say this was the least favourite activity, particularly with the potential Yeomen group, would be a huge understatement. However, as I have previously mentioned, it was very easy and non-stressful for me, so I lapped it up. My boots were always like glass, and I spent even more time at the ironing board than normal; I figured you should never look a gift horse in the mouth. The other guys in my group were less willing to give of their time to achieve the easy life, but as bright, technically capable soldiers, they were always looking for shortcuts to make life more bearable.

Willie Riding and Steve Roden decided that the bulling of boots was a particularly tedious activity and concocted an idea to bypass the hard work involved. They went into the Garrison centre to a hardware shop where they purchased a can of black gloss paint. On arrival back in the accommodation block, they then proceeded to paint their best boots top to bottom with the spray paint. The boots we all used were what were referred to as ammunition boots: very tough, hard leather with metal studs in the sole and heel. I must admit, the paint appeared to take rather well, with both pairs gleaming after they had been sprayed. Happy with their work, Willie and Steve placed their boots close to the radiator to dry and headed off to bed for a good night's kip.

Sadly, they had not anticipated the effect of the direct heat on their freshly painted boots, which by the morning had settled to a rather dull, deep grey. With no time to attempt a rescue, as drill was the first activity of the day, they accepted their fate, laced up their boots and we all headed off to the drill square.

As you would anticipate, the grey boots did stand out a bit and a very agitated Kenny Morris asked what had happened to their boots, no doubt expecting a long-winded set of excuses to pour forth. I'm pretty sure he didn't expect Willie to say, "We painted them with gloss paint, Staff, but we clearly got the wrong shade…"

As most of us nearly wet ourselves laughing, Kenny just shook his head and moved on past them. There was never any doubt in my mind as to Kenny's total despair with some of the characters on our course.

We went on to undertake the final exercise which is held on Warcop ranges in Northumbria, a cold and intimidating place at the best of times, but just not great in March. It was a well-structured, well-run exercise that tested every one of us to the limit; physically demanding in extremely tough conditions and as real a combat environment as it is possible to create. We yomped for mile upon mile, night and day, regularly used live ammunition, and undertook superb range work. There are so many great memories from that time, but I will tell two quick stories.

During a range activity, we were being taught how to prepare and throw L2A2 anti-personnel hand grenades. Following the initial lesson and safety briefing, we were called forward into the individual grenade bays and under instruction, we prepared and threw live grenades over the bay wall towards incoming enemy. We then waited and hoped it would explode, otherwise it was the student's responsibility to go forward with some prepared explosive, crawling on your stomach all the way, and blow the grenade up. As I threw my grenade, thanking God that it safely cleared the wall, I heard the terrifying noise of a second grenade hitting concrete and saw it drop right into my bay.

"Holy shit!" I thought. "Not again!" because unbeknown to my colleagues, this had happened to me years before on my Detachment Commander's course. Who said lightening doesn't strike twice! I was definitely better prepared this time though and almost in a single action, I bent down, grabbed the grenade, and lobbed it up and over the bay wall. I then heard two *thump, thumps* very close together, and was genuinely in shock for five to ten minutes. The craziest thing of all is that I hadn't noticed who had entered the bays either side of me, but as my instructor and I left the bay, I noticed the guy to my right was Dave Cox, a Sergeant on the other course. We both just stared at each other; he was the guy who had thrown the grenade on my Detachment Commander's course with the same result, ending up in my bay! You couldn't make it up! Dave and I became very close friends later in our service and as only squaddies can, had a lot of laughs telling that incredible story over a beer. I did make sure that we were never on the same range detail again, just as a self-protection measure, of course…

The second little gem of a story occurred as we were undertaking the command task element of the final exercise. The weather was awful; it was pouring with rain, freezing, and by the time it came to my turn to do my task, it was pretty dark. This was one of the parts where we were using live ammunition and I had said to my guys that they needed to lay down some firepower to demonstrate our confidence and competence. Everything seemed to be going well despite the conditions, when suddenly live ammunition was coming straight at us from high ground to our left. I do like a bit of realism, but this was too much; 7.62 mm rounds can cut you in half, so I must admit to a bit of flapping! What had happened is our own gun group, with Robbie Davies on the gun, had become disorientated in the driving rain and as they moved forward, they had effectively turned through 180 degrees, at which point they just kept shooting, not realising they were putting rounds down on us. When I later spoke to Robbie, he said it was raining so hard he couldn't see through his glasses. I can still visualise it, like a sketch out of *Dad's Army*; anyway, nobody died, luckily!

Having completed the Final Exercise successfully, it was back off to Catterick to finalise the last few bits and pieces, enjoy the formal end of course dinner and head off home by the end of the week. Everybody passed on my course and so we were in great spirits as we attended the mess dinner on the Wednesday night.

As always in such situations, we ripped the arse out of it and headed off back to bed around 3.30/4 am. I knew that Dai would struggle to get up in the morning and that if he didn't, he would certainly not be ready for the room inspection, so as soon as my alarm went off, I headed to his room to wake him up; but he wasn't there. Knowing that something must be wrong, particularly as his bed was already made and room tidied, I checked his mattress; you're right, he had pissed the bed. He knew that Kenny Morris would take the opportunity to put him on orders for it and took the decision to leg it before the inspection to avoid that outcome. OK, it was part of a plan, not bad when you are three sheets to the wind, but lacking in a reason for his early departure, which just might be spotted.

I was still racking my brain for what I could use as an excuse when I heard the inspection team at the other end of the corridor. In those days, we didn't have mobile phones so I couldn't call Dai and agree a story as to why he had left early. Just as Kenny was approaching Dai's door, I stepped forward and said that he wasn't in his room as he had dropped the bed on his foot whilst cleaning it. Kenny looked at me and said, "Did he piss himself at the same time?" pointing to the rather large puddle that had formed under his bed. Surprisingly, Kenny just strode past the room and carried on with his inspection. For the life of me, I don't know how Dai got away with that incident. To give Kenny his due, he knew that if Dai had been charged, he would probably have been kicked off the Yeoman's course, so he cut him a bit of slack, but we will never know.

R Signals SSgt's Course (RSSSC) 1985.
I am 1st on R, centre row.

Yeoman of Signals Course 37A

After a week's leave to recover from the stress and strain of such a physically demanding course, we were all back together in the School of Signals, on Day 1 of our career course to become a qualified Yeoman of Signals. This was an intense, residential course lasting 12 months, with homework every day and each weekend, and constant tests and assessment throughout the period.

As we were introduced to our Chief Instructor, Major Derek "Bergen Belly" Wallace, he made a play to be the real hard case who wouldn't stand for any nonsense; actually, most of us knew he was just a great bloke who would do his best to help and support you. The course Yeoman was WO1 Glenn Bartliff, a Teessider with a much worse bark than his bite. The other main player was a civilian instructor called Amos. He was an ex-Naval man who was a doppelgänger for Captain Birdseye, but a great old bloke who was a walking encyclopaedia of communications knowledge. At the start of the course, there were 18 of us, all fully committed to giving it everything we had to achieve our career dream.

It really was a never-ending sequence of lectures, tests, homework projects and exercises conducted to confirm what we were being taught had been learned. There wasn't a huge amount of time to enjoy ourselves, but we did belong to a very active sergeants' mess and there were functions on most weekends, so we could get dressed up with our ladies and go and let some steam off; it was very welcome. We knew we were to be Derek Wallace's last course, but didn't focus on that point at all, until the arrival of his successor, Major Jim Ross.

Jim was a dour Scot who was extremely career focused and clearly saw this role as the perfect opportunity to secure his promotion to Lt Col; as a Late Entry Officer, that was the highest rank to which he could aspire, and he certainly did that. Being very conscious of Derek's reputation for not removing anybody from the course, Jim was at great pains to point out that he would have no hesitation in doing so if anybody failed to achieve the required standard and that any interview where you were advised to bring your briefcase equated to goodbye. In my opinion, it became an instant obsession for Jim to see who he could get out of the door quickest, and that honour fell to Sgt Albert Allison, a big friendly giant of a Geordie.

The annoying thing about Albert's removal was the fact that he genuinely wasn't struggling. For whatever reason, Jim didn't take to Albert and seemed to single him out as a target. Perhaps it was because Albert was always laughing, or he wasn't particularly smart, but in my opinion that wasn't an acceptable reason to shatter the guy's career dream; Albert was a good communicator and had only ever wanted to become a Yeoman; our course felt that he could and should have been allowed to do so. We lost another four lads during the course, of which two subsequently attended the following course and passed, so in reality, 15 of the 18 actually achieved their goal. It may seem that I am highly critical of Jim Ross' style, but that's really not the case. I have little doubt that on arrival, he was directed to shake things up a bit, and that it was needed, as nobody had been removed from the course for about seven years; I'm just simply saying that I would have handled it differently.

Having my best friend, Dai Jones, on the course made the whole experience much more enjoyable. When things got tough, we would always find a way to get through it, normally involving a great deal of laughter. Even when things weren't tough, we laughed a lot. Having three young boys, he had less time than me to focus on some of the more mundane matters, like homework. Dai often called for me in the morning on the way to work and his first question would be, "Did you do the homework?" followed by, "Can I have a look?" He would then spend the next 30 minutes copying it at the speed of light because failure to submit completed homework was seen as a major transgression. Oh well, we were a team!

Dai made me laugh so much with some of his capers, that I still struggle to think of some of them without practically wetting myself. We had one particular civilian instructor who wasn't very robust, to put it mildly. Therefore, Dai felt that his lessons were an opportunity to undertake extra-curricular activities. In one particular lesson, the instructor was randomly throwing questions around the class and Dai appeared to be diligently reading his precis, holding it directly in front of his face.

As one of us struggled for an answer, the instructor shouted out, "Sgt Jones, give us the answer from your precis." When Dai offered no response, the instructor stomped up behind him and grabbed the book, only to find Dai had been reading that week's *Viz* comic which he had tucked inside the precis! The instructor's reaction was little short of hysterical, and Dai was duly sent to see Glenn Bartliff for the inevitable bollocking.

As the end of our course drew closer, we were all looking forward to a visit to HMS *Mercury* (a naval shore establishment), which was the home of the Royal Navy

Signal School. This visit was a long-standing tradition undertaken at the end of each Yeoman's course; given the inter-service rivalries, it saw many competitive events over the years, most of which involved copious quantities of alcohol. On arrival at Mercury, we quickly dropped off our kit and were immediately taken to the harbour side and split up into groups. Each group was then loaded onto a rigid raider with a couple of Booties (Royal Marines) as the crew. Once on board, each boat was off at full speed, and let me confirm that in a rigid raider, that's fast (or too fast for your normal landlubber)! We were all pretty sure this was a Team Mercury tactic to give us a good shake up before the inevitable drinking competition that evening; not to worry, we still rinsed them.

The Navy and Royal Marines were great hosts, and we were chaperoned around all sorts of interesting demonstrations which we thoroughly enjoyed, even the rigid raider trip. Our performance, following the formal dinner, took them by surprise, as did the eating of several of their plants, even if Mick Drewett did spread mayonnaise on them first! To be fair, our team did have quite an eclectic mix of SAS, Para, Royal Marine, and general monsters, so their chances were quite slim from the outset.

The Mercury visit completed, we headed back home to Blandford with only a week to go before the Christmas and New Year break, following which we had to return for a few days in early January 1986 before reporting to our allocated units across the Corps. My heart was bursting with pride as I prepared to report to my first unit as a fully qualified Yeoman at the ripe old age of 24 !

Yeoman of Signals Course 37A, 1985.

Rear rank (from left): Andrew Fraser, Terry Crosby, Paul Curley, Steve Roden, Andy McIver, Albert Allison, Ginge Wheatley, Bob Wallace RM, Martin Wedge.

Front rank (from left): Mick Dawson, Phil White, Mick Drewett, Willie Riding, me, Maj (Tfc) Derek Wallis, Steve Catterall, Robbie Davies, Dai Jones, Dave Leyland.

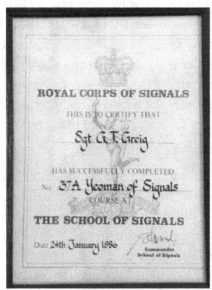

YofS Course Certificate.
A lot of work went into this little certificate.

POSTING 5
7 Sig Regiment
(Herford, W Germany)

"Home" to Germany

I wasn't particularly happy with my posting to 7th Signal Regiment, but at least it was back to Germany where we had been so happy previously. 7th Signal Regiment was stationed in Herford, alongside the 4th Armoured Division Headquarters and Signal Regiment, so there was a big Corps presence in the town. I think perhaps that was part of the turn-off for me, too much of a military presence in one location.

On arrival in Herford, we were quite happy with the quarter allocated to us; yes, it was small but compared to the house in Blandford, it was well-maintained. I had been given a role in 6 Squadron, but it was within a small, highly specialised team that was responsible for delivering a Defensive Electronic Warfare capability across 1 (BR) Corps. If nothing else, it meant that I was going to be busy, with an average of three out of every four weeks on exercise year-on-year. The team was commanded by a Traffic Officer (commissioned Yeoman), Major Bill Cheeseman, who was a bit eccentric to say the least. Sue went round to visit his wife one day and Bill came to the door, which opened onto a very busy road, wearing only a pair of Y-fronts! I think she was a bit traumatised.

I liked Bill because he was very open and honest, sometimes too much so. I gave him a lift to the Brigade and Battlegroup Trainer (BBGT) on one exercise, where I used my own car which was allowed as it was a static training facility. The weather was very poor with a lot of snow on the ground. Unfortunately, I hit a patch of ice and spun off the road into a fir tree and although I had not been travelling fast, a tree does tend to put a few dents in a car when bringing it to a halt. I immediately checked that Bill was OK and he said yes, albeit he had a bit of neck pain. He then proceeded to tell me that he would have to lodge a claim against me for his injuries. I was astounded; here he was as a passenger in my brand-new car as his hadn't been available, my car was wrapped round a tree and we were in the middle of nowhere waiting for recovery, yet Bill's mind was on suing me! My car was eventually recovered and happily it was deemed repairable, although it would be off the road for several weeks. Bill and I were picked up by one of the team and given a lift the remainder of the way to the BBGT in Sennelager.

Understandably, Sue wasn't overly impressed that we had no car for weeks and rightly so. She didn't drive and our normal process of doing a major shop on the few days I was at home was no longer an option. As always, she overcame that nightmare and used to take Mark in his buggy all the way to the NAAFI shop two miles away, do her shopping and wheel it all back home again.

Bill was eventually posted and replaced, to my complete surprise and delight, by Captain Glenn Bartliff, who had been the WO1 on my Yeoman's course. He had just been commissioned and was far more up for the challenge than Bill, who was focused on seeing his time out. It wasn't long before we were informed that the team was to be relocated to Celle, where it would become part of 14 Signal Regiment, the Corps specialist Electric Warfare (EW) Regiment. This made absolute sense from an organisational perspective, but immediately opened up the usual bag of bolts on availability of married quarters.

I had to tell Sue that she was going to be stuck with our little boy by herself in Herford whilst I moved up to Celle, about two hours away, for an undefined number of weeks, or maybe even months. This was made even more difficult by the fact that her dad, Jimmy, had been taken seriously ill with lung cancer, with a very bad prognosis. Susan showed her strength in that scenario, as she always did, and just got on with what had been thrown at us. I managed to get home most weekends but it's a long week by yourself with a little one and I felt desperately guilty; I also missed them both terribly.

Sadly, about four weeks into this enforced separation, Sue got a call to tell her that her dad had become even worse and wasn't expected to live, so we needed to get home quickly if we were to see him before he passed away. Many things are levelled against the army and their handling of compassionate cases, but Sue and I both believe they couldn't have acted faster or done anymore to help us recover to the UK. We made it back to Arbroath where my parents-in-law lived, but Jimmy was extremely unwell and didn't regain consciousness. We all swear though that he reacted to Sue's voice and seemed to become calmer before he passed away with his family by his side. Sue had always been a daddy's girl but in exactly the right way, and I loved him to bits because of the way he was. As people say, losing a parent is a terrible experience but at least being there at the end provides comfort; we will always be grateful to the MOD for making that possible.

Following my father-in-law's funeral, we spent a few days with the family before setting off back to Germany, a journey that we had completed dozens of times, but rarely in such a quiet, reflective mood. I was extremely pleased to be given the keys to a married quarter on my first day back to work. It wasn't a coincidence; everybody knew what we had just been through and wanted to get Sue and Mark up to join me in Celle as soon as possible. That's one of the things that makes the army, indeed the Services, so special; we look after our own and just make things happen. So, about two weeks after we got back from leave, I was able to pick my family up and bring them north to Celle.

POSTING 6
14 Sig Regiment (EW)
(Celle, W Germany)

Incredibly Beautiful Celle

Our quarter was a very tidy apartment on the Nordfeld Estate, but it was just good to be back together again permanently. For anyone that hasn't visited Northern Germany, Celle is a uniquely beautiful medieval town on the banks of the River Aller. It had every facility you could want and was within easy reach of Hannover, a substantial city should you wish to explore further afield.

The job remained the same and with such a small team (there were only eight of us including the boss and myself), we were extremely self-contained. A lot of our time was spent on Soltau-Lüneburg Training Area (SLTA) an hour or so north of Celle, so that did make life a little easier. With Glenn at the helm, we were able to really build the team, its equipment, capabilities and reputation. The Formation Headquarters and Units that we supported rated us very highly and although I often wondered if the OC of the squadron we were administered by had any interest in us whatsoever, I knew that the CO really rated us. Given that the CO was one of the best I ever served with, that was good enough for me. As a young Yeoman, I really didn't want my career to drift off into obscurity because I was employed in a small specialist team, but I needn't have worried; my annual report was fed by senior officers and Battlegroup (BG) Commanders, so lack of interest from the OC of my parent squadron made no difference whatsoever.

Whilst Glenn was with us, we undertook a great piece of adventure training, where we hired the Corps Yacht which was anchored in the port of Kiel in Northern Germany. We decided that we would travel up to Kiel the night before our hire started, with a view to storing our equipment and preparing the boat so that we could get underway at a sensible time the following morning.

It didn't take us long after arrival to get the task completed, so we went off for a couple of beers together before grabbing an early night at our mooring. Included with the hire was a suitably qualified instructor who was responsible for initial training, skippering the boat and on-board safety, and he turned up bright and early next morning. He delivered his initial briefing and made the point that as he was the only qualified guy on-board, the fact he was a serving L/Cpl in the Corps had no relevance, he was the boss at all times. To make this easier to accept for everyone, he suggested that ranks were dropped, and first names used throughout the trip; after all, we were on an adventure training expedition. His name was Gerry. Nobody had any issues with his suggestion and as we sailed out of the harbour entrance on that fine summer day, we were all very relaxed.

However, on exiting the harbour, the yacht immediately tilted to an angle of thirty degrees or less in a fierce wind that seemed to come from nowhere. Assuming we were about to drown, I heard Glenn asking a panicking member of the team, Neil Duncan, where Gerry was.

"He's still in bed, having a kip," said Neil, followed by the first challenge to the "let's drop ranks" rule as Glenn yelled, "Cpl Downs, get your fucking arse out of bed now, we're sinking!"

I was absolutely crapping myself but just couldn't stop laughing as "Gerry" raced past me to get to the wheel. Well, he was in charge of safety… but had appeared to forget his role. Steadying the boat relatively quickly, Gerry pointed out that he had expected the crew to have rectified the situation without his input, implying that we had flapped and that he would have stepped in if we couldn't right the boat within a certain time. My honest view is that the two hours of training prior to sailing was a little bit shy of what was needed, and that the tip of the mast touching the water is not a sight for complete novices; call me old-fashioned!!

The rest of our sailing trip was great fun. We sailed around the Danish coast, travelling by day and tying up overnight in some superb little Danish ports. We had many memorable meals, enjoyed the lager and checked out a lot of good nightspots. However, what happens on the Corps Yacht stays on the Corps Yacht. Let's just say it was one of the best expeditions I have ever been on, the bonus being we managed to return the yacht to Kiel in one piece, a true miracle.

A Trip to See the "Spooks"

I decided that I would take the team Cpl, Billy Bothroyd, with me when I was given the opportunity to attend a seminar at GCHQ in Cheltenham. He was still new to the team and I wanted to get to know him a little better and see him in an environment where he would be asked to contribute to the specialist subject and need to draw upon his experience.

It was only a few days back in UK and was a chance to do something quite different for a change; exercising on Soltau-Lüneburg Training Area (SLTA) week after week did become a bit tedious at times, so the change was welcome.

We flew to Birmingham and then caught a train to Cheltenham in Gloucestershire where we were booked into a local B&B. It was a lovely place with clean, spacious and well-appointed rooms, probably as good as most hotels in the town, but the lack of a bar meant we had to head into town for a bit of relaxation. On the first night, we visited several pubs and grabbed a kebab on the way back, not something that I would normally do, but Billy was from a different generation to me and convinced me it was a good idea. I must admit, I quite enjoyed the kebab, although it would never replace a bag of fish and chips for me.

The next morning, Billy didn't turn up for breakfast and I figured he was just grabbing a bit of extra sleep after a long day travelling the day before and the few beers we consumed in the evening. To be fair, he was up and ready to go at the agreed time which was all I was interested in; he was an adult and a full screw, so he deserved some respect.

As we walked along the road towards GCHQ, I asked if he hadn't fancied any breakfast.

"I knew I had some ready to eat on the way to work," he said, scooping a half-eaten kebab out of his pocket and proceeding to eat it… Having never tried last night's cold kebab in place of a cooked breakfast, I just smiled and continued walking. The seminar proved to be a remarkably interesting event with a range of diverse participants from across the globe, both military and academics. Billy showed himself to be a knowledgeable professional who was very happy to get stuck in, which was both pleasing to witness and justification for bringing him along. We headed home a couple of days later, having thoroughly enjoyed our visit and the event itself.

Exercise Dangers Are Very Real

With the 1997 exercise season in full flight, we were almost continually in the field, but often supporting the Infantry and Armoured units as opposed to our own Corps' exercises.

On one occasion, we had just completed an exercise and were heading home to Celle when we passed a military sign for 2nd Division Headquarters and Signal Regiment. Knowing that two guys off my Yeomans' course were with the Regiment, we decided to drop in to say hello; Glenn knew them as well, as he had been our WO1 on the course. The two lads, Robbie and Mick, were both SSgt Yeoman of Signals, like me; Mick had qualified at the same time whilst Robbie was removed from our course but completed the subsequent one. Their Regiment was UK-based (York) but wouldn't be heading back for two to three days, so they had some downtime. Robbie and Mick were in great spirits, bolstered by having completed an excellent exercise very successfully.

Whilst we were with our colleagues from 2 Div, we witnessed an extremely bizarre incident. The Regiment had set up in a relatively well-protected area of low ground, avoiding the wind and making good use of the land. However, whoever sited their Portaloos hadn't thought things through and had put a couple up on the ridge in the full face of the gusting wind. Whilst chatting to some of the 2 Div guys, we heard laughter erupt from the site and looking up, we saw one of the Portaloos had blown over. Unfortunately, somebody had been daft enough to use it and could be heard shouting and banging on the sides of the toilet, as it had fallen door first onto the ground. "Oh dear," I thought as a few of the lads lifted the toilet upright and out stepped the padre, looking very distressed and not a little wet and smelly!

We had a brew and chatted for a while before the lads suggested that we stay overnight and attend a bit of a party they were having that evening. Glenn and I were both up for it but had made promises to our wives that we would be back for the weekend. If we did stay, that would have effectively written Saturday off. Given the sheer volume of time we were spending in the field, we both agreed that we should head home. The lads understood; we shook hands, wished them a safe trip home, and drove off. Needless to say, we didn't seek out any spiritual guidance from the padre before departing the site, poor bloke.

The next day around 11 am, Glenn called and asked if I had heard about the fire at the location we visited the day before. I hadn't, but it suddenly got a whole lot worse when he told me that Robbie and Mick had been directly involved and both had been badly injured. Whilst he didn't have any real detail, he knew that both had been taken to hospital, probably BMH Hannover, so we agreed to try and get some information and to see what we could do to help in any way.

I rang their Regiment in the field but there wasn't a lot they could tell me other than it had been an unbelievably bad fire, probably caused by a gas leak inside a tent where they had been sleeping. From what they knew, Robbie was very badly injured, whilst Mick had severe burns to his hands and arms.

I don't know how much more I would have got out of the system, but I had a call mid-afternoon from Robbie's wife, Ute, a lovely German lass and good friend. I'll never forget that conversation, it was a real heartbreaker. Ute was stuck in the UK not knowing what to do and understandably praying that it wasn't as bad as it seemed. She was a Berliner with no family in the part of Germany concerned, so I told her that she could stay with us for as long as it took once she travelled to Germany. The truth is, I just wanted to hug her because she was so lost. I told her that I would ask the hospital if I could visit the guys, together with Glenn, but they wouldn't allow it because we weren't family, which I fully understood. I'm not sure what family members made it over to Germany, but Robbie died very shortly after my call to Ute; I was genuinely devastated and equally concerned for Mick because of his injuries.

Robbie was a genuine lad; he was married to the love of his life, and he had shown so much drive and determination in overcoming the knock-back of being removed from his initial Yeomans' course, to pass the next one. Life really isn't fair.

Robbie's funeral was held in Berlin, and Glenn and I were able to attend. The music included *The Power of Love* by Jennifer Rush, and I don't mind admitting I haven't been able to listen to that song again to this day. I'm not keen on funerals, but it was a fitting service for a top lad, and I had the privilege of meeting Robbie's family to pass on my condolences. Ute returned to Berlin sometime later and I believe still lives in the city, with Robbie close by. Whether she remarried or not, I don't know, but if she did, I hope she has had a long and happy marriage; I think that's what Robbie would have wanted.

Glenn Bartliff was a great boss, letting me get on with things and run the team on a day-to-day basis without any interference. That said, he was always there for advice and guidance if I wanted it. As an ex-para from 216 (Para) Signal Squadron, he maintained a fantastic level of fitness which was another bonus, as we just built PT into our daily lives wherever we were. We became remarkably close professionally and as genuine friends, I always knew he had my back and that is a great feeling. We were both strong characters though, so it wasn't always sweetness and light, but at the end of the day, he was the boss and I always accepted that.

During the tour, we did so many thoroughly enjoyable things together and with our team, I will always be grateful to Glenn for letting me be myself and for the excellent top cover he always provided.

Susan and I have always loved kids and we wanted some siblings for Mark; he was our pride and joy and would have been the perfect big brother. Whilst in Celle, we were overjoyed to learn that Sue was pregnant again and we were really looking forward to the baby's arrival, particularly having lost her dad a few months before. It was a real pick-me-up for both of us. Sue was a daddy's girl and I thought he was a truly great guy, so losing him was very difficult; her mum was a widow at 53 which was way too young and, of course, lived a very long way away in Scotland. My own mum had been widowed at 42, so I genuinely knew some of what my mother-in-law's future held. They bred them tough up there, but they also tend to marry once, with most never seeking to re-marry. Again, my mum had been the same, but she did like to travel to Germany fairly regularly to see us, which made her life a little more bearable.

Family Heartbreak

My tour with 14 Sigs was probably the busiest I have ever been; we were on exercise for around 40 weeks of the year which was tough on the family. As a very wise old Sgt Maj had warned me many years before, pick the right girl because this is a hard life, and it was. Luckily, I got that bit right.

We also had a good social life when I was at home. There were a lot of great characters in the Regiment who knew how to party, so that also helped to overcome stress and constantly being in the field. As Yeomen, we also had separate parties (any excuse, really!), and on one specific occasion, we had been invited round to Dave and Judy's. He was our Regimental Traffic Officer, so a commissioned Yeoman. They were a pair of characters, being heavily into the commissioned officer lifestyle. They were also lovely people and did everything to ensure they gave us a great night.

Midway through the evening, Sue started to feel ill, with extreme pains in her tummy and feeling generally very unwell. I was so glad that the other wives were there as ladies are so much better at dealing with this type of situation. Judy was amazing and did so much to help; I will always be grateful to her for her kindness.

Judy recognised all the signs as she herself had been through the same nightmare; Sue was miscarrying the baby. I got her into the car and drove her to Celle Medical Centre as quickly as I could. Such places were on minimum staff at night times and whilst it took some time for the doctor to arrive, the nurse did everything he could whilst we waited. The doctor was quickly able to diagnose the miscarriage, but worse was to come; Sue was carrying twins.

We were devastated. We didn't know we were having twins, but we had numerous sets in both families, so it wasn't a total surprise. The only thing that made it a little easier to live with is the fact that it was a relatively early miscarriage but please don't misinterpret that comment; our lives were completely turned upside down. I can't imagine how much more painful it would have been if it had happened in the last few weeks. I'm not sure how we would have handled such trauma. The saddest thing of all, besides the fact that we had lost two children, is that Sue was a fantastic mother, and this would have completed our family. When these things happen, both of you need to pull together and support one another, otherwise it could tear you apart.

We never gave up on having more children, it just never happened; that's why we are so proud of Mark and thank God we have him.

Another New Boss

Glenn, or "His Bollocking Majesty" as the lads often referred to him, eventually moved on and his replacement was a chap called Carl, another genuine character but very, very different from his predecessor. Change is a good thing and to be honest, Carl was quite happy for me to get on with things, shouting if I needed any top cover. That suits my style and we got on exceptionally well. Carl did like a beer; indeed, he was a bit of a beer monster and sailed close to the wind on several occasions.

I recall one occasion when we were called to 7th Signal Regiment to brief Commander 1 (BR) Cops, Brigadier Tim Waugh. The plan was to finish our exercise on Thursday, drive up to Herford where we would overnight, and brief the Brigadier at 10 am the following morning.

The problem with this type of away day is that you inevitably bump into old mates who invite you for food and a few beers the night before. Never being one to refuse a few ales (OK, so I have the willpower of a gnat), Carl had already accepted an offer within five minutes of parking up in the barracks. We dropped off our kit, got changed and headed off downtown within the hour. We went to an outstanding Balkan restaurant where we ate some excellent meat dishes and drank rather a lot of Pilsner, along with a couple of shots. Making it back to barracks at a rather later hour than originally planned, we headed off to bed.

"See you in the Training Wing at 8.00 am, boss," I said to Carl, but I wasn't sure it registered since he had lost most of his power of speech…

I am lucky in that I have never had a problem getting out of bed, irrespective of how much beer is involved, and I was up, washed, dressed, and breakfasted by 7.30 and in the Training Room by 8 am, sorting out our equipment and preparing for a rehearsal. Unfortunately, I had run through everything twice by 9am and there was still no sign of Carl. Getting worried, I decided to nip down to the officers' accommodation to check that he was awake. I knocked hard on the bunk door, but there was no reply, so assuming he must be at breakfast, I headed back to the presentation room.

Everything was good to go; all I needed was the presenter, my boss, but he wasn't there. I knew Brigadier Tim Waugh as he had been my CO at 3 Div HQ & Sig Regt some years previously. He was a good guy but not one to be mucked around by anybody, so when he strode into the room early, I had images of Carl being loaded into a very large catapult and launched over the fence as his penance for non-attendance.

"Where is the Traffic Officer, Yeoman?" asked Brigadier Tim.

With nothing to lose, I replied, "I think he injured a muscle in his leg yesterday, Sir, and may well have gone to see the doctor."

"Bollocks!" said the Brigadier. "Go and find him and tell him he has 10 minutes to get here, or he is toast!"

"Yes, Sir!" I said and legged it down to the officers' mess where nobody had seen him that morning. I therefore decided to try his accommodation again.

This time I dispensed with the knocking approach and nearly kicked a hole in the door, accompanied by shouting his name very loudly.

After a few seconds, the door swung open, and a clearly still inebriated Carl appeared, looking like he had been dragged through a hedge backwards. "Is it 8 o'clock?" he asked.

"Er no, it's 10 am, the Brigadier is here and has sent me to summons you!" I just didn't have the time to explain my earlier visit, all the preparation that I had done or anything else. "I think you need to get dressed quickly and get your arse over to the Training Wing. I have told the Brigadier that I think you injured a leg yesterday, so you could try to expand on that story!" I then headed back to the presentation room.

"Did you find him?" asked the Brigadier.

"Yes, Sir, he is still in a lot of pain from his leg but I didn't ask for the full story."

"Um," mused the Brigadier, "get going with the presentation."

Given I had written the presentation top to bottom, I was very comfortable delivering it, so when Carl burst into the room some 10 minutes into it, I was pleased that Brigadier Tim motioned him to sit down and let me complete it. I think things would have ended very differently had Carl been tasked to take over; he hadn't done any rehearsal and although he would have been OK with a couple of run-throughs, without them and still pissed, it may have been game over.

After Q&A, the Brigadier thanked me for the presentation, turned to Carl and invited him to a private discussion. I was genuinely very worried about the outcome of that meeting, so I was very relieved when Carl came out and said we should pack up and get on the road back to Celle. He was still a Captain, didn't appear to have been sacked, and the Brigadier seemed to be quite relaxed.

"How the fuck did he get out of that one?" I thought to myself, whilst packing at the speed of light in an attempt to get the hell out of there. I knew how tough Tim Waugh could be, so I was intrigued to understand how Carl had survived, seemingly unscathed although still half-cut, which made the journey home uncomfortable for him. Carl did say that he had received a painful tongue-lashing, but the Brigadier was going to let it go.

Personally, I have always believed that he saw Carl as a character and recognised the sheer number of days we were doing in the field, which doesn't mix too well with a skinful the night before! If I had been a more experienced Yeoman, I probably wouldn't have been too concerned about making a lot of noise in the officers' mess and kicking his door in on my first visit, but you must put that down to the fact that I was a very young SSgt. Anyway, I was happy he wasn't in deep doo-doo; he was a good bloke.

We were part of 3 Squadron in 14th Signal Regiment but because we were a specialist team, working across all of the units in BAOR, we had a separate and much heavier exercise schedule than they did. Unfortunately, this did lead to a bit of tension occasionally, which really wasn't necessary. The OC of the squadron used to get jealous of the fact that we were regularly visited by senior officers and he and his wider squadron weren't involved. His SSM would quite often pick on my guys, but never when I was around; this was probably because he was following his boss's lead.

SLTA – Our Home From Home

A lot of our time was spent on Soltau-Lüneburg Training Area (SLTA), which was one of the British Army's busiest training locations in Germany. There was always some unit or other undertaking exercises, and our role was to monitor and report on the quality of their communication security; we would listen to hours of radio traffic, recording and transcribing the information, from which we had to present a report at ENDEX (End of Exercise). These reports would be copied to Corps HQ in Bielefeld and were taken very seriously; a bad report could definitely create problems for a CO or BG Comd, which did not enhance their chances of promotion.

We spent so much time on the Heath that we were allocated permanent use of the main building on Reinsehlen Camp in the heart of the training area. Not wishing to paint too comfortable a picture, the building was an absolute dump and hadn't been used for years, but it gave us a roof over our heads which was better than canvas, particularly when you are spending up to nine months of the year there.

I guess none of us will ever forget Wolfgang "The Bratty Man", who was a Cold War hero to the many thousands of troops that used the training area over the years. A local German who had built a very profitable business by miraculously tracking the units down in his food wagon, even when they were operating on a fully tactical basis, with everything camouflaged and no lights at night, his knowledge of SLTA was unsurpassed. Whilst there is no doubt that it drove senior officers mad, they realised that the easiest thing to do was just let Wolfgang sell his tea/coffee and various sausages, to get him on his way as quickly as possible. It did make for some strange pauses during exercises, but they do say an army marches on its stomach! I would hazard a guess that Wolfgang was probably better known than any other German, even the Chancellor. He was also a very wealthy man.

Losing a Mate

It was during this tour that I entered a terrible period, where I lost some incredible friends, starting with my crewman from 3 Armd Div HQ & Sig Regt, Del Wood.

When Derek (Del) Wood arrived at 3 Div HQ & Sig Regt in Soest, he joined 3 Squadron and was allocated to my Detachment, G3 Ops. Del was a bit of a cockney wide boy, but I really liked him. He had a good sense of humour, excellent work ethic and was a team player in every way. As he learned his trade and I prepared for my forthcoming YofS Course, we became firm friends and I always felt I was helping him shape his career.

Before I left, he asked me whether he should consider an EOD (Explosive Ordnance Disposal) role in Northern Ireland (NI). My advice was to apply if he fancied a very different role, which he duly did. Del went to Northern Ireland and thoroughly enjoyed that tour. In fact, he got hooked on working in that environment and it wasn't long before he returned to the Province to undertake another completely different role. During this second tour, he was brutally murdered by the IRA.

177

On the weekend of 19th to 20th March 1988, my best friend, Dai Jones, and his family had driven up from Krefeld for a BBQ and a bit of a break. We didn't have too many chances to spend time together at that point because of the distance involved, so we took the chance to spend the majority of Saturday outside in the early spring sunshine.

Dai, Kathy and the kids set off home around midday on the Sunday, so I settled down to watch the news on BFBS (British Forces Broadcasting Service). I can't begin to explain how I felt as a report on the murder of two R Signals Cpls began to unfold and to my absolute horror, the reporter announced their names: Derek Wood and David Howes.

I recognised Del from the TV footage, so the reporter only confirmed what I feared, but hoped I had got wrong. Of all the terrible things I had seen before or since, this was the most barbaric, inhuman, and sadistic killing I had ever seen. I will never accept that any cause could justify such actions, nor indeed that such brutality could be inflicted by members of the human race on others. To my mind, the perpetrators are, and always will be, sub-human monsters. Del was just 24 years old, whilst Dave Howes, known as Bob, was 23.

Dai phoned to say they were home safely, and I then had to tell him what had happened. He too knew Del very well from our time in Soest, and had also recently returned from a tour with 39 (Inf Bde) Sig Squadron in NI, so he was no stranger to the horrors that unfolded there.

I had spoken to Del just a few weeks before he returned to NI on his second tour and I told him that it should be his last tour in the Province, and that he should focus on gaining more experience in a traditional Corps unit. He never got that chance...

Vast Canadian Plain

The British Army Training Unit in Suffield (BATUS), Canada, is a fascinating place. Set in the province of Alberta, it is the British Army's largest armoured training area, capable of accommodating live firing (yes, real bullets and shells!) and what is known as tactical effect simulation (TES) exercises up to battlegroup level. Incomparable as a capability, it has been in use since 1971 and has seen many thousands of UK forces pass through over the decades. To give a feel for the geographical size of the vast terrain available, the area is seven times the size of Salisbury Plain Training Area (SPTA) and 19% of the size of Northern Ireland.

Unsurprisingly, it is a huge favourite amongst soldiers, not just because of the location which clearly does have a certain attraction, but because of the sheer quality and realism from a battle simulation perspective. The training in this environment is second to none. Given the ferocity of the Canadian winters, exercises are conducted from May to October each year, with an annual turnover of four to six battlegroups (BG) each exercising for around 24 days at a time. BATUS has both permanent and temporary staff, together with a dedicated enemy; the latter being provided by a nominated regiment.

As my team spent so much of our time at this level on Soltau-Lüneburg Training Area (SLTA) in Germany, it was decided that we should also provide support to BATUS. Normally, additional workload wasn't well received, but for some reason the lads were very accepting of this task; I wonder what swung it?

We flew into the city of Calgary and then undertook a very tedious road trip to the small town of Suffield, some 162 miles away to the south-east. On arrival, we quickly settled in and after a series of briefings, we got our equipment set up and tested prior to the main exercise deployment.

We were working from the main base, so didn't get an opportunity to join the main exercise, which was a shame. Whilst the monitoring tasks were a bit 'same old, same old', the weather was good, and we did get a fair bit of time to look around. The hamlet of Suffield had very little to offer, so if you wanted any entertainment, it meant travelling 30 odd miles into Medicine Hat which was a bit of a drive for a couple of beers. It was home to a nightclub called The Pink Cadillac and had a life-sized model in the centre of the dance floor. I am reliably informed that it wasn't a great place to hang out when the whole BG was in town, which I find quite easy to believe. A mixture of very tired, bored soldiers and some Canadian cowboys just doesn't bear thinking about!

At the end of the visit, we managed to do a bit of a short tour, taking in a local Blackfoot Indian village at the Siksika Nation Reserve, east of Calgary. Whilst quite commercialised, it showed the way of life for their ancestors, complete with tepees, totem poles, and entertainment with mock battles and tribal dancing. Inevitably, trinkets, headdress and the like were on sale at vastly inflated prices, but fascinating, nonetheless. Returning to Calgary for our flight back to the UK, we also managed to get a couple of nights in a local hotel and an opportunity to look around the city.

For those who haven't been to Canada, particularly the western side, I would definitely recommend it; at around 1.5m people, Calgary is the country's third largest city. Situated at the confluence of the Bow and Elbow rivers in the south of the province, in the transitional area between the Rocky Mountain foothills and the Canadian Prairies, it is extremely beautiful. The city has a lot of great steak restaurants and bars, some of which still have traditional batwing doors, so great for the cowboys amongst us! I would also recommend eating at the top of the Calgary Tower in the Sky 360 Restaurant and Lounge, where the revolving restaurant provides magnificent views of the city and the Rocky Mountains.

Following the trip to Canada, our stints on the SLTA and other Northern German plains never felt quite the same again.

Getting on with Life

As a family, Celle was a great posting for us, with the exception of the exercise load, of course. The other guys within the Def EW team lived close by and Sue got on well with them, and she also had several other friends to spend time with whilst I was out on exercise. Mark loved it there and seemed to be enjoying school.

We were also spoilt for choice in terms of facilities, with the superb Heide Park just up the road and fabulous sporting venues all around us. We were within a couple of hours of several international airports (Hannover, Hamburg, and Munster), providing great flexibility on travel, and we also had access to an American PX facility north of us in Bremerhaven. The Americans take exceptionally good care of their service families and the PX was their version of

Aladdin's cave, so having one located relatively close was a godsend. I spent longer in the Defensive EW Team than I wanted but I thoroughly enjoyed the job, had some great bosses and the lads within the team were some of the best I served with.

We didn't often exercise as part of our parent Regiment, but on the special communication-only exercises, such as the annual Ex FLYING FALCON, it happened occasionally. Given that we were so self-contained when deployed alone, it could be quite painful to join the Regiment on exercise, and unsurprisingly it wasn't something our small team overly enjoyed. It seemed that a lot went wrong in these situations, with everything being much slower and simply less dynamic than when we were with the Teeth Arm units.

On one occasion, the Regiment had sited the team with a German Signal Unit and we were at the top of a steep hill which was covered in snow and ice. For anybody that is unaware, it can get unbelievably cold in Northern Germany in February, so the resupply of rations and fuel was a real challenge in this particular location. As if that wasn't bad enough, we were required to use Portaloos rented from a local contractor and getting up and down the hill was extremely difficult for the toilet servicing vehicle. This was obviously of serious concern to all of us as time went past, with several postponed visits, but eventually the service vehicle made it to the site. However, our relief was short-lived as having completed its work, the wagon set off down the hill; unfortunately, the operator had forgotten to close off the suction pump, resulting in deposits being left all the way down the hill... Unpleasant doesn't cover it, and we were certainly incredibly pleased when ordered to move to a new location.

We were an exceptionally fit group and trained religiously as a team, often joining our squadron and regiment groupings on their runs. The River Aller ran close to the barracks, so it was quite normal for these runs to follow the riverbank for at least part of the route. On one run, we joined the squadron, and despite heavy snow and the river being iced over, we followed one of the popular routes along its banks. I kind of suspected it might be somewhat dangerous, as it was very difficult to discern the edge of the river.

As we trotted along, Russ Jardine, a pretty tall member of my team, made the mistake of stepping outside the leading footprints and immediately disappeared through a hole in the ice; it was a bit like the scene from *The Vicar of Dibley*, with Russ taking Dawn French's role in that famous skit. It was terrifying and a great relief when a few seconds later. he popped back up and we hauled him out. Scary, but as you will appreciate, it appealed to the sense of humour of all his colleagues.

We took the opportunity to travel quite extensively whilst there and enjoyed many holidays. Usually travelling south towards the Mediterranean, we just took our time, stopping overnight in places like the Black Forest or Vienna, grabbing dinner and a few beers, accompanied by a bit of yodelling. Life was pretty special.

We went on holiday regularly with friends to countries such as Denmark, which was relatively close, or made significant journeys south to locations like France, Spain or Italy. On one occasion, we visited Denmark with our friends Mick and Debbie McKenna, hiring a beautiful farmhouse that was big enough for the four adults and three kids. We had a lovely break in great weather, barbecues galore and

Defensive EW Team 1988.
A fantastic group of lads!

some very enjoyable visits. On a day out to a local zoo, we were making our way around the various animal enclosures and eventually reached the hippo house which had a very pungent smell indeed. Knowing that Mick wasn't great with such things, I gave him a shout to come and have a look at these magnificent animals. I will never forget him walking in and retreating at breakneck speed, retching as he made his getaway.

When I got notified of my posting to 1 Armd Div HQ and Sig Regiment, I was pleased to be staying in Germany, but a bit apprehensive about going to Verden, which had a rather poor reputation. I took the opportunity to visit Verden and my new unit before my move date. I was to be the 3 Squadron Yeoman.

My time in Celle drew to a close and I eventually headed to Verden, an hour and a half further north on the River Aller. Professionally, I was delighted to go to Verden at that point, as I was just about to enter the promotion bracket and it was exactly the right unit in which to make my push.

POSTING 7
1 Armd Div HQ & Sig Regt
(Verden, W Germany)

Back to Life in Armour

Moving from the Corps EW Regiment to a Divisional Signal Regiment was always going to be a change of pace. I was allocated to 3 Squadron, who provided one of the two Armoured Headquarters; they swapped roles regularly during exercise and operations, allowing one to command the division whilst the other moved location.

My old pal Guy Benson from 249 Sig Sqn days was the Yeoman in the other headquarters, run by 2 Squadron and to my further delight, Martin Fielding was the 1 Squadron Yeoman. His job was to provide the tactical trunk network across the division. I couldn't help but think how strong this group of Yeoman would be with Guy, Martin, and myself, and I am pretty sure anybody serving with us in the year that followed would agree.

The bloke from whom I was taking over was SSgt Yeoman Bob Tait. I had been in Harrogate with Bob so I knew him, but not well. He was a bright and capable individual, who had hit really hard times whilst in Verden.

I'm unlikely to forget my first visit to the office Bob shared with the Squadron Foreman of Signals, Chuddy, another one of my intake from Harrogate. I liken the state of the office to the home of a famous hoarder, Mr Trebus, and I imagine the smell wouldn't have been too different either. Chuddy was one of the most laid-back characters I have ever met, so I wasn't surprised that he had just accepted the situation. Time for change!

During my first afternoon, Bob informed me that we needed to visit the Regimental HQ, so I could be introduced to the RSM. It was only about 100m between the buildings but to my surprise, Bob pulled up sharply outside the HQ and told me that I would have to head in by myself, as he was banned! I'd never come across something like that in my life but just headed in, located the RSM's office and knocked on the door.

"Come in, Yeoman," the RSM called.

I marched in, employing my best drill. Stamped my foot as hard as possible and presented myself. It became clear within a nanosecond that the RSM's main concern was to ensure I wasn't a like-for-like swap for Bob. As he explained some of his concerns, it became extremely clear why. Once he had regaled me with tales of woe relating to Bob, he drew things to a close by asking me why I was wearing the shirt I had on. This threw me a little, but I briefly explained to him that it was a formally issued KF (khaki flannel) shirt, albeit it was a brown one. He let me know that he never wanted to see the shirt again and dismissed me to my work. Strange, I thought, what's his beef with my shirt, but given it had been issued to me by a Quartermaster's department and I liked it, I decided to wear another shirt for a while before returning to my favourite. I assumed that Bob had driven him to the point of insanity, and therefore he simply wanted to stamp his authority on me nice and early.

From there, Bob and I headed over to the other barracks across the road. This was where the divisional staff were based and our Comcen was co-located. The Yeomen within the Regiment, of which there were three SSgts and a WO1, were responsible for looking after the Comcen, with the WO1 providing permanent oversight, whilst the more junior SSgts did the real management for one week in every three. Blow me, but Bob again came to a halt outside the Comcen to inform me that he was also barred from there! He wouldn't share the whys or wherefores on his expulsion, but I had little doubt that my fellow Yeomen would bring me up to speed.

After an introduction to the Comcen staff, who were largely female, I left and picked Bob up as we headed back to the office. I needed to start getting my head around the bizarre incidents I had witnessed, and to do something to try and tidy up the shithole of an office so that I could get some work done.

As I had another two formal introductions that afternoon, to the OC and the SSM, I encouraged Bob to get back to the sergeants' mess and start his own packing for departure at the end of the week.

"No problem," he said. "We've got another four days to complete the handover."

I just shook my head in despair.

The OC was Major Scott Ewing, another ex-249 man that I knew and got on well with, and the SSM, WO2 Ian Kirkpatrick, was straightforward, albeit his trials and tribulations with Bob had taken their toll and he wasn't a great supporter of the Yeoman fraternity. I just accepted him for who and what he was; we didn't clash, and our working relationship was professional.

At the end of Day 1, I was able to head home and let Sue know that this should be the job to get me promoted, although I anticipated some real challenges in the handover and expected some hostility because of the bad feeling Bob had created. Our quarter, in Niedersachsen Ring, was reasonably decent, but if I achieved my aim we would only be there for a year anyway, so we were quite relaxed about that aspect.

As I settled into my squadron, I uncovered some more pals were there with me. SSgt Kev Froggett, my first Cpl Detachment Commander at 249, ran one troop, whilst SSgt Pete Griffin, again part of the 249 gang, ran another. This was seriously good news, as these were two of the best guys I had ever served with. Unfortunately, Kev was posted to Northern Ireland a few months later; he was awfully close to his end-of-service date, so the location didn't appeal to him understandably. Being Kev, he took it on the chin and moved on when the time came. "It's only a year," I remember him saying the day he left. But it wasn't a year because he was shot and killed whilst conducting maintenance on a mast in Coal Island by an IRA sniper. What a loss.

But on to happier times. One of the funniest memories of Verden relates to my old buddy Ronny Allan who had been

Bob's predecessor as 3 Squadron Yeoman. Obviously, it happened long before I got there, but it involved a guy that I knew and indeed, was a fellow Yeoman. His name was SSgt Frank McCubbin and he lived in the same married quarter block of flats as Ronny. Frank was an easy-going, happy-go-lucky bloke, very placid by nature, who just got on with things. His wife, on the other hand, was, shall we say, the complete opposite!

As many people with army connections will know, when living in blocks of flats, it is customary practice for the senior rank to be nominated as block leader. The base responsibility is to ensure that the building and communal areas are kept clean and that the various jobs are cycled between the occupants in a fair manner. I think primarily because both Frank and Ronny were SSgts, his wife couldn't or wouldn't accept that Ronny had been made block senior and made this clear to him at every opportunity. She had a wide and varied range of profanities that she enjoyed aiming at Ronny whenever the chance arose. Frank knew through experience not to get involved, as the outcome might turn out to be a little tricky….

A specific visit by a senior officer had been arranged and as was normal, the need to ensure the blocks were immaculately presented was repeated on various orders and briefings. Not liking the tasks allocated to her by Ronny, her response was to wait until the night before the inspection and then paint a giant face with a huge brown nose, annotating it, "Ronny Allan – arse licker," on a wall in the stairwell of the block.

Clearly, there was no time in which to remove this piece of art and I am informed that the visiting dignitary wasn't particularly impressed. Poor old Frank almost certainly took the flack for the action, but as previously mentioned, I very much doubt he made any attempt to remonstrate with her. Ronny and I still laugh about this to this day.

Guy Benson's OC in 2 Squadron was Major Geoff "Scary" Carey. To be fair, they were a good team but Martin, the 1 Squadron Yeoman, and I just couldn't resist taking the piss out of them at every opportunity. Geoff was quite a highly-strung individual, but I liked him because he would stand up for himself and his squadron, no matter who it was he was talking to. Guy, just like me, and Martin to be fair, was always pushing to be the best, but in the right way; we always had each other's back. Any Yeoman will do what it takes to deliver the best quality communications to his unit, that's the way we were made, but Guy used to try and have his cake and eat it.

As I mentioned, I had one of the divisional headquarters whilst Guy had the other. Radio communications were bread and butter for both of us, but the delivery of secure trunk wasn't under our direct control. We relied upon Martin's squadron to provide a fully connected network, into which we could link our respective headquarters. The links to us on that system were a combination of UHF (Ultra High Frequency) and SHF (Super High Frequency) and of course, we had to contend with the fact that the headquarters were always trying to tuck themselves away from a tactical perspective, out of sight of the enemy.

There were three bands of frequencies available to us for the trunk network, Bands 1-3 and as you incremented from 1, it became progressively more difficult to establish a link as the geography played more and more of a part in the Line of Sight (LOS) requirement. Guy would almost have paid for allocation of Band 1 frequencies to ensure success and we ribbed him about it mercilessly, to the point that we dubbed him Band 1 Benson. Being Guy, he loved it and as always, he just returned the stick he got. Those were happy days for me, working with two of the most professional men and best friends I made throughout my service.

Our first Traffic Officer was Major Tony Lomax, a really lovely bloke who stood up for his Yeomen and was always there for us. He was also always up for a laugh, and I recall one specific incident where Martin and I were in his office, but Guy hadn't been able to attend as he was giving a squadron briefing at the time. As usual, we were taking the mickey out of each other when Tony noticed my rather large Filofax, which I carried everywhere with me.

"I hope everything in there is unclassified?" says Tony, "otherwise I will have to charge you for breaching security."

Because he was into amateur dramatics, he was a very polished actor, so Martin and I stared at each other before Tony burst out laughing, saying "Gotcha!"

When we left the office, we decided that was too good a prank to let go, especially since Guy hadn't been there to witness it. We quickly headed back to Martin's office and phoned Guy. When he answered, Martin told him that I had been charged by the Traffic Officer for not ensuring my notebook was appropriately classified. He then said that Major Lomax had stated that as Guy wasn't present at the time, he would have to report to him to have his daybook checked.

Flapping, Guy quickly visited his secure room and applied a RESTRICTED stamp to the top and bottom of every page of his book, before heading off to see the Traffic Officer. Of course, we hadn't told Tony Lomax about this stitch-up but typically, he recognised the scam as soon as Guy turned up at his office with the classified notebook. Martin and I made Guy suffer for that one, and Tony really enjoyed his part too.

The work hard/play hard approach was very much part of life in Verden and I think myself, Guy and Martin worked at 100 miles an hour every day, so it was very pleasing when all three of us were successful on the same promotion board to WO2. I had absolutely no hesitation in telling my CO that I wanted to go to 201 (22 Armd Bde) HQ & Sig Sqn, which was down the road in Bergen-Hohne. It was part of 1st Armoured Division and was the only "square" Brigade in the British Army; by square, I mean it had two infantry battalions and two Armoured Regiments – the usual mix was two and one.

It had been one of my career aspirations to be the 22nd Brigade Yeoman and that, I hoped, may take me through to another promotion, where I would be posted to one of the other division's as a WO1 eventually. The fact that it kept me in Germany was a bonus, but the icing on the cake was that the squadron was commanded by Major Andy Forster. I knew he was one of the best before I worked with him and he proved to be even better than I had heard. Anyway, I was delighted to get the job and after a matter of weeks, I made my merry way to Hohne Camp which was pretty close to our old haunt in Celle.

POSTING 8
201 (22 Armd Bde) Sig Sqn
(Bergen-Hohne, W Germany)

My Dream Job

Hohne was an exceptionally large camp, with everything, including a huge number of married quarters behind the wire. Sue and I were a bit taken aback with the name of our allocated house, 'OB 4/2' which stood for Obersturmbannführer, Row 4, House 2. The reason for our shock is that Obersturmbannführer was an SS rank in the German army during the war, so it was a bit strange, particularly as Bergen-Belsen concentration camp was literally four miles down the road...

Our quarter was fairly small but had the benefit of having a usable cellar, which we turned into a playroom for Mark, where he had things like his pool table, football table, pet rabbits and all the usual stuff. The house had a door directly into a 100ft long garden which was handy. The garden, unfortunately, had a lot of very tall pine trees, so it spoilt some of its usage. On the first day in the house, we noticed that next door, number 4/1, was empty and it had a superb hand-built brick BBQ, so I quickly lifted Mark over the wall to pass it to me brick by brick! This was a good move as that BBQ served us well for nearly four years. In Germany, BBQs were a big thing, so it got a lot of use.

From the day I stepped into the squadron HQ, I knew this was the unit for me; everything just felt right. The bloke I was taking over from, Mick Boxall, was a big solid guy that I knew from various functions; he was a jovial, likeable fella who was popular with everybody, so that was helpful. I had seen just how difficult handovers could be the last time around, and Mick had most things under control. We were quite different characters, largely due to the significant age difference, but also our personal traits and ambitions. That said, as is normally the case with Yeomen, we had each other's backs; Mick had done a fair bit of detailed preparation, so time spent with him was hugely beneficial. Our handover lasted the full five-day working week and when I finally shook Mick's hand on completion, I was absolutely up to speed on 22 Brigade Signal Squadron.

Out of the Mist…

One of the things I will never forget during that week is that we had a unit assessment on the Wednesday, which included a Basic Fitness Test (BFT) for everybody. In essence, this is a mile and a half march/jog, immediately followed by another mile and a half run on an individual best-effort basis. Dependent on age, completion pass times were incremented upwards. This was the type of thing I thoroughly enjoyed and was rather good at, but I realised it probably wasn't Mick's favourite pastime.

On the day of the run, it was cold, wet and intermittently foggy, which I was to learn was quite a regular set of conditions in Hohne. We all set off at a steady pace led by a Physical Training Instructor (PTI) and got to the halfway point without any casualties, but a few guys blowing like steam trains. The second half just followed the same route but at your own pace, so at the whistle, off we went.

Part of the route was around a big sports field and the fog had descended yet again. Unfortunately, the fog dispersed very quickly, and a few desperate souls were uncovered in the middle of the sports field as they took a shortcut. Mick was amongst them and as you can imagine, that went down like a lead balloon, but it was very, very funny. Post-handover, Mick headed off in the reverse direction to me, as he had been selected for promotion to WO1 and was heading up to Verden as the Regimental Yeoman. I liked Mick and was pleased that we would be working together in the future.

As I settled into the squadron, it was clear to me that we had a lot of excellent people right across the board. As mentioned, the OC was everything I had hoped he would be and more, whilst the other Officers and SNCOs were a solid, competent and happy group.

My only concern was the SSM, whom I had bumped into previously back in Soest. He and I were both WO2s and he was one of those people that thought because he was an RD (Regimental Duty) man, he ran the show. However, the way he addressed people, even SNCOs, was very odd. I shared an office with my technical counterpart, the Squadron Foreman of Signals; on arrival, it was a guy called Jay Allen. The SSM knew perfectly well that he should refer to the appointment and not the rank when addressing Jay, yet he insisted on calling him Staff, undermining and embarrassing him. This was like a red rag to a bull with me; knowing the SSM, I was aware that he had been a technician previously and as such, had attempted to become a Foreman and failed. His treatment of Jay fell far below the standards, quality, and common decency that the army expects, so I quite deliberately ensured that each time he referred to Jay in this manner, I pulled him up on it.

Not long after my arrival, I was watching from the office window as the squadron were on morning parade. The SSM was conducting an inspection on the guys and just generally being obnoxious as he did so. He stood in front of a LCpl called Jason Raybould and asked him very loudly if he had shaved that morning. When Jason confirmed that he had, the SSM pointed out that he had left some shaving foam behind his ear, whereby Jason reached forward behind the SSM's ear and wiped a huge lump of shaving foam from it, saying, "That's two of us then, Sir!" That demonstrated perfectly why, in my opinion, that SSM would never attain the required standard for the appointment.

Meeting Freddie Mercury

Our Chief Clerk, a Scottish guy called Dougie, or as he was known "Duncan Disorderly", was a real madcap character. Outside of work, Dougie spent most of his life in the bar, often morphing into his alter-ego Freddie Mercury, particularly at mess or squadron functions. His costume consisted of a pair of enormous plastic teeth and a stick-on hairy chest. Although it was extremely funny first time around, by the time you had seen it a dozen times, it had lost its shine!

The lads had devised several ways to deal with his antics and these were often far funnier than the appearance of "Freddie" himself.

One particularly hilarious example was during a squadron event held in the cellar bar, where we were being entertained by the aptly named "Fat Bastard", a UK act doing the rounds across BAOR (you do have to wonder sometimes). I'll refer to the "artist" as FB, for the sake of brevity and to avoid too much random swearing. FB was quite funny, and the majority of the audience were enjoying his act, but as with most acts, he needed to take a mid-way break. Unfortunately, this gave our own "artist" his opportunity and as soon as FB had left the stage, Freddie burst through the curtain belting out his favourite hit. The guys quickly decided this was one appearance too many, so Dougie was hoisted onto the shoulders of a few lads, carried across the room, and physically thrown upwards and outwards from a cellar window. Luckily it had been snowing for most of the day which meant he had a reasonably soft landing. Happy with Freddie's expulsion, the window was quickly secured to ensure he didn't fall back in again!

I saw this performance often during my time with the squadron, but even the extremely tolerant group of SNCOs eventually got so fed up with it that he was barred from the mess. Funnily enough, Dougie was a competent Chief Clerk and a good, fit and capable soldier. The demon drink just transformed him into a complete pain in the arse!

POSTING 9
Gulf War 1 Operation GRANBY
(Saudi Arabia, Iraq & Kuwait)

Operation GRANBY

A few short months after my arrival in Hohne, the first Gulf War started to brew and pretty quickly our Sister Brigade, 7th Armoured Brigade, based just up the road in Soltau, was placed on standby to deploy. We were soon drawn into their preparation cycle, helping on different areas of training and general support. However, I was called into my OC's office a couple of weeks later to be told that the deployment would now also include 1 Div HQ & Sig Regiment, and that the CO had decided that I would be recalled to the Regiment to do my old job with 3 Squadron.

To say I was disappointed would be an understatement, as I knew that my own squadron would eventually become involved and given this was an appointment I had worked towards all my career, I didn't want somebody else to take them to war in my place. Andy Forster knew exactly where

I was coming from, but the CO at Div had made it clear he wanted me with them, so there wasn't a lot he could do.

As with all war scenarios, things change quickly as the situation unfolds and the intelligence improves. Luckily for me, the Order of Battle (ORBAT) changed yet again, and the CO decided that I was still needed but that the whole squadron would be going with me. I know it was selfish, but I was absolutely elated, particularly as we had been chosen to provide a second or alternative HQ for the division, something I personally knew inside out and had every confidence we would do very well.

Breaking these things to your family is just part of the job but it's never easy. This was a war that was building up under the spotlight of the world's press and on the TV every day, so they knew it was pretty serious. We swung from our position of assisting 7 Bde in their preparation to commencing our own pre-deployment training programme. The lads were great right from the outset, but we did need some additional resources to make our numbers up and these were drawn from across the wider Corps.

We were a very tight knit unit, so it must have been a fairly daunting experience just being pitched into it from elsewhere. It did prove too much for some of our reinforcements, with one guy deliberately dropping a very heavy tiled table on his foot and breaking it, in order not to deploy. Whether this was because he was finding it difficult to integrate, or he was scared, will never be known, but I can't see anybody having a problem mixing with our guys because they were pretty much the salt of the earth and very welcoming. That said, there is nothing wrong with being scared. In fact, being honest, we all were. It's just human nature to be afraid of the unknown; it's part of a soldier's life and needs to be managed accordingly.

New Year's Eve in the Sun

Our preparation and training culminated just prior to Christmas 1991, and we were allowed to enjoy the holiday with our families, before deploying by air just before New Year. That was a sensible move, as it would have proved trickier gathering people up post-New Year; we are talking about soldiers, remember!

There is nothing quite as tough as standing on your doorstep, saying goodbye to your family. My little boy was only eight years old and I was leaving him and Sue on their own in a foreign country, with no close family around them. That's a tough ask for any father and you simply don't know if you will be coming home. Remaining calm is essential but extremely hard.

The flight out to Saudi Arabia was mundane, leaving most of us to consider what lay ahead and, of course, what it held for each of us individually. On arrival, we were bussed onwards to the port of Al Jubail, the world's largest industrial city, where our equipment would arrive by sea. Here we were, New Year in the Persian Gulf, where the weather was scorching and there wasn't a beer in sight, or likely to be for quite some time. Ah well, it was bloody cold in Hohne so that was at least one benefit.

As part of 1 (UK) Armd Div, we were placed under the command of 7 (US) Corps, commanded by Lt Gen Freddie Franks Jr (call sign *"Jayhawk"*); now it really was starting to gather momentum.

Having completed the in-country vehicle and equipment preparation cycle, we were ordered to move up country into the desert, along what was known as the Tapline Road. It was quite a sight to behold, a full armoured division moving through the desert on a road as straight as an arrow. To be honest, I thought we were pretty exposed to enemy aircraft at this point. Although the war hadn't actually started, we would have been in trouble had the Iraqis decided to launch an attack early. That worry didn't last long, however, as our air cover soon hovered into view and suddenly there were US and UK attack helicopters everywhere. For those that have seen the AH-64 Apache up close, it is intimidating, but when you see it fully loaded and bristling with the latest weaponry, flying at 150 to 200m above your head and there are more of them than you knew existed, it does give you immense confidence.

The enemy decided not to attend the party and we eventually arrived at our initial desert locations. This is where we were put through our paces big time. We undertook a long, arduous sequence of activities in preparation for battle, including some exhausting but very real exercises with our various allies. There is no doubt in my mind that our squadron very quickly established themselves as a massively competent Division Alternate HQ. As a Brigade HQ, we were just that bit sharper in our movement and drills than our Divisional Signal Regiment counterparts.

The morning after our arrival up-country, the Divisional Traffic Officer asked me if I could attend a briefing at 7 (US) Corps HQ and whilst there, pick up some secure items.

"No problem, Sir, but have we got a map that I can use?"

"Of course, George," he said, handing me a 1:500,000 map of the desert. This isn't going to be easy, I thought, given the scale of the map made it appear more akin to a piece of heavyweight sandpaper; at least there weren't any roads to get lost on, I thought!

My driver, Cpl Ally McKitterick, and I set off about 30 minutes later with our piece of sandpaper in my hand; Ally found it quite funny, as I did, but the reality was that's all we had at that point. We were sitting ducks if the enemy had any recce troops anywhere near us, but I think Ally and I were both much more concerned about our US allies, who aren't the best at vehicle recognition and tend to ask their questions after they start shooting.

There were very few waypoints on which to focus my route planning, so it was a bit haphazard, but we took our time and many, many hours later, I told Ally to slow down, as I had noticed some troop movements just beyond some dunes. We got out of the vehicle just as these American wagons came screaming towards us. Luckily, we could see the US markings so we were waving a Union Flag to let them know we were friendlies.

Unbelievably, they stopped just short of us and approached on foot, when within voice range, the Captain leading them asked me, "Are you guys Syrians, man?" I didn't know whether to laugh or cry! At about 30m, he couldn't identify two blokes in British uniform, in a British Land Rover with UK and coalition markings for what it was. I'm just surprised and relieved that they didn't just open up on us.

Once I had advised him that I wasn't a Syrian and indeed was there to attend a 7 US Corps briefing, he and his team escorted us for the last few miles. The briefing only took around an hour, after which we collected the equipment and set off back to our own HQ. Sadly, it wasn't as simple as following our own tracks on the way back. There were tracks everywhere outside of 7 (US) Corps HQ – not very professional when you consider what could have been seen from an aircraft should the enemy undertake air recce. So, it was pretty much a replay of getting there on the way back, taking time to actually plot our route as best we could. The round trip took the entire day but at least we got it done and weren't shot up by the enemy, or the Americans (bonus on the latter!).

Whilst we were getting ready for war, we realised the normal life went on and things like Valentine's Day would occur wherever we happened to be. It was a morale booster though when a couple of boxes of Valentine's cards were donated to us, so that we could at least write a note to our wives and girlfriends. The boss decided the boxes should sit in my area, so that we could control the distribution of the cards, albeit you would think one card per person should work... ! But, no. Jay, the Squadron Foreman, was living proof of the fact that Scotsmen like myself are considered tight but this is a cover story created by Yorkshiremen such as Jay! To demonstrate this point, I was sitting in my vehicle with Titch Anderson, the Detachment Commander, when we noticed a shadowy character sneaking past the door. Intrigued, Titch and I jumped out of the wagon to find Jay stuffing Valentine's cards down his jacket. He knew that there were more than enough to go around, so he thought he would stock up for future years. Unbelievable!

Throughout the deployment we received all sorts of fantastic gifts from organisations such as the Royal British Legion, usually filled with food, soft drinks, books, and so forth. On top of that, our families were constantly sending tuck boxes with food and so much more. It became like a game of cat and mouse to stop Jay from constantly dipping his hands into the boxes. Some said he was sending it back home; talk about tight!

Taking Care of the General… or Not!

One of my closest friends in the squadron was the SQMS, Dave Cox. You may remember the name as he is the guy who had tried to blow me up a couple of times several years previously by throwing grenades into my training bay – but I didn't hold it against him! We couldn't really spare enough guys to help Dave run the squadron stores so inevitably he ended up with the misfits and miscreants as they became available.

As an example of this, one day I heard a shout from Titch when he was on top of the vehicle. "Yeoman take a look at this!" I popped up onto the roof and he passed me some binos. "Take a look at what Sig Norman is doing!" he said, with a grin on his face.

As I looked through the binos, I just couldn't believe my eyes. Sig Norman, a total nightmare at the best of times, had built a bonfire and was busily burning a load of clothes. This was somewhat bizarre, but as I looked closer, I could see name tags on some of the jackets and shirts which said 'Smith'. I immediately looked at the epaulettes, and low and behold, Sig Norman was burning the Gen's clothes! This was **not** going to end well.

I rang Dave on the trunk system and asked if he knew Norman was glibly burning the General's kit on a bonfire. Unsurprisingly, it took Dave a few minutes to compose himself and reply, "No, he's burning the rubbish." I advised Dave to go and look immediately, which he did, and the rest is history as they say. Sig Norman had been asked to burn the rubbish, which, very unfortunately, had been stacked alongside the outgoing laundry. Never one to split hairs, Norman decided that it was all rubbish and burned the lot. He might just have thought twice as the clothes he burned were largely in very good condition, and as mentioned, many having Smith as the name tag and those with rank showing, displayed Maj Gen slides. But no, not Sig Norman…

The Dolly Files

Thinking about characters, one that can't escape without a mention is Cpl Dave "Dolly" Jowett. Dolly was my Crypto Cpl and worked directly for Sgt Andy Millard, who ran my Comcen and crypto account back in Hohne. Whatever people may say about Dolly Jowett, he had been around a long time and knew his stuff and was also very loyal and diligent.

Unfortunately, he also possessed a cartoon voice and was the most accident-prone guy in the unit. The guys used to rib him a lot but he handled it well, giving as good as he got on most occasions. There are too many Dolly-related tales to recite but as a flavour, I will share some of them.

The first time we put our tent complex for my Comms Ops together in the desert, it was a bit windy, with sand swirling and getting into every orifice. Dolly had decided he would set up a 9 x 9 foot tent by himself, as the rest of the team focused on the heavy nylon penthouse tents that were attached to the armoured vehicles. With Dolly's tent being much lighter and not anchored to anything, it wasn't a surprise as he was lifted off his feet and then crashed to the floor, whereby he was then dragged along the ground. As if that wasn't funny enough, listening to the high pitched "Help me with the fucking tent…!" was just too much for the lads to bear as they fell about laughing.

A couple of days later, the team were having a bit of trouble with the Billy burner (heater) as they wanted to get some hot water for washing. The intrepid Dolly decided they were all incompetent and took over the attempts to get it working again. These burners were unpredictable and to be fair, dangerous if mishandled, so it was of little surprise when Dolly stuck his head in the tent about ten minutes later looking like Mr Magoo. He had pumped it too hard with the result it blew up, burning his tache and eyebrows off. I probably laughed more than the lads because he looked such a wally, but I did make sure he was OK whilst laughing!

My final offering on this subject relates to the delivery of a cake from home. It was Dolly's birthday, so his wife had made him a big chocolate cake and sent it out by post. Receiving post was a big deal for everybody so it was quite common for those not on shift to gather in the Admin area whilst it was offloaded and distributed. Roger Dummett, our Pioneer Sgt, was driving the lorry and when everything was offloaded, he backed it up, narrowly missing everything except Dolly's cake, which seemed to explode everywhere covering those closest, including Dolly, in chocolate sponge and filling.

As Roger jumped out of the vehicle to investigate what had happened, Dolly turned into a screaming banshee and attacked Roger, claiming the act had been deliberate. It wasn't; Roger was one of the nicest guys you could ever meet and simply wouldn't do that. The fight was funny though!

Young Officer Nightmares

Having mentioned my admiration for Andy Forster earlier, he had proven to be even better than I had hoped for as a boss. Our mutual respect was never in question, but he had an enormous amount of pressure on his shoulders with the General and the COS to deal with, never mind the remainder of the HQ staff. Andy never flinched once, he just took a grip on the relationship with this key group and led his squadron in such a way that they constantly delivered high-quality support and solid communications throughout the campaign. That doesn't mean he didn't have some serious trials and tribulations to endure.

One of the troop commanders definitely tried his patience on several occasions. The young officer in question didn't quite have the sequence for engaging his brain at that stage. One unforgettable example of this was when he was told to go to a local supplier of AstroTurf, which was to be placed on the ground inside the HQ tent to help stop the desert sand continually rising and causing people to choke. Most people would have thought about the requirement and accepted that the size of the tent (18 x 36 feet) would need to be covered in a single sheet of AstroTurf, or at worst two pieces, if only to prevent the sand rising between the joints.

Unfortunately, this particular individual decided to apply young officer logic and felt that it would be a good move to chop the material into individual one metre squares, as they would be easier to transport! Best to say the end result did not impress Andy Forster nor anybody else involved with the HQ. Who paid for the replacement was never confirmed but I have my suspicions as to who may have contributed…

Final Preparations for War

There are many complex and often highly dangerous heavy armour manoeuvres called for during warfare, even between those on the same side. One of these is a "Passage of Lines", where one entity is called upon to move through another so as to achieve a relocation on the battlefield.

On the first one of these that we encountered, we were all relieved that it wasn't going to include the typically gung-ho Americans. However, everybody's heart sank when we were informed it was… the Syrians! We would have been concerned if it were to be conducted during broad daylight, but given we were in full tactical mode, it was planned for the middle of the night.

On the night of the Passage of Lines, I was in my vehicle and remember the ever-increasing rumble of heavy armour moving at speed across the desert. I'm sure there was a significant element of luck in the fact they didn't hit any of the HQ vehicles as they passed within a few metres of us. Unfortunately, the same couldn't be said in relation to several of our wooden portable toilets, several of which were completely destroyed as a tank rolled over them. The fact that nobody got killed is pretty much a miracle; these toilets were usually well occupied even at night, but I guess nobody felt the need, knowing the Passage of Lines was going to happen at some stage during the hours of darkness.

On a professional note, I was sorry that Guy Benson and Martin Fielding had moved on prior to the deployment and that's no slight on either Andy Trask or Al Haresign, who had taken over from them, respectively. The only reason I mention this point is simply because I had worked with Guy and Martin for some time, and we were a very slick, strong team; building that teamwork is difficult and doing so during a war makes it significantly more so. However, I needn't have been concerned, Andy and Al were great lads and proved themselves during the war without any shadow of a doubt; both remain friends to this day and will always be so. After all, you don't go to war every day.

After we had completed Ex DIBDIBAH DRIVE with 1 (US) Division, we moved forward through a huge concentration area, but unfortunately the RMP, who were meant to stop each convoy and direct them off the route into the concentration area, simply waved us through and we kept on going. The fog of war, I guess.

We eventually arrived at Wadi al-Batin, a dry riverbed/gully, and realising something wasn't right, we pulled over and contacted the divisional HQ. I will never forget my CO's words when I asked whether he wanted us to turn around or stay where we were until the move forward recommenced. "Set up where you are; there are only five enemy divisions facing you on the other side of the border..."; food for thought when you are trying to grab some kip!

It wasn't so much the idea of the enemy strength facing us, but more likely the fact that all we had to defend us was an Infantry platoon and our own Signal Squadron guys, a total of about 50 people! Our staff, who had travelled in vehicles that the RMP did turn off the road and into the concentration area, were driven forward to join us and to take control of Ex DIBDIBAH CHARGE which effectively moved the whole division into an Assembly Area, prior to another step into a Staging Area on the Saudi/Iraqi border. Once that had happened, we handed control of the division to the other squadron and moved forward to join up with everyone else.

We were all aware that the next stage for us meant breaching a very deep Iraqi minefield that ran for miles along the border, and from there we would actively engage the enemy to try and drive them back towards Kuwait. On the evening of 23rd February, the Div COS called a briefing and as we all stood under the desert sky, he proceeded to give us his 'Eve of Battle' speech. Personally, I would have preferred it if he hadn't because I don't think he had genuinely thought through the impact of what he said. He included some very enlightening thoughts, such as, "Look at the guys to your left and right, because tomorrow they might both be dead." I got his point and some of the other rather unsubtle tales of doom, but we didn't need that style of address; we needed real positivity, confidence building, and assurance that we were going to be victorious. Whether we believe it or not, telling people they are going to die the next day is not good for morale.

I hadn't had a lot of sleep over the months since our arrival, but that was my style in any case. I was responsible for the communication planning, delivery and management and knowing that lost communications could render the HQ unable to effectively command the division at war, potentially resulting in a huge loss of life, provided all the adrenalin I needed to stay awake. However, I do remember the Divisional Traffic Officer, Captain Alf Thomas, peering into my Comms Ops vehicle later that evening saying, "You've got eyes like piss holes in the snow! Go and grab some kip and I'll cover for you; it could be some time before we get another chance." I liked and respected Alf, so I just grabbed my sleeping bag and went outside and lay down in the sand alongside the track of the armoured vehicle; very comfortable!

The War Starts

When the Allied bombardment started on the night of 16th February 1991, it was a real cacophony of noise. I had never heard anything like it, even when attending one of the fire power demonstrations held for VIPs and foreign dignitaries back in the UK. The difference, of course, was the sheer number and types of weapons being used, with multi launch rocket systems (MLRS), heavy artillery, nuclear missiles, and even the USS Missouri out in the Gulf joining in. She had been brought out of retirement to put her enormous guns into use whilst accompanying six US aircraft carriers.

It went on for an awfully long time and even when you consider it was targeting the enemy, as a human being it is impossible not to think of those on the other side, and the carnage that must be unfolding. Whilst military planners will always try to minimise civilian casualties, the simple facts are that some of the civilian population will inevitably end up as collateral damage. Soldiers are human beings, and, in my experience, they are largely decent, caring people who hate war. However, it is part of their role, and self-preservation will always kick-in; they are sons, daughters, and parents, so the fact that they want to return home after the conflict is an absolutely understandable human emotion.

Nobody wants to see a loss of life, whether it is civilians or indeed the enemy. We were aware that a large proportion of the Iraqis were conscripts, there against their will and often on the back of threats made against their families being targeted if they did not support the regime. In other words, they could risk their own lives, or that of all their family members, a horrific choice that most folk will have sympathy with. In my mind, the thought that there would be nobody left alive as and when we entered Iraq started to form. I was later to realise that I was very wrong on that point.

Having been very rudely awakened from my slumber by sounds so loud I thought we were under attack, I was extremely thankful that it was the start of our artillery raids to soften the enemy up prior to the minefield breach. Not many people will have heard a fire mission in which five regiments are engaged; it must literally have been hell on earth for the Iraqis. To say the earth moved during our assault is nothing more than fact; for those on the receiving end, it spelt death. I decided that there was no way I could try to sleep so I relieved Alf and took control of my little kingdom once again. For the remainder of the night, I was poring over my various plans, repacking my kit on the vehicle so that it was safely stowed, and just generally fidgeting around waiting for the off.

Cpl Titch Anderson brought me a brew nice and early on and we had a chinwag as to how we would play things during the breach. Titch was a fantastic lad and a friend that I had known for years; in truth, there isn't another bloke I would rather have with me than him. He was also the driver of the vehicle, which was usually commanded by my Crypto Sgt, Andy Millard. During the breach itself, I would be in the back of the wagon, monitoring the various radio nets.

Once we were all lined up and ready to move, 1 was desperately trying to get comfortable in the wagon but couldn't find a decent place to sit. Looking to my right, I noticed a decent sized box, so I moved it into a small space and sat down on top of it. I didn't notice the contents at the time, but on a later inspection I found the box to be full of L2A2 anti-personnel grenades, so if we had taken a serious hit, I would have gone up like a rocket off my "seat"!

There were a few incidents in the various lanes as we made our way through the minefield, a lorry lost a wheel, vehicle breakdowns and so forth, but nothing serious. As you would expect, the first units though were in contact with the enemy quickly, but the Iraqis, having had a very sleepless night, were on the back-foot quickly and withdrawing, albeit in contact. 7 Brigade were all over the enemy and their forward units were giving them a real kicking; whilst the Iraqis had a lot of armour, it was very inferior to ours and to be blunt, we were shooting holes in their T55 tanks with small arms, which demonstrates the capability gap. But I wasn't complaining.

The Coalition Commander, General Norman Schwarzkopf, or "Stormin' Norman" to give him his nickname, and his staff had very cleverly decided on an elaborate deception plan, convincing Saddam Hussein and his military leaders to believe that an attack would most likely be launched via a huge amphibious operation from the Gulf. Whilst this story was being peddled, a huge force of American, French and British troops and equipment was deployed to Western Saudi Arabia, so that they would be in position to conduct flanking manoeuvres deep into Iraq to cut off and destroy the Republican Guard.

As the strategic decision to invade was being weighed up, it was decided to offer all our troops the opportunity to be vaccinated against the potential threat of anthrax which intelligence suggested was very real. It wasn't a decision that was forced upon us but was an individual choice in view of the known facts. Having come this far, I decided not to take unnecessary risks and accepted anthrax injections one, two and three. It's a decision I regretted in later life, but as they say, hindsight is a wonderful thing.

The ground war was launched at 04:00 on 24th February 1991, with our division forming part of the 7th US Corps, the most powerful military formation I have ever been part of. Thankfully, allied supremacy in the air kept Iraq's 43 Divisions pinned down so that they could not move to meet the attacking forces. Knowing we were already hugely outnumbered, this was a source of great relief.

The advance was incredibly fast, with our armour pushing forward at full speed, engaging and destroying the enemy in great numbers as they did so. The Iraqis had a lot of old Soviet T-55 tanks which our much smaller Warrior IFVs (infantry fighting vehicles) were able to engage with their 30 mm RARDEN cannons, blowing holes in the antiquated T-55 armour with ease.

The attack, which saw a pincer movement to cut the Iraqi forces off as they headed north, was incessant with only relatively short breaks, even for the Divisional HQ. We would push on, often in the dark of night and with drivers who were so tired that they slept as they held the vehicle tillers (steering mechanism) back. Luckily, maintaining a straight line in the desert isn't too difficult!

As the advance into Iraq continued, we were aware that a decision would be taken at some point as to whether we turned towards Baghdad to finish the conflict by ousting Saddam completely, or towards Kuwait to secure the country and cease hostilities at the earliest opportunity. The ground assault is often referred to as the "hundred-hour war" and I am convinced that many people have no real understanding of what took place during this period.

We were outnumbered in combat troops, tanks and artillery. Many will know that there were a lot of tanks deployed in the desert, but how many would recognise the fact that the world's greatest ever pitched tank battle was fought in the Iraqi desert, not against the Nazis in WWII. Conservative estimates tell us that between 25,000 and 50,000 Iraqi soldiers lost their lives, whilst 80,000 were captured. Tragically, many thousands of civilian lives were also lost. Coalition losses were contained to 292 and whilst we thanked God for that, the huge loss of life on the enemy side wasn't lost on us. We were all soldiers and there is always a mutual respect between opposing forces. I also felt very sorry for those of our troops detailed to help bury the dead. This is a soldier's worst nightmare and something that lingers with those personnel, often for the rest of their lives.

The battle was amazingly fast moving, and as a Divisional HQ, we were having to chase our forward units in order to keep up with them. This made communications very difficult to maintain and I had no choice but to roll my VHF rebroadcast stations forward continuously to extend cover. The way the battle was unfolding, we were spread across a large area with very little depth; sometimes we were immediately behind the 7 Brigade vehicles who, in turn, were remarkably close to their battlegroups (BGs).

It really was a case of 'stop, start' at a high pace and the outcome of that was we got almost no sleep, so people were becoming completely worn out. The Recce Officer, Captain Neil Griffiths, was flat out finding and guiding the HQ to its next location. I remember arriving at one berm (a large pre-prepared hole in the desert sand), to discover that Neil was nowhere to be found. Whilst we shouldn't have been giggling at things, the OC running around waving his arms, shouting, "Quick, hunt for Neil!" was actually very funny and almost worthy of John Cleese himself.

This incessant pursuit across the Iraqi desert, stopping only to engage the enemy, continued unabated, as did the need to continually project my RRB stations so far forward they were at times even ahead of our recce troops. This worried me deeply because this placed these crews in tremendous danger from both sides. From a friendly forces' perspective, if they were spotted and incorrectly identified, the possibility of a 'Blue on Blue' situation was very real. Conversely, if the enemy engaged them, they would easily have been overwhelmed, given they were lightly armed and small in number. It was difficult enough for the guys in the HQ to get any sleep, but I doubt the RRB crews got any. We were all aware that in our pursuit of the enemy, we had swung north and east, heading towards Kuwait itself, but whether that would alter, nobody was telling us, probably because they simply didn't know.

Continuing in the same general direction, we eventually came to the Basra Highway sitting elevated above the desert floor. I think we were all aware that dependent on which way we turned would signify whether we were heading to Baghdad, left, or Kuwait City, right. On a personal note, I have always believed that if Maggie Thatcher had still been

PM, it would have been hard left! Who is to say that would have been the wrong decision, it would almost certainly have resolved the situation once and for all, as opposed to letting things fester and result in a needless second Gulf War. However, Mr Major was certainly no Maggie Thatcher, so a right turn it was.

The war ended on 28th February 1991; a short but brutal conflict that claimed a lot of Iraqi lives because of a dictator. That said, of course, I was delighted it was over and grateful that we didn't lose a single soldier from the squadron.

The War Is Over!

The desert roads, or at least the highways, are usually elevated up off the desert floor with culverts installed to drain the water in times, albeit irregular, of heavy rainfall. As we took our turn to move up over the rise onto the road, I reminded Titch to be very careful and keep his eyes open for snipers. We didn't actually get over the rise fully before I heard Titch say, "Oh, fuck!" and when I asked him what was wrong, he said that as his track went over, he saw a body at the last minute and couldn't stop. As you can imagine, that was quite traumatic.

Once on the road, I noticed what looked like a sniper in one of the culverts further down on our left, so I stopped the convoy and we debussed into a defensive position. As I kept eyes on it, it struck me that the sniper was very still and not reacting to noise or movement around him, which was very strange. Rather than just hold our position and wait for somebody to deal with it, I asked the guys to provide cover as I moved forward to check it out. It wasn't an attempt to be a hero, just a desire to get moving as we were sitting ducks where we had stopped. It only took me 30 to 40 metres before I knew the guy was either very gravely injured or dead.

As I got to the culvert, it was clearly the latter. As I pulled him out, I could see he had been dead a while, given half of his chest was missing. He looked like a little manikin; taut, shiny skin, and jet-black hair; he couldn't have been more than 18 at the most. It's impossible to look at something like that and not wonder if he had been given any choice regarding being there; I doubted it. Like many of the Iraqi conscripts, he had the choice of taking part or his family would be jailed, or even worse.

With the "sniper" out of the way, we continued along the highway for a few miles before spotting what looked like the M25 on a Friday evening rush hour – a total traffic jam. There was a British checkpoint at the head of the jam. I can't remember which unit they were from, but they informed us that the highway was impassable and that we should be extremely careful approaching any of the vehicles because of potential booby trap risks. We were then marshalled down off the highway back onto the desert floor where we were held for a while until we could be escorted the rest of the way to our destination, a fruit orchard north of Kuwait City.

Inevitably, the lads took the opportunity to have a look at the traffic jam a little closer and even they, as experienced soldiers, were totally disgusted by what they saw. The exodus along the highway had created an enormous traffic jam, whereby the Iraqi forces had simply walked between the vehicles killing the unarmed, fleeing civilians. There were whole families, most still strapped into their cars, sitting upright in their seats, having been shot dead where they sat. Nobody had been spared in the cars I witnessed; men, women, or children; it was disgusting and shocking.

Once our guide arrived, we set off for our next HQ site where we were to set up pretty much opposite the other Divisional HQ once they arrived, with little more than a dirt road separating us. Knowing this was likely to be our home for quite a while, we set up thoroughly to ensure a quiet life and just maybe catch up on some much-needed sleep whilst not on shift. Given the war had just ended, of course, we remained on a high state of alert whilst going about our job. This proved to be a smart move, as the lads were stumbling across enemy soldiers, both injured and otherwise, for quite a few days after our arrival. Most of them were terrified but once they realised our only interest in them was to provide medical care and place them in secure custody, they were more than happy.

Soldiers are innovative by nature and quickly constructed large washing pools to enable them to do a bulk dobby of their masses of dirty uniform. When the SSM fell into one in the dark, you can imagine the hours of amusement it provided for the lads; given his nickname was Flipper, it seemed quite unfortunate.

The General, Rupert Smith, and his COS, Colonel John Wreath, were both Paras and as such, they had a thing for spending time with the soldiers. They liked to share the hardships in many ways and decided that everybody, including themselves and all the staff officers, should sleep under the main HQ camouflage net. I admire the thought process but always felt that it could lead to trouble somewhere along the line. With everybody sleeping in the same place, it was sometimes difficult for the lads coming off guard to find their replacements. It gets very cold at night in the desert, so if your replacement doesn't turn up to take over, it's a massive pain. As people caught on, I am sure some deliberately slept on in the hope they wouldn't be found amongst all the bodies. This, understandably, caused a lot of irritation in the ranks and gave rise to some memorable stories.

Stoker and the Joker

One of my all-time favourites involves our youngest Sig on the deployment, Andy Stoker, a young Makem from Sunderland. Given his incredibly young age when we deployed, he learned more than most during the conflict. Couple that to the fact that Makems are usually not easily put upon, something was always going to get his goat at some point.

As his end of shift came round at 2 am one particularly freezing morning, he wasn't best pleased to find himself in a position for the third time where his replacement didn't turn up. He clearly thought enough is enough and decided to find his replacement and tell him to get his arse out of bed; who wouldn't? The trouble is, when you have literally dozens of people sleeping in the open in military issue sleeping bags, they all look pretty much the same.

Undeterred by this issue, young Stoker makes his way to the spot where he believes the culprit is sleeping. Trying not to wake anybody else, he gives the sleeping bag a gentle shake and whispers, "Howay, mate, y'er on shift now!" but with no success. Angered further by this piss-taking person, he grabs the bag and shakes it violently, shouting, "Get y'er arse out of bed, ye lazy bastard!"

Normally, squaddies would not have a problem with that, but when the bag opened, out popped Gen Rupert Smith's head. "What do you want?" he asked calmly.

"Oh, sorry, like, I thought ye were on shift!"

"I don't think so," says General Rupert, as he rolls over and goes back to sleep.

Stoker decided this was too dangerous a method to employ, so he went back on shift until the next replacement arrived. This story demonstrates the benefits of having a Para General, who later that day was heard regaling the story whilst laughing his head off. I hope Stoker realised that would not have been the reaction of most two-star officers.

Although the war was over, the HQ was still a hive of activity with the staff putting together the planning for our eventual recovery to Germany. This, of course, meant the lads had to adjust to a quite different routine which some found quite boring in contrast to the adrenalin rush of battle. Standing guard at the HQ entrance is hardly the stuff of dreams and it eventually shows itself, normally through some act of rebellion, or indeed petulance. Sig Jock Sloane, known to everybody as Ted Bovis, due to his striking resemblance to the comedy character (of *Hi-de-Hi!* fame), was always somebody who was likely to crack first.

There was an electric water boiler positioned just outside the main entrance to the Div HQ tent, and it was supposed to be maintained (filled, switched on/off at the appropriate times, and so on) by the person on guard at the entrance. The staff were given specific brew times at which they would go outside and make themselves a tea or coffee. At these times, the sentry would ensure everything was ready for them. Whilst Ted knew the plan, he had become worn down by what he considered a bunch of Hoorah Henrys so he decided it was payback time.

Just before a morning brew session, he filled the heater up with cold water and stood there smirking as the officers wondered why their coffee was just floating on top of the water. When they started whinging at him, he said the boiler must have blown a fuse, which strangely went unchallenged, particularly as I could see a red light shining on the side of it. I did my duty as a responsible WO and informed Ted that I knew what had happened, but seeing how much tension he had released, I just told him to bring it back to the boil and give the Ruperts a shout; but once out of sight, I nearly wet myself laughing.

Step forward Sig Andy Stoker, again! Having learned a lesson from his brush with the General over trying to put him on stag (shift), life had more or less returned to normal for our youngest soldier. He was still doing his fair share of guard duties, of course, but his colleagues had started to respect the fact that if he wasn't replaced at the right time, he would come after somebody!

This particular night, he had picked up a guard duty and I had briefed him to ensure that two of my RRBs left the HQ at 5 am, showing him where they were parked. The RRB crews had been fully briefed and were getting their heads down for an early night. Sig Stoker was determined that he shouldn't be blamed for the RRBs not deploying at the right time, so when he spotted the two vehicles still standing there at 5 am, he wasn't happy. Indeed, seeing a couple of guys sleeping in the open by the side of their vehicles on American camp cots enraged him, to the point that he ran across the open desert and delivered a boot to the underside of the first bed, shouting that he was pissed off taking the blame for the mistakes of others.

We have all been young once, but just a cursory check would have made him realise that these were different wagons that had clearly pulled into the spaces vacated by the RRBs. Almost unbelievably, and certainly very worryingly, the person who emerged from the sleeping bag was none other than Gen Rupert Smith; recognising his victim instantly, Stoker turned and legged it across the sand as fast as his legs could take him, which in this instance was extremely fast indeed! With nobody in sight as he came round from his slumber, Gen Rupert just rolled over and went back to sleep; I'm fairly sure that Stoker has no lives left. That said, once we were back in Hohne, he did borrow my No1 Dress uniform and has yet to return it. Perhaps he still hasn't learned his lesson...

Not On My Watch

At one point, I started to notice that the attached US team who provided tropospheric scatter, a fairly old technology that the UK didn't utilise, were consistently missing in the early part of the mornings. As I started to investigate what they were doing, it soon became clear that they were going out onto the Basra Highway to "collect souvenirs" which to put things mildly, was completely unacceptable in my book (and most other people's too).

I decided to wait for them to return, which took around 15 minutes. I grabbed the "Lootenant" (I can't hide the fact that their misuse of our language has irritated me all of my life) and asked him where they had been. Just as he was launching into some cock and bull story, I noticed one of his guys had a couple of photos in his hand, so I stepped over to him and asked what he was holding. He showed me and it was evident those in the photos were of Middle Eastern descent. Stupidly, he then said he had picked them up at the side of the road which convinced me that my suspicions were correct; they had been trophy hunting. I asked the officer to step to one side and then just gave him a simple choice: pack up and bugger off, otherwise my next discussion would be with the COS or Gen, either of whom were likely to chin him, then sack him. He made the right choice, and I gave him a cover story that said because they weren't actually doing anything, we had agreed that he could leave the HQ, giving us some additional space. They were gone within the hour.

Time to Go Home

I really liked the Gen and his COS. They were typical Para officers; straight to the point, happy to be alongside the lads and pretty clear when they wanted something. I have always responded well to that style of engagement. With my boss, Andy Forster, being the way he was, I couldn't have asked for better support from my superiors, and I guess that's why I got such a career boost from that period of my service.

As the guys started to recover from the short but very demanding period of war fighting, they started to relax and look forward to the eventual return home. Sadly, my boss Andy had to head home a little bit early, as his wife Frances wasn't well. I felt for him because he didn't want to leave his men but knew he had to get home as quickly as possible for Frances. They were and are a fabulous couple and were very well-loved by everybody in the squadron, so we all completely understood. The truth is the remaining days were just mundane, with continuous maintenance on the vehicles, packing and, of course, checking for contraband that had been stashed on the armoured vehicles. It's amazing how many hiding places there are on these big old lumps of steel. Mostly, of course, the lads couldn't really be bothered looking too far and settled for hiding anything they wanted under the belly plates. Unfortunately, that's the first place everybody goes for when conducting a search...

Having recovered a mountain of weapons, including thousands of small arms, hand grenades, land mines and missile launchers, which we destroyed through the formal route, we were ready and eager to go on the first leg of the journey home. Iraqi insurgents were still making a nuisance of themselves, of course, and had set fire to many of the oil wells across a wide area. The result was extremely dramatic and a bit of a problem to deal with as the oil fires had rendered the skies black, filled with acrid smoke which made breathing quite difficult for most people. It also didn't do much for navigation as it was difficult to see more than a couple of metres in front of yourself. But you don't let petty things like that get in the way of going home to your family, so we just bumbled along in our convoy; making sure you could see the guy in front, there was nothing else we could do. At one point we came to a halt as an RMP on the side of the road let us know we could take 15 minutes to have a brew, go to the toilet and such like.

Jumping down from my wagon, I desperately needed a pee, so given it was almost pitch black (at 12.30 pm!), I took my 9 mm pistol out, cocked it, and moved to one side to find a suitable spot close by.

"Alright, Yeoman," came the voice as a hand tapped my shoulder. It was lucky he was so close as I jumped out of my skin and had the pistol in his face ready to blow his head off. It was an old friend, Major Pete "Quiff" Barron.

"Fucking hell, Pete, I nearly shot you!" I gasped. "I didn't see you there!" He just chuckled and headed on. Pete isn't with us anymore and I didn't get the chance to take the mickey out of him after the war, but it would have been a good one to tell after a few beers.

We eventually made it to the drop-off location for our vehicles after an exceptionally long drive in the dark, most of us with sore eyes and throats from the smoke. We were all pleased to get a bit of shut-eye until the morning when the next stage of our recovery journey would start. The trip to the airport went quickly and the feeling of getting on the aircraft was amazing, but not quite as amazing as the fact that the flight crew were happily dishing out cold beers! Whilst they tasted superb after all these months, the fact that we were all drinking probably carried more risk than an Iraqi T-55 tank! I'm relieved to say the lads behaved themselves well and after drinking **every** beer on board, most just drifted off to sleep, me included.

Arriving into Hannover International Airport, we tumbled off the plane and made our way to the awaiting buses to take us back to Hohne. Needless to say, there was no beer on the buses.

As we turned into Hohne Camp, it was a great feeling; war over and everybody home safely; you can't ask for any more than that. The wives and kids had made up a load of 'Welcome Home' banners and were waiting for us as the coaches pulled up outside the squadron HQ. I couldn't wait to see Sue and Mark; we have always been a very close little family and I had missed them terribly. As I got off the bus, I saw my new Ford Sierra coming straight towards me and thought, "Who the hell is driving that?!" To my complete amazement, it was Sue, who to my knowledge didn't have a driving licence and most certainly couldn't drive! As she pulled up and got out of the car, I think my mouth must have been hanging open; she had never once shown any interest in driving!

"Surprise!" she said as I gave her a kiss. "I decided I wanted to learn to drive so I could get around but didn't want to worry you, so I kept it a secret until you got home." I was absolutely delighted that she had done it and so proud of her when she passed her test first time a few weeks later.

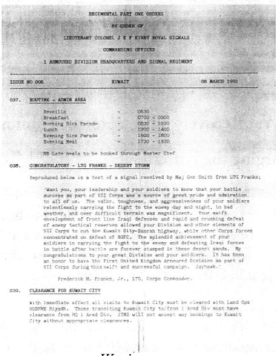

War is over –
Thanks from Jayhawk (LTG Freddie Franks Jnr, US Army).

Me on shift in Comms Ops during the Gulf War 1

Post War Recovery – Back Home in Hohne

Recharging the Batteries

We spent the next few days sorting a few things out before being granted a bit of leave, and we decided to head off to the Costa Brava with some friends, Dave Cox and his wife Jacqui and son Darren. More sunshine, oh yeah, but it was only March in Europe so not too warm.

We set off from Hohne with my son Mark deciding he wanted to travel in Dave's car, something he must have regretted about an hour later when it broke down on the autobahn. With repairs completed, we headed off again, hoping to hit our hotel in Heidelberg around seven to eight hours later, which amazingly, we did. Just as well, as I think Mark's ability to listen to any more of Billy Ray Cyrus' *Achy Breaky Heart* had completely evaporated. I did warn him!

The hotel was a beautiful, old wooden building, typical of the Black Forest; they also sold superb beer and edible German local food. I've always loved German fast food, but their more formal and traditional dishes are a bit of a gamble on occasion. We faced another seven to eight-hour journey in the morning, so it was an early night all round. Up with the larks, we all enjoyed a beautiful continental breakfast before setting off on the second leg.

Driving through France is never enjoyable to my mind; the French are aggressive, rude drivers and really don't seem to mind the occasional bump. We deliberately didn't hang around in France, preferring to get through and out the other side into Spain. It isn't a huge distance to L'Estartit from the border, but we did stop for a drink and a sandwich to keep our strength up. Cracking on from there, we arrived at our rented villa around 4.30 pm, which was spot on.

After checking out the villa, which was perfectly fine, we unloaded the cars and then headed off into the town centre for a stroll, inevitably ending up in a lovely but extremely quiet little pub for a decent meal and a nightcap before bed. Personally, I should have realised how quiet a resort such as L'Estartit would be in March which is well out of season, but to be honest, I just wanted to spend some quality time with my family and friends.

Life was never boring with Dave in any case; he was a happy-go-lucky character and always full of fun. Dave thought he would quickly learn Spanish during the holiday and as far as he was concerned, he did quite a good job; just stick an "io" on the end of everything and you are halfway there. As an example, his attempt to purchase some sausage from a local butcher went along the lines of "sausageio por favour". As you might expect, the butcher thought he was a half-wit and completely ignored him whilst shaking his head vigorously.

The point of the visit to the butchers was to stock up for a BBQ which we managed to do despite Dave, and we built a brick and wire BBQ in a safe place in the garden of the villa. Sitting with our feet up in the garden, enjoying tasty food and a lovely bottle of wine, I thanked the lord we didn't send Dave to the butchers by himself, otherwise this might have been a very different experience altogether.

Despite the relatively low temperatures, we did manage to fit in some beach time and some swimming, albeit with wet suits, just to ensure we avoided pneumonia! The holiday shot past, but we did get out and about, visiting Barcelona, in which driving is not recommended, Gerona and other nearby small towns. It certainly did the trick, providing the break and family time that we all needed and became another great memory. The drive home went smoothly, no breakdowns, and unsurprisingly, Mark chose to travel in our car.

Following our return to work, we set about regaining our focus in providing a HQ for 22 Armd Bde, our real job. The Bde staff, many of whom had been on standby for the war as BCRs (Battlefield Casualty Replacements), didn't deploy, but they were very understanding of our position post-return and gave us the support we needed to get back up to speed.

Our vehicles and equipment made it back safely and we duly collected them from the German port at Emden, west of Wilhelmshaven.

Once back in Hohne, the detailed maintenance started, returning the vehicles to the right colours, and general vehicle and communications equipment servicing. The lads also took the opportunity to renew the many items of damaged personal gear, such as clothing. We were soon back in the swing of things conducting Bde exercises and generally just getting on with life. It was good to enjoy mess life again and we certainly did that. As we were a minor unit at squadron level, we belonged to the Garrison WOs and Sergeants' mess as opposed to having our own. It was a good mess and we had regular entertainment at weekends and quite a few things laid on for the families, celebrity visits and the like. We also had our own squadron bar though and many a brilliant night was held in there with groups, comedians and other acts entertaining the lads.

The Pain of Loss

201 Sig Squadron was my dream job and I had so many great times, but the truth is, heartbreak is only ever just around the corner as a soldier.

I lost two tremendous friends during my time there. The first of these was WO2 (SSM) Pete Griffin, a friend from both 249 Sig Squadron and 1 Div HQ & Sig Regiment. The second was Sgt Mick Newman, my close pal from my time in Soest, whose wife and daughter had spent so much time with Susan and Mark whilst we were away on exercise. The fact that neither of these guys were in the squadron but serving in the UK at the time of their deaths didn't lessen the pain of their loss.

Pete's death was a terrible accident, but in some ways that made it even harder to overcome. A keen runner, Pete had been out training around Blandford Camp in Dorset, where he was serving at that time. Anyone who knows that part of the country will tell you that there are some very dangerous roads in the county and that played its part in the tragedy. It happened to be quite a bright, sunny summer day on 26th August 1991 and should have been a good day for a run. As Pete and a colleague were breasting a hill, a driver came over the top and was blinded by the sun, at which point he hit and killed Pete. When I heard what had happened, I was completely gutted. Our careers had followed a remarkably similar path since our time together in Bulford, a first posting for both of us, and we had a great respect for each other. Pete was an outstanding soldier, and I am totally convinced that he would have been a superb RSM and gained a commission from there. He was only a young man, 33 years old with so much yet to do. He also left behind a loving wife and children. Pete was a great loss to his family and to our Corps, and to have died in the way he did just amplified the loss.

I had lost three close friends in the space of four years and unfortunately, there was yet more to come. Mick Newman, whom I served with in 3 Div HQ and Sig Regiment, had been promoted to Sgt and posted home to Derby. He was working in the Army Recruitment Office and was probably expecting a quiet tour in his home city. Sadly, at that time there was a very real terrorist threat on mainland UK. The Derby office had been bombed 19 months earlier, so I am quite sure there would have been no complacency.

Mick finished work on 14th April 1992 and was walking back to his car in civilian clothes when he was approached and shot multiple times in the head. This was a cold-blooded murder, an execution of an unarmed man. We had been close friends, so finding out about this killing was yet another massive blow. That made four mates lost in four years, three to terrorists and one to a tragic accident. In all honesty, being killed in action (KIA) is something all soldiers accept is a risk they must take, but to see three murdered is exceedingly difficult to deal with.

Cpl Del Wood, R Signals. Del was murdered by IRA sympathisers along with Cpl Dave Howes, R Signals.   *Sgt Mick Newman, R Signals. Murdered outside the Army Recruiting Office in Derby. A really lovely bloke and great friend.*

SSgt Kev Froggett, R Signals. My first Det Comd, mentor and close friend. Shot by the IRA whilst repairing a mast in Coal Island.

233

Time for Reflection

War is a horrific experience even for professional soldiers; hence they have an extraordinarily strong sense of remembrance. Living inside the camp perimeter in Hohne, we were always very aware of the various grave sites strewn across the camp and its very strong connection to WWII, during which it was a Nazi Kaserne (Barracks). Our local NAAFI store, referred to as the Roundhouse, had at one point had its main entrance hall floor lifted, only to discover a very elaborate Nazi swastika tiled below it.

The most graphic reminder of Nazi atrocities, of course, was the Bergen-Belsen concentration camp, just 8 km down the road from the main gate. We visited on several occasions and having just returned from a war in the desert and lost a number of friends in such a short space of time, I found myself visiting yet again. Despite the horror of what took place there, it is now beautifully kept and manicured, has a museum, and is a place of learning to educate humanity on the need to ensure such events must never again be allowed to occur. It is undoubtedly a place for reflection and is very serene, although the stories of a lack of birds flying overhead seemed to hold weight. The mass graves, some containing upwards of 20,000 bodies, can't fail to touch anyone who visits. The fact that any element of humankind can hate others enough to submit them to the horrors committed in that place is simply inhuman.

Work Hard / Play Hard

Andy left some time before me and was replaced by a chap called Chris Wakerley, who was rejoining the Corps having spent several years as a pilot with the AAC. I had never met

Chris but appreciated that he had big boots to fill. From a personal perspective, the job had been everything I had dreamed of and with the best Brigade Commander I had ever served under, I couldn't have been more committed to keeping things at the standard we had achieved. Chris' appointment would be crucial to this and I was really keen to meet him.

My mindset had always been, if the boss failed, so did I and I had been so very lucky with Andy. However, loyalty and integrity have always been at the heart of what I am about, so having never met Chris previously was actually irrelevant to me; I was his Yeoman and we would succeed or fail together. I knew within five minutes of meeting Chris that we would make a great team and that was the start of an outstanding period for me. Chris was simply amazing and the kind of boss who always took the time to engage, mentor and guide me. When you add the degree of support and trust he placed in me, life simply doesn't get better than that for a WO2 (YofS). I am also very proud to say it was the start of a double act that allowed me to flourish in a way that I could only have dreamed about, and the commencement of a lifelong friendship.

We had also changed SSM a few months before Chris arrived. "Flipper" left on promotion to WO1 and was replaced by WO2 Dave Stachiney. Dave was a young SSM and very much a team player. I can honestly say that he helped me in several ways. If I had a briefing, he would automatically take control of attendance, getting the room set up and all the administrative tasks. The role of a Brigade Yeoman is particularly busy and whilst I would happily have organised these things myself, it genuinely helped to know Dave was on it and would deal with it, leaving me to get the communications planning, training and documentation sorted. That's how mature WOs should behave, and Dave knew if he needed anything from me, he only had to ask. The balance across the squadron improved and I think it became a happier place from the soldier's perspective.

Character Building – The Haute Route

The round of exercises at division and brigade level rolled on but we did actually get an opportunity to do some excellent adventure training along the way. I believe that leading the Haute Route, from Chamonix in France to Zermatt in Switzerland, was superb experience and would test most mountain leaders. Indeed, whilst I led the expedition heading one way, the Squadron 2IC, Captain Chris McIntosh, led a team in the opposite direction at the same time. Our intention had been to rendezvous in the middle, but I will cover that later.

My team consisted of an RMP Major from Brigade HQ plus seven lads from the squadron; it was a good group of people of mixed ability, but all of them strong enough to face an arduous adventure. Chris had a similar type of group, all fit and healthy, but he also recognised that being at high altitude was a serious challenge which was likely to stretch everybody. We walked long days and really struck it lucky with the weather. We also covered some of the most beautiful countryside I have ever seen. We initially climbed up onto the Balcony du Mont Blanc and traversed that for a while. The view from there is stunning.

Arriving at the Col de la Forclaz at the end of Day 1, I think the lads had realised just what we had taken on; I had been very open with them prior to our departure. To succeed, we would need to be comfortable with hiking approximately 25 km a day, and climbing 1,200m (i.e., walking 15 miles a day and climbing 4,000 ft). Given acclimatisation takes two to three days, we would need to start slowly until our bodies adjusted to having 25% less oxygen in the air. So yes, it hurt! But we all slept well, of course.

After a very hearty breakfast, during which their numerous outbursts of "Oooh, aaah," and "My back hurts!", we limped off heading for Champex; a relatively easy start but which gets much more serious as you breast the Fenêtre d'Arpette and descend down to Champex. The tents went up incredibly quickly and after some hot food and a couple of beers, all that could be heard across the valley was a contented rumble of snoring in unison; we were whacked.

The next morning was a replay of the previous day – aches, and pains but a good, healthy breakfast to fuel us up for a long, hard trek to the very glamorous overnight stop in Verbier. Amazingly, we were provided with free accommodation in the town's nuclear bunker. This was such a wonderful thing for the local council to offer, but they probably realised that we would spend most of our money in the various bars in any case, so it was a win for them too. I must admit, we did spend a few hours in some very nice eateries/bars in this spectacularly beautiful Swiss village; it would have been rude not too, right?

The next couple of days saw us travel through some of the most dramatically gorgeous scenery in Europe, if not the world. Up past the Glacier de Mont Fort, to the Cabane de Prafleuri, with the team getting stronger and better acclimatised by the day. As I touched upon earlier, part of our plan included hooking up with Chris McIntosh's party travelling in the opposite direction to my group. There is always a competition in something like this; we had deliberately chosen a central location at which to rendezvous (RV) and both teams were determined to get there first for bragging rights.

When we arrived at that RV point, it was obvious that we were first and that nobody had been at the location for some time. Whilst we laughed and joked about kicking the other team's backside, we started to get pretty nervous when they hadn't arrived by nightfall. Even though it was summer, it still throws a lot of challenges at you when you are going up and down 10-12,000 feet mountains and certainly sees a wicked drop in temperature overnight. Chris was an experienced mountain leader and a sensible officer, so I figured they would have gone to ground overnight and would continue the journey in the morning. With that, we all turned in.

When we set off in the morning, I assumed that we would probably cross their path within a couple of hours, so when we didn't, I decided to head for the closest village to contact the squadron HQ to see if they had heard anything. This took us off our route, but the safety of the other group was now worrying me, and I needed to confirm the situation or raise an alarm. The good news was that they had called in and explained their situation; having failed to reach the RV, they decided to bed down, as I had suspected. What I didn't expect was them to have left their sleeping bags with their admin vehicle, with the intention that they would meet at the RV. When they decided to bed down the night before, the drop in temperature left them freezing and as a result they headed to the nearest farm and slept in a barn. That action was acceptable but setting off without their sleeping bags was a complete nonsense; that's how people end up dying of hypothermia. We were just glad the other team were OK and although we wouldn't sget a chance to meet up, that was good enough.

I had been a mountain leader for quite a few years before this trip, but to be honest, my favoured environment was snow and ice. However, the Haute Route was definitely providing an enormous challenge. We would cover over 200 km on the trip, with a pattern of 10,000 feet up and down on an almost daily basis; yes, it was summer and exceedingly beautiful, but when you hit areas such as the Glacier du Monte Fort, there is certainly a serious risk to be overcome.

To recount one such memory; we had just arrived at the Arolla ladders at the Pas de Chèvres. Whilst not the longest vertical climb, with two sections of 30 and 15 feet respectively, it is very tiring with 45 to 50-pound packs on your back. For absolute clarity, when I say vertical, that's exactly what I mean, with the ladder bolted to the rock face. I stressed several safety points to the team before setting off up the ladder and once at the top, I called them up individually.

All was going well until Cpl Titch Anderson reached the top. As he stepped off and without thinking, he leant backwards… I don't think I have ever reacted so quickly in my life, hooking and pulling him towards me with every ounce of strength in my body. Titch looked at me as if I had lost the plot. "Bloody hell, Yeoman, what's happening?" he said, not realising how close he had come to toppling off the last rung. I was too shocked to say anything, but I had seen the impact of such a fall before and it wasn't pretty.

Haute Route – 12,000 feet.
One of Europe's great trekking challenges.

Haute Route –
Don't loose your footing!

With Titch still a bit confused at my mad grab at him, we had a quick brew and set off again. Given how close Titch and I were, I was pretty relieved that he hadn't fallen to his death on my watch!

The route traverses below the summits of 10 out of the 12 highest peaks in the Alps, and crosses several extremely high passes, the highest of which is at 2,964m (9,800 ft). At this point, the view opens up to some of the most spectacular views in the Swiss Alps. The final pass is the Augstbordpass (2,894m), beyond which you descend steeply to the wonderful viewpoint known as the Twära. From here, it is an even steeper descent that takes you to the hamlet of Jungu, perched on the side of the mountain. Most people that have participated in trekking at a reasonable level will understand the pain that we were experiencing in our knees at this point, so I didn't have the heart to tell the guys, it wasn't over just yet!

As we headed down from Jungu to St Niklaus, I saw everyone at their most vulnerable, all of us suffering from excruciating knee pain. We rested a while and enjoyed the amazing views of the Matterhorn Mountain itself, one of Europe's most recognisable peaks, before setting off for the Matter Valley floor. The lads that had joined me on the trip were some of the best I served with, strong and determined soldiers who just kept going. We must have looked like a load of old men as we hobbled down that mountain, but I was immensely proud that every one of them made it.

Walking along the flat valley bottom made an enormous difference to all of us, allowing us to enjoy our final stroll into the town of Zermatt, by which time we were ready for a bit of fun. Having checked into our lovely Swiss mountain hotel, we proceeded to eat copious amounts of cheese fondue, washed down by exceptionally large, cold beers. One of the lads, known affectionately to his mates as the "Pie Man", certainly amazed the locals with his capacity to consume his own body weight in food, but he had earned it in my book. The guys were in seventh heaven, until the next morning! What a trip.

I have always been a huge fan of the rock band Queen and at that time my favourite song was *Barcelona*, a duet between Freddie Mercury and Montserrat Caballé. Throughout the trip, I had played it every night to help me drop off to sleep. I hadn't realised that the RMP Major, who was sharing a tent with me, had to put up with this every night after I fell asleep, until the tape stopped some hours later. He did share this at the end though, where he informed me that if he ever heard that tune again, he would not be responsible for his actions. I just told him he had obviously not worked hard enough and clearly did not appreciate great music. For the life of me, I can't remember his name, but he was a good bloke and a great team player.

I still have the training report that I had to produce at the end of the trip and to this day, I don't think I have ever seen anything quite as beautiful as the sight of the Lac des Dix from the Cabane des Dix at 10,000 feet; the turquoise water is completely mind-boggling.

The Chamonix to Zermatt "Haute Route" is one of the best multi-day trekking journeys in the world, and here we were doing it for free as part of our job; how can you beat that? For those that enjoy such things, I recommend you put it on your bucket list!

No Peace for the Wicked

In a Bde Sqn, it was a regular task to undertake simulator-driven training at the Bde and BG Trainer in Sennelager. It was a bit dull for the squadron guys, but undoubtedly great training for our Staff Officers. Our main activity was to set up our HQ complex and feed communications into the training hall where the staff worked. Other than that, it was just a case of doing shifts in the mock-up vehicles and tearing it all down at the end.

One of our SNCOs, Sgt Nick "Noriega" Middleton, was a talented cartoonist who when bored, would normally be observed sitting in a corner staring intently at somebody. If it was you, you just knew that very shortly a ridiculous caricature of you would emerge. They were very funny and helped to lighten the atmosphere of boredom on this type of deployment. Unfortunately, the boss didn't like them and got pretty cross on one occasion when he was depicted sitting reading *The Beano* in the middle of the Bde staff. To be fair, it probably didn't give the best impression of a hugely capable officer looking for his next step on the ladder, but the Brigadier loved it! I still look at my copy and smile.

Of all the crews in the squadron, the Lineys were the ones that took best care of me. They were all real grafters, pulling heavy cable and carrying huge cable drums around the HQ. I think they had a lot of respect for the hours I worked and it was mutual. The line truck was superbly set up with real beds fitted along the inside of the rear cargo area, with one reserved for me. I was honoured by this and to be honest, the quality of sleep I was able to grab kept me sane on many occasions. They were a great bunch and were the first to

201 (22 Armd Bde) Sig Sqn cartoon. Simply the best.

be deployed to a new HQ site ahead of the main body, so that they could lay the required cabling ahead of our arrival. Equally, they were the last to leave a previous location as they had to recover the cable once the HQ vehicles had moved. These guys did this for every move and without them, the HQ would have taken very much longer to establish and tear down, with a huge amount of additional pressure on the individual detachments. A good Line Tp was an absolute godsend and in 201 Sig Squadron, we had one of the absolute best.

I have to admit though, there were a few sticky moments for our Lineys. On an exercise on SLTA, we had "stepped up" the HQ to a new location and we were awaiting the arrival of the line crew from the last site, having picked up all the cable. The weather was terrible with torrential rain falling, high winds and to make things even more challenging, very poor light. The Land Rover carrying the incoming crew came screaming into the HQ and whilst the Lineys were known to speed on occasion, they were usually cute enough to drive very calmly when coming into a site.

L/Cpl Dave Jack immediately jumped out of the wagon and started regaling us with tales of how much worse the weather had become once most of us had left the last location. He seemed somewhat overexcited, and it quickly became clear why. The site was suddenly bathed in bright light as a Mercedes car roared into camp and a very irate driver got out and started gesticulating at the line pole sticking out of his windscreen. Now it was clear as to why the arrival of the Line crew had been at such speed; they were trying to shake the Mercedes off their tail! The Mercedes driver was duly placated and compensated for the damage to his car, whilst the line pole was extracted. I still cringe when I think of the additional damage that could have been inflicted had the pole struck a body on its way through the cab. The moral of that story is to ensure your line poles are properly tied down on the roof before you move off…

Holiday Time

As I was coming towards the end of the tour, we decided with Dave and Jacqui Cox that we should have a holiday in Venice. It was a fair drive but if you stopped midway, it was very doable.

We decided to stop off in Austria, which was more than halfway, but we calculated we could get there by late afternoon, which we did amazingly. The hotel was a beautiful old Tyrolean building with lots of flowers all around it; inside, it was picture postcard stuff and, of course, it had an excellent selection of local beer, wine, and food. We were all quite tired, so we enjoyed some food and a couple of beers before turning in early.

We took a detour into Innsbruck the following morning, having a quick tour of the city centre and then taking a walk up the mountainside where Dave took some video recordings. Those were the days when a mobile video camera weighed about 6-7 kg, so we were all laughing our heads off as Dave made his way up the mountain as though he was carrying a heavy box of tools. He did get some good video though, so he wasn't too hacked off.

By mid-afternoon, we were back on the motorway heading south towards Northern Italy. The drive through Italy is beautiful, particularly as you head down past Lake Garda; we had been to Venice a few times but as you head around the Lido di Jesolo, it is truly heart-stopping scenery. Arriving at our campsite, we were shown to our individual caravans which were a little small but otherwise amazingly comfortable. Once set up, we went for a stroll around the site and down onto the beach. The view across the lagoon to the city was absolutely stunning.

We did all the tourist things but having been there before was a definite bonus. Visiting the islands in the lagoon is a must, but often costs tourists an arm and a leg. Don't take the expensive tours, just wander along the outer limits of the city and you will regularly be asked if you want a free ferry to the islands of Morano, Burano and Torcello. There are many more islands but the three mentioned are famous for glass, lace and beautiful churches, and tend to be the tourist focus. We stayed in Burano for lunch, which was fantastic, if a little bit expensive. Perhaps I should have emphasised how expensive Italy can be, but I thought Dave was going to have a seizure when the waiter delivered the bill. Restaurant alla Vecchia Pescheria in Murano is without a doubt a superb fish restaurant, but at £300 for lunch, I thought we had purchased it rather than just a meal!

At the end of a lovely week, we headed home, stopping off in Austria in a small village outside Salzburg on the way. The hotel was very old, beautiful and had the biggest set of doors I have ever seen. It was very picturesque, but also a little bit creepy; with lots of creaky floorboards and connecting doors, it was a bit like a haunted castle. The staff were very friendly, and the food and drink were excellent, so we quickly forgot about the ghost concerns that had started to emerge.

The evening passed and after a very squeaky night's sleep, we enjoyed a hearty breakfast and got on our way. The drive home was long but uneventful. Luckily, we arrived early enough to catch the Grill Stop at the camp entrance still open. They sold the best gyros in that area of Germany, and it was great to eat just as we arrived home, rather than have to start cooking ourselves after such a long drive.

Cheating Never Pays!

The week after we got back, the squadron was tasked with running some young officer training on behalf of the Bde HQ. It was a job that we did regularly, and I was used to running the exercise or JOTES (Junior Officer Training and Education Scheme) as they called it, but it had a high profile and needed to be right. We also had some officers from the squadron and the Divisional Signal Regiment who were participating in the event as students. This is always a period of tension for the young officers as it forms part of their promotion cycle, so it's good to see them work hard and succeed.

When I took one of our own young officers through the communications element, I was impressed as to the accuracy of his answers, but when I pressed him for supporting detail, he really struggled to expand in any way. I thought it was a bit strange but thought he was regurgitating his revised work whilst suffering from nerves.

By the end of Day 1, I thought no more about it as we closed everything up for the evening and headed back to camp. Day 2 kicked off and seemed to be going well until the Bde COS came to my stand and pulled me to one side.

"Did you notice anything strange about any of the candidates and their performance yesterday?" he asked.

"No, not anything that genuinely troubled me," I responded.

"It has been reported by three of the staff that a specific officer has been submitting absolutely verbatim answers to exam questions, and if that isn't suspicious enough, we changed a question, yet the verbatim answer to the previous one was given!" I then told the COS about my issue the day before but at that point we hadn't mentioned any names.

"Who was the candidate?" he asked and when I told him, he immediately turned on his heel and strode off.

My boss, Chris Wakerley, had the task of explaining this very embarrassing bit of dishonest behaviour to the Brigade Commander, and whilst I don't know what was said or by whom, by 5 pm the individual was on his way back to our parent Regiment in Verden, never to return. That was the only low point of what was a dream tour for me, providing communications and support to a truly outstanding headquarters, in which we were held in the very highest regard.

Some Fun Needed – Real Skiing

Like me, the new boss Chris Wakerley was a great adventure training fan; he was also an excellent skier. He asked me one day if I fancied leading a trip to my old haunts in Norway as the expedition for that year. He didn't need to ask twice, and it was a mark of the man that he was the first to volunteer.

I must admit, I was a little concerned as to how the guys who stepped forward would fare in the harsh Norwegian mountain conditions, and even more as to how they would cope with Nordic ski touring. I hoped that they hadn't assumed that they were signing up for a downhill "slipper city" exercise; ski touring is a very, very different style and experience. The places for the trip filled up quickly, and Chris mentioned that a Major from the Bde HQ wanted to tag along. His name was Pat Chapman.

When I met Pat, I was absolutely delighted. He was an ex-Royal Marine who had been commissioned into the Royal Logistics Corps (RLC), as there were no vacancies in the Marines. He had spent many years in Norway whilst with his previous Corps and was both an excellent skier and Arctic Warfare trained. The team was starting to shape up nicely but still the majority had never worn cross-country skis in their lives.

As Pat Chapman oversaw the Bde HQ vehicle fleet, he was able to arrange for two minibuses to be loaned to us for the expedition, which was an immense help.

The departure day duly arrived, and we headed off to the Danish port of Hirtshals for our crossing to Stavanger. Inevitably, the trip was a little rough, but the guys made the best of it, enjoying the on-board disco and a few beers before we arrived and set off for the Hardangervidda mountain range in south central Norway. Although it had been some years since I had been to this area, I had remembered how much I liked the Haukeliseter Fjellstue, a small hotel at the bottom of the plateau. I had therefore rung the hotel during expedition preparation in Hohne and to my delight, it was still being run by Morten.

Amazingly, his dad had taught me to ski many years ago when I first joined 249 Sig Sqn, and he was our Norwegian Liaison Officer (LO). Even more surprisingly, I asked him if Carlos the waiter from all those years ago was still there and was chuffed to find out that he was! Carlos was the ex-Portuguese sailor who somehow ended up in Norway via Wolverhampton after leaving the Navy; back in my 249 days, the lads took him to their heart and always looked out for him. I guess everybody has heard how expensive Norway is, and was even back then, so knowing the owner and staff certainly assisted my bartering on prices. Carlos' only question was "Will you bring it?" I will explain this random query later on...

We rolled into Haukeliseter a few hours after our arrival in Stavanger, and I could tell that most of the guys had never seen snow quite like it before. We were greeted by our host and quickly dispatched to our cabins which sat around the main building. After dinner and a few beers, we all headed off to bed, it had been quite a long trip.

Bright and early next morning, I lined the guys up on the flat ground outside the hotel. The snow was very deep, but the sky was bright and there was no wind, so the -18°C didn't feel too bad as we had all brought sensible clothing. I spent the next five days teaching the team how to ski, assisted by Chris, Pat and Dave Alexander, our Foreman, all of whom had previous experience. Most of the time was spent in and around the hotel, with a few longer trips into the bondu to get everybody acclimatised. What none of the guys knew was that most of our training area was a huge lake that was frozen and covered in snow. I did, of course, teach them what actions to take if they fell through the ice whilst crossing a frozen lake, but I figured they didn't need to know they were training on one!

Our second week was the actual expedition, where we circumvented the Hardanger, first climbing up onto the main plateau which was immediately above the hotel. The climb was undertaken on skis, of course; after all, this was ski touring. Although Pat was 55 years old, he was like a mountain goat and demonstrated the benefits of his time in the Marines; the younger lads immediately knew they were in the presence of an elite soldier, despite his age.

The plateau is vast and has a range of tourist huts dotted across it which can be used throughout the year; in the winter, the challenge is to find them. With snow drifts many metres deep, these huts are often completely buried, so good map reading is critical. As a mountain leader, that's a good thing as your students soon learn to trust their map and compass, a skill which is usually more difficult to embed. When the sun is out and the wind is light, even temperatures of -20°C are relatively easy to deal with, but on the Hardanger it can change in an instant; from bright blue skies, to a total white-out. In such situations, the only option is to take cover and often by simply digging into the snow; albeit care must be taken to avoid digging in the wrong places, which could be disastrous.

Our first two nights were spent in the relative luxury of the huts. These amazing sanctuaries had beds with bedding, cooking utensils, firewood and the like available for use by those lucky enough to find them. The deal was that you paid for what you used by putting cash in an "honesty box" which was left in a prominent position in the hut and made sure that you prepared the hut for the next user on your departure. Several of the lads commented that they didn't consider this system would be entirely successful in the UK; I made the point that it's pretty much life or death in this scenario, but I did agree that it wouldn't work everywhere.

The next morning as we set off, it was windy and cold, and something told me that we were in for a really testing day. It quickly went from bad to worse, with visibility being extremely low. After a gruelling period, we eventually hit some clear ski tracks, and Chris, who was leading at that point, was elated that we had stumbled into somebody else's trail. His joy was short-lived though as he quickly realised that they were actually our own tracks and we had gone round in a circle!

We decided to adopt first principles and very carefully moved forward, sending a front man out as far as we could see on a bearing and then closing up on his position. It was slow progress but it was our only option to keep moving.

I figured that if we didn't arrive at the hut within an hour and the weather remained the same, we would dig in at that particular point. I'm glad to say that my reputation remained intact as we arrived at our destination 45 minutes later, after a sterling effort on the map by Chris. I would like to think that it was experience but in truth, there is always a bit of luck in those situations. Anyway, we quickly dug our way into the hut and got settled in for the night.

Sadly, the weather didn't pick up much the next day, so I decided to take a shorter route and we set off in the knowledge that we might have to endure another night in a snow hole. The guys were doing really well but the weather was truly awful, so after about four hours, I was looking for a decent place to dig, when one of the lads noticed the top of a hut popping up out of the snow. I knew it wasn't one of the tourist huts but also that where the weather was treacherous, it was accepted practice to force open a private hut for shelter; so that's what we did.

Unlike the other huts, it only had beds but no bedding, and very little tinned food. That wasn't a problem though, as we were carrying emergency rations, sleeping bags and other supplies. Here we were, having forced entry into somebody's mountain cabin without permission, but at least we were dry and warm. We had a whip round the next morning and left the money with a short note that I had written, explaining what had occurred and apologising, with my name and contact details. One of the lads had a padlock in his pack, so we managed to secure the door on leaving, which made us all feel better; breaking and entering didn't sit well with any of us.

We made it safely back to Haukeliseter the next afternoon and set about cleaning up and packing up our kit. Carlos had been keeping a very close eye on my movements, clearly anticipating something. Eventually, he strolled over to me and asked, "George, you bring it?"

"Of course, Carlos!" I said, reaching into a box by my side from which I produced a bottle of Whyte & Mackay whisky. We had brought a few with us from Germany, as I had remembered the bartering we used to conduct with the locals all those years ago when I first visited the country. His eyes lit up as I passed it over and shook his hand; how much was it worth nowadays, I thought.

I had promised the team a few day in Hovden, a town around 12 miles south; the downhillers amongst them were hugely excited as the town had an Olympic standard slope and after being beasted in the mountains, they really fancied some posing. We sat down for dinner at Haukeliseter one final time and Carlos duly started to bring the food out, although he seemed to be walking strangely. I guessed the whisky had taken a bit of a hit! I knew the lads would be hungry, but our old friend, the Pie Man, who had again volunteered for the trip, decided that the first loaf delivered to the table was his and duly demolished all of it. Scouse, as we normally called him, was a big lad and hadn't realised it was for all of us. He was a great guy and the youngest on the trip, so we let him off.

Hovden was like a Christmas card; beautiful houses, and shops with snow up to the windowsills and lots of people moving about, all of whom were very welcoming. I couldn't believe it as we arrived at the bottom of the ski slope to find the guy operating the lift was my old mate, Raggy, who I had last seen 10 years earlier when he was one of our Norwegian ski instructors. He was a monster of a man, easily 6'3" and 18-19 stones, and he nearly crushed me to death when he recognised me.

"George!" he shouted, "you come back!" The best was yet to come though. Raggy wasn't just the lift operator; he owned the resort, including several very nice huts on-site! I asked him if there was any chance of hiring four of them for a couple of days. "No, you can't hire them," he said. "They are free for you to use!" Astounded by his generosity, I shook his hand and told the lads to get their gear and settle in.

The next couple of days were superb fun, downhilling on an Olympic slope free of charge; happy days indeed. We did have a bit of an issue first night and to be honest, it was down to me. I decided to repay Raggy's kindness by giving him the last three bottles of whisky we had brought from Germany, but stupidly I had forgotten an old Norwegian custom, which was to come back to haunt me.

We had all arranged to meet up in the best hotel in Hovden for an end-of-expedition meal on the night before we headed home. Once I was dressed, I asked Pat if he wanted to come along to thank Raggy for his kindness before we went to dinner. Raggy's house was quite a plush building that was just above the rental huts, so it only took a couple of minutes to get there. Raggy opened the door and invited us both in. He was absolutely delighted when I handed over the whisky and immediately asked if we would join him for a drink. That was my mistake; forgetting that if you crack a bottle of whisky with a Norwegian mountain man, you are expected to help him finish the bottle.

Mindful that Chris and the lads would be waiting for us, Pat and I kept our part of the bargain and helped Raggy empty the bottle, rather too quickly. I don't remember getting in the taxi that was to take us to the hotel for dinner, but I am glad that the roads in town were deep in snow. Both Pat and I fell out of the cab as it approached the hotel, laughing hysterically as we rolled about in the road. We hadn't delayed dinner, which was a bonus, but I don't think the boss appreciated two rubber men turning up to join him at the table. I left Pat to explain what had gone on the next morning!

The journey back was uneventful, although I am glad that Chris had flown back and not joined us on the ferry; I was feeling a little guilty, to be honest. I declined the lads' invitation to join them in the bar/disco and decided to have an early night.

On the Move Again

About 18 months after our return from the Middle East, I was called in to see the OC, who let me know that I had been selected for promotion to WO1, which was one of the highlights of my life. He then told me that I was to be posted to Liverpool to join HQ 11 (ARRC) Sig Be. Almost in one foul swoop my dream had been realised and shattered at the same time.

"I can't go to Liverpool. Sir, there is nothing of any significance there; that will kill my career!" I said.

The boss was concerned that I was so anti-Liverpool but understood my career worries. "Come back in an hour," he said. "There's somebody I think you need to talk to."

"OK, Sir, see you in an hour," I said, turning on my heel and wondering who on earth the call would be with.

The hour literally flew past. The whole thing was a mystery to me because I had been promoted a year before I even entered the formal promotion age bracket, so there was clearly somebody rooting for me. I knocked on the OC's door and he called me in. "I'll leave you to it," he said, and left the room!

The phone rang a few minutes later and when I answered, I got a bit of a shock when the caller identified himself.

"Yeoman, it's Brigadier Bill Backhouse from 11 Sig Bde. I understand you have concerns about coming to Liverpool?"

Recovering from the initial shock, I explained my worries to the Brigadier, and he very kindly answered all of my questions. The upside was that he had been selected to take command of 11 Bde as part of a major reorganisation within the army and de facto, the Corps. The Bde would consist of a regular Sig Regt and four TA Sig Regts, three of which would be issued with the Ptarmigan secure, tactical trunk system which represented a multimillion-pound investment in the Bde.

The latter point made it clear as to why the role I had been offered had an extremely high profile and in fairness, represented a big enough challenge for anybody, no matter how career minded. Just in case I had missed the point, Brigadier Bill reminded me that he had chaired that year's promotion board and had hand selected his Brigade Yeoman, hence the early promotion had been offered.

So, Liverpool it was then, and that proved to be one of the best decisions of my life. The boss returned to the office

WO & Sgts' Mess, Hohne –
My LSGC Presentation with
Sue and Mark by my side.

and was pleased that it had all been sorted. Little did he know that he would be joining me in Liverpool inside nine months.

As my time in Hohne came to an end, I was truly sorry to leave; it was one of the highlights of my career and indeed my life. To be Yeoman 22 Brigade was an experience and honour I will never forget.

On top of that, I had worked for two of the finest officers in the Corps – Andy Forster and Chris Wakerley – both of whom I am lucky enough to still call my friends. After a round of leaving functions and presents I will treasure for ever, I completed my handover to WO2 (YofS) Paul Sexby and shortly thereafter, I was on my way to Liverpool.

POSTING 10
HQ 11 (ARRC) Sig Bde
(West Derby, Liverpool)

Welcome Home – How Things Had Changed

The ferry crossing from Zeebrugge to Hull was a bit rough which Sue really didn't like, so we spent most of the time in our cabin trying to sleep. Mark was so used to travelling, he just got on with things and never whinged once; to be fair, he wasn't that type of kid and never complained about much.

We got off the boat in the morning and for a change we didn't have a monster drive ahead of us. It was straight across the country to Liverpool as we weren't heading for Scotland as we normally did when travelling back to UK.

As we came off the M62, we decided to have a quick look at my new place of work, Deysbrook Barracks in West Derby. Travelling down Princess Drive through Huyton into West Derby, I decided to stop for fuel and duly pulled over into a petrol station. I jumped out of the car and grabbed the pump handle to find it padlocked. I thought it a bit strange, and I could see an old bloke in the shop gesticulating wildly in my general direction.

The tannoy sparked up and a voice said, "Hang on there, lad, I do that," and a couple of minutes later, the old guy came out, locking the door behind him.

I was a little concerned by this strange process, so as he approached and unlocked the pump, I asked him what was going on. "I don't take any chances here, lad, I'm sick of getting robbed," he mumbled. "How much do you want?"

"Just fill it up," I said, a bit perplexed and wondering what sort of place this was.

"You normally pay for that first," he said, "but since you're not from round here, I'll let you off," and he proceeded to deliver the fuel.

On completion I automatically followed him to the shop, but when he got to the door, he told me I wasn't allowed in and had to pay at the window.

"But I want to buy some stuff," I said to him and was completely shocked when he said, "Just tell me and I'll get it for you." I was beginning to think I had arrived in Beirut, not a city in the UK!

"Where are you heading?" he asked, looking genuinely interested.

"Just down the road to Deysbrook Barracks," I replied.

"Oh, God, you're not going to be living down there, are you?" he responded. "It's like the Wild West!"

After thanking him for his very insightful but worrying view, I jumped in the car and we were outside the barracks five minutes later.

My first impressions were not good. It looked like some kind of community hospital, all low-level red brick with a very dodgy-looking pub across the road. The only good thing about it was it was right next to Melwood, the Liverpool FC training ground. We noticed a row of what were clearly military quarters next to the barracks and genuinely thanked God not to have been allocated one of those. Somewhat depressed, we set off for our house which was a few miles outside the city in the village of Formby.

Neither of us had ever heard of Formby, so we spent the next 20minutes of the drive praying it wasn't anything like West Derby. Thankfully, it was the polar opposite and an exceptionally pretty place. Sadly though, the MOD had managed to acquire some pretty tatty semi-detached houses, and in our case, 39 Kirklake Road was a huge disappointment. Here I was, a brand new WO1, moving into a quarter that resembled a rabbit hutch and quite frankly neither met my basic needs, or more importantly, an allocation in line with my rank.

Given it was a Friday afternoon and quite late, we decided to head off to Blackpool and relax for the weekend. We had been in Germany for 12 years with only a 14-month break when we returned to UK for my Yeoman's course, so what a let-down this was! We had a week's leave before I started work in any case, and perhaps I could get something better sorted out next week; anyway, off to Blackers!

My brand-new red Toyota Corolla estate was having a few challenges travelling at my normal speed, which was probably a blessing in disguise, as I was used to autobahn travel with no speed restrictions. Eventually, we arrived in Blackpool and managed to secure the weekend in a reasonable hotel on the seafront. We hadn't been to Blackpool previously and were a bit surprised at how run-down everything was, but equally how cheap things were from a pricing point of view. Mark was quite happy, like most children would be; the sandcastles, an indoor leisure complex and the fairground had everything he wanted, so we just relaxed for the weekend. I fully understand that there are a lot of families, especially Scots, who swear by holidaying in Blackpool, but I decided there and then that I would not be tying up any accommodation there in future years; it really wasn't my scene.

We travelled back to Formby on Monday so that I could make a few calls to see what/if any alternative options there were on the housing front. Despite people being very understanding and willing to help, the simple truth is that the only options were for us to move some way south if we wanted a married quarter in line to my position and I really didn't fancy a lengthy commute every day, so we decided to stay in Formby; at least the village looked very good. As a compromise, I was told that another house just behind where we were would become vacant in around six months' time and I could have first refusal; that seemed very fair.

New Job, New World

My first day at work was quite different to anything I had previously experienced during my service. The officers were quite a weird bunch, largely hangovers from the TA HQ that was now being re-tasked to take up a very key role within the Corps and, I guess, having never served with TA in the past,

I knew it would be very different. There was little doubt they would be thinned out and replaced as we got up and running in the new role. I had my interview with the Brigadier in the afternoon and he was absolutely buzzing about the future; he sold the whole concept to me very easily. Brigadier Bill was an outstanding man, and I will always be grateful and proud that I was his Brigade Yeoman.

There were lots of strange occurrences in the first couple of weeks, getting used to the HQ team being the strangest of all. It was going to take time to get a handle on the real characters; a COS who was a complete blusterer, a Captain who visited the mess at lunchtime and imbibed a bit too readily, whom I regularly saw asleep at his desk with a lit fag hanging out of his mouth, and a QM (Quartermaster), who spent his life trying to be taken seriously. The latter had a habit of using words he didn't understand, usually completely out of context, and he collected things he once heard the Brigadier mention he liked; a real plonker. I worked for a Traffic Officer called Geoff Downie who was an absolute gentleman; I'd known him for a few years as he was, of course, a commissioned Yeoman. In addition, I had a WO2 Yeoman, Jerry Hughes and a Crypto SNCO, SSgt Mick Allcock, working directly to me who were extremely hard-working and very competent.

I got to know the TA guys and girls as they came through the HQ either on their drill nights or when they were offered additional hours and did the odd few extra days. There were some, of course, that were working on full-time contracts, such as Sgt Archie Reid, our MT SNCO; boy, was he a character.! When you then consider that our Superintendent Clerk made my old mate "Duncan Disorderly" look teetotal, you will be starting to get a feel for the personnel.

The WOs and sergeants' mess was on-site and was run by my old adversary Rod Whatley who was now a WO1 (RSM). Rod had been posted to 33 Sig Regt (TA), and as they didn't have their own regimental mess, their RSM always ran the HQ mess. He lived up to my expectations during his tour and managed to fall off the stage during a mess presentation, caught two SNCOs fighting outside the mess and on ordering them to "stop fighting", got punched for his troubles. Some things never change.

My boss Geoff Downey wasn't around for long as he took redundancy and retired to spend more time watching his beloved Everton. I was absolutely delighted to meet his replacement, Captain Ronny Allan, my old close friend from 3rd Armoured Division Headquarters & Signal Regiment many years before. In a lot of ways, Ronny and I were very similar; highly focused perfectionists who would stop at nothing to achieve the very best results possible. That said, we both enjoyed a laugh, cared for our guys and girls, and tried to help them in any way possible. Despite being old friends, we both towed the line and always acted in a professional manner; we never used first names unless we were by ourselves, and we always set an example to others.

My Introduction to the TA

The TA can be an organisation where standards are allowed to drop by the regular personnel posted to their units as permanent instructors, who should know better. I always felt the TA soldiers deserved to be shown more respect. In truth, I really didn't expect to see the levels of commitment some of the TA soldiers showed.

I can think of a married couple who owned their own business, both SSgts, who attended every drill night, every exercise and would happily volunteer more time if we were ever in need. It's hard enough to run your own business, never mind do all this additional stuff. I quickly gained a lot of respect for the good ones, of which there were many. The TA Officers, on the other hand, were largely a burden, with very little talent and an irritating habit of trying to play games to demonstrate they were contributing. I've always been quite a robust character and just wouldn't let them take any liberties. I had to be respectful, of course, and generally was, but if they were behaving inappropriately, or just getting in the way, I would certainly not hesitate to get amongst them. I knew the Brigadier had my back and to be fair, we were a very busy group of people with an enormous task on our hands and simply couldn't afford to carry passengers.

When you consider that we were taking receipt of the multimillion-pound secure Ptarmigan tactical trunk fleet across the Bde and handing this key combat communication resource over to the TA, that will highlight the challenge we faced. The key vehicles were classified and as such, had to be accommodated in suitable buildings of the same classification. It won't surprise anybody that in our TA locations, including Huyton, Leeds, Middlesbrough and Birmingham, to name but a few, there were no garages capable of holding such highly classified vehicles with these types of installation. It was therefore down to us to design and contract the new garage builds, design and contract new training facilities, and design, produce and deliver the requisite training to soldiers across the Bde.

I am sure it won't be a surprise to hear that this enormous task kept us extremely busy, with any spare time spent planning, deploying, undertaking, and recovering from a range of exercises. This also included an annual two-week exercise that is central to TA bounty payments, so there were no free lunches. Far from the "slipper city" environment that had worried me when I was first notified of my posting to the Bde, it was panning out as one of the hardest tours of my life, but I did realise that I was in a very privileged role and was so grateful that the Brigadier had offered me the job.

Amazingly, and very happily for me, my old boss from 22 Bde, Chris Wakerley, was posted into the HQ to replace the COS. I did say we were upgrading but that is equivalent to swapping a Mini for an Aston Martin! It was necessary to make such changes as this previously backwater-style HQ was now at the heart of the UK's deployable military communications capability.

Training a TA Brigade

Finding an appropriate area in which to deploy a full Bde in the UK is a very challenging task, unless you want to use the same training areas year on year. With most of the Bde made up of TA units, that would be disastrous, in that the location of their annual major exercise is understandably very important to them. In years gone by, it would normally be somewhere abroad or in a very holiday-like venue in the UK. In truth, that was when they were largely focused on having a good time, as opposed to undertaking relevant training suitable for a formation that owned, maintained and could be called upon at any time to deploy the army's critical tactical trunk communications in support of peacekeeping or war fighting operations.

I don't make this point to try and denigrate the TA; far from it. I had built up a healthy respect for these folk and could certainly understand why they previously had enjoyed a light-hearted "annual camp", as they referred to it. They willingly gave up their own time throughout the year on drill nights and weekend exercises, on top of holding down a real full-time job. In my view, they had every right to expect a well-planned annual exercise focused on adventure training, sports, and leadership training that included some fun as payback. Unfortunately, the MOD's decision to equip and train them on such a core element of our military capability had consigned that option to the history books.

As the person responsible for planning and managing the Brigade's deployments, I had the task of identifying suitable locations to train on and the constraints outlined the above complicated things, particularly in the UK. However, as finding suitable locations is a bit easier in Scotland because of the large swathes of land belonging to individual landowners, I decided to focus there. It is significantly easier to agree the use rights with one person who controls tenant farmers, than to engage dozens of individual farmers directly. In Scotland, the major estate owners tend to have a "Factor" or Estate Manager that can act on their behalf. These individuals will be empowered to agree use across the full estate and to simply tell their tenants that this is the case and direct them to support the exercise; job done.

On an initial recce for the annual exercise in 1994, I came across an old RAF airfield at Castle Kennedy, just off the A75 in Dumfries and Galloway, near Stranraer. It was enormous with a huge runway on which we could set up hundreds of vehicles. That fact was hugely important, as the main task for this camp was to train the TA on the use of the highly complex Ptarmigan tactical trunk system with which they had been equipped. The exercise would be split into a week of detailed training on the system within a controlled environment, followed by a week with the units deployed across the entirety of the southwest of Scotland to reinforce the training.

I quickly discovered that the disused airfield belonged to the Earl of Stair, as indeed did most of the county, so I made an appointment to meet with his Factor to start the clearance for use process. The Factor was exactly as I had imagined he would be; a big bear of a man in a Harris tweed suit who would easily pass for a retired full Col. Mr Woolsley-Brinton was a charming chap who was delighted to see us and stated that as "His Lordship" was an old soldier, he would be more than happy to support the use of his land for exercise purposes.

This was an amazing result, but only the start of an enormous task, with every site that we would use having to be formally recced and a signature obtained to approve its use. This started a round of recce visits by personnel from across the Bde and was a huge undertaking. Personally, I made several return visits to pull the plan together at the highest level, before opening it up to individual unit recces. During these visits, we stayed at a lovely old Scottish manor house hotel, the Glen Tachur, just outside the village of Barrhill. Most amazingly, the family who ran it were Mancunians. They were great people, and the quality of the food and rooms was simply outstanding; we even spent a Burns Night there, which was one of the best I have ever attended. I like to think the family enjoyed a substantial upturn in their revenues during the periods in which we stayed; they certainly deserved to.

I have many, many memories of this specific period and the enormous effort that went into the exercise preparation. One memory that just makes me laugh out loud relates to a particular recce with my boss and great friend Ronny, who was the Bde Traffic Officer. For absolute clarity, the traffic I refer to is signal message traffic, just in case anybody is thinking Ronny was some kind of traffic warden!

Feeling particularly hungry one day whilst on a recce, we decided to pop into the small town of Newton Stewart, to visit a good Scottish chippy. We decided that as Northern Scots, we should appreciate an opportunity to enjoy a Scotch pie supper.

As we turned up at the chippy, we were both a bit taken aback to see it had a serving hatch window through which you could order your food. Although this was the kind of thing we had come across before, it was quite unusual for a chippy in Scotland! As we looked in, a rather rotund bloke asked very gruffly, "Whit ye want?"

"Two pie suppers," said Ronny, in his best Dundonian twang, only to reel back in abject horror as the big fella threw the two pies straight into the bubbling oil.

Astounded by this reaction, I asked Ronny how he had expected the pies would be cooked.

"Baked!" retorted Ronny. "We bake our pies in Dundee!"

Now, I'm not one to be embarrassed by my working-class background but where I come from, that simply didn't compute! Only posh people baked their pies in Scotland; the rest of us were fully signed up to the chippy staff chucking them in the oil, or indeed beef dripping in my day. Despite knowing Ronny for decades, I started to wonder if he was descended from Scottish royalty, or maybe they were just posh in Dundee. We laughed ourselves silly over this incident and I am certain the chippy guy, who had clearly eaten most of the pies, thought we were insane. I have to say, the pie supper was fantastic as expected, but I am uncertain of Ronny's true perspective!

Enjoying Life

Everything that Brigadier Bill had sold to me about this tour came to fruition. Far from being a backwater, it was one of the biggest challenges I had ever faced. I was trusted, appreciated, and given a level of responsibility rarely afforded to a WO1. The Brigadier was a great advocate of our Corps being 'communicators', not just support staff that simply built and serviced Formation HQs. The latter did sadly fall to R Signals in many instances, purely by virtue that as we provided the HQ vehicles together with the communications facilities used by the HQ staff, it was easy to make us responsible for everything else. Brigadier Bill believed that our explicit role was to set up, deliver, and maintain communications, and therefore he was a huge supporter of the specialist roles of Yeomen and their technician counterparts, Foremen.

My personal view was that I had joined the Corps to be the best I could be in my trade; that was achieving qualification as a Yeoman and going on to be commissioned as a Traffic Officer. My commissioning was something I had dreamed of and worked extremely hard to achieve, so it is fair to say it made my military journey seem completely worthwhile when it was confirmed. Incredibly, that was after only 18 months in post as a WO1 (YofS), so I had to accept that once again, my age would delay my promotion as the system wanted its pound of flesh. Truthfully, I didn't mind because I knew that this was a very special role and it was a genuine privilege to fill it. I also knew that I wouldn't have time to dwell on the delay; we were so busy.

Whilst living in Formby, we took the opportunity to buy a puppy, something I had wanted to do for years but avoided because of the very stringent regulations on moving a dog between countries at that time. It just didn't seem fair to have the animal placed in kennels for months on end as they went through quarantine. Searching the local papers, we found a breeder in Formby offering Labrador puppies for sale. As a family, we decided that was the breed for us. As a child we always had dogs in the house, and I had always been a dog lover.

On the day we went to select our pup, I remember the breeder taking us into the yard to see the parents and puppies together. "Which one would you like?" she asked as we laughed at the various black and chocolate dogs running around.

From the corner of my eye, I saw a little black pup peeping out from behind a tree, so I went over to investigate. It was a little boy with the most beautiful face and a very easy-going temperament. The three of us were hooked; he was the one.

We went back to pick him up a week later and "Benjy" became a huge part of our family from that moment forward. I took time to research his background and found out he was a Sandylands Labrador, which enthusiasts will recognise as a very famous bloodline. I was never interested in showing him, but I am sure he would have done well if I had. He certainly had the pedigree for it, with lots of champions in his family.

Brigadier Bill eventually took the decision to retire on redundancy and his replacement was a former OC of mine at 249 Sig Squadron, now Brigadier, Mike Shaw. This was another chalk and cheese moment, with the two Brigs being completely different. We also knew that Brigadier Mike had already accepted a redundancy package, so his would be a relatively short tour.

He was a monster of a man but strangely quite shy, and as I knew him, I was able to provide some counter to stories circulating about him. He was a very deep thinker who didn't appreciate bluffers and if that was his view of you, then he was difficult to be around. If you showed him the qualities he was looking for, then he had your back and showed tremendous downward loyalty. Luckily, I had always got on well with him. He was also a massive adventure training enthusiast, so that boded well for a bit of downtime which we all needed.

It didn't take the Brigadier long before he decided that I should take everyone walking or climbing at least once a month which to be honest, I was delighted to do. We did lots of hill walking in the local area – the Peaks and the Lake District – but we soon found out that it was a big mistake to walk too close to the Brigadier; he was an intellectual and knew a bit about everything. Those who failed to keep their distance were questioned unmercifully about all sorts of random trivia, and following failure to provide the correct answer, were the subjected to an extremely in-depth series of lectures to try and increase their knowledge. This was not good for some and particularly painful for others, such as Sgt Archie Reid (KOSB) whose brain used to contract and render him speechless! The Brigadier enjoyed these trips so much, he decided that the pair of us should revisit our youth and go back to Norway to do some Nordic ski touring. Again, I was really happy to do this, including all the planning and preparation. My first task, of course, was to decide on the groups and given we only had one other qualified instructor, Major Simon Purser, I quickly ensured that he had the Brigadier in his party.

I decided that we would undertake a circumnavigation of the Hardangervidda, much as I had done in 201 Sig Sqn back in Hohne. It was a place I knew well and I was sure Morten would once again take care of me on the cost side, amongst other things. Simon was happy with the choice, and we decided between us that we would run two camps of 10 days, and I would lead the first. The Brigadier was ecstatic about the choice as he had spent some time there with 249. I was a bit worried about his enthusiasm though; given he was now 20 years older and at 6 foot 4 inches tall and 18 stone, he might just feel a bit of pain. Anyway, I was sure Simon could sort any issues out!

I quite deliberately opened the trip up to as many people within the Bde as necessary, hoping to get TA personnel on board if possible. Unfortunately, I didn't get any TA takers for the trip, but to be fair, unless they were unemployed or willing to sacrifice annual leave from work, it was very difficult for them to participate which was a real shame. I doubt that too many TA soldiers had been given such an opportunity.

To a professional soldier, TA officers can be a huge challenge; I used to equate it to a fully qualified tradesman being lectured by a labourer. Of course, there is good and bad in all walks of life, and I certainly met some of the former, but being talked down to by an individual that you knew was only

Hardangervidda Expedition in 1995 –
Ready to go!

in the TA for the kudos, was hard to stomach. Inevitably, this type of individual would be an over-privileged, snotty-nosed wally, with as much leadership potential as a house fly and no real commitment to the role.

I remember one particular herbert, wearing the rank of Major, who simply could not get his head around the fact that I, as a WO1 (YofS), was empowered to plan Bde deployments, run Bde communications, and generally lead Bde Ops, despite being fully backed and trusted by the Bde Comd and the COS. This was because I was not an officer, but a WO; the guy was completely insignificant in every way but took it upon himself to try and get in my face. At the end of one Bde briefing prior to an overseas exercise, he tried to undermine a communications point I had made, but rather than embarrass him which would have been particularly easy, as he couldn't even spell Comms, I decided to bring it up with him privately.

After the briefing had concluded, I asked the guy if we could have a private chat to one side and we stepped into a small office. I explained that my briefing had been pre-approved by the Brigadier and why his communication point was incorrect. He instantly flew into a rage and in a high-pitched rant, he asked me who I thought I was. I replied that I was the Brigade Yeoman and that I was delivering the brief as directed by the Comd and he was at liberty to challenge the Brigadier's plan if he thought that was the appropriate way forward.

He then started screaming again, so I decided his behaviour was irrational and that it was time to leave the room. As I walked down the corridor, I could hear this shrill, rather silly voice, literally screaming, "Mr Greiiiiiig...!" I could see Ronny Allan at the end of the corridor laughing his head off. I managed to hold back my laughter and headed straight past Ronny and knocked on the Brigadier's door.

When he called me, in he was also chuckling, and told me he had been informed about this Major's behaviour and to leave it with him.

As I left the office, Ronny nodded at me and again burst out laughing. The officer in question never came near me again. I understand that he had a rather stressful 'discussion' with the Brigadier, so I just forgot about it. It does stick in my mind though, as every time I see or talk to Ronny, it starts with him shouting, "Mr Greiiiiig!" and laughing uncontrollably.

Ronny and I used to split shifts in the Brigade Ops vehicle on exercise, with WO2 (YofS) Jerry Hughes and SSgt Mick Allcock supporting us. One night, I had gone off to bed after my shift, leaving Ronny, Mick and Major Nick Leviseur, a TA Watchkeeper, on shift overnight. It was a dark, wet night, so I was glad to be getting my head down.

About an hour later, I was woken by Mick Allcock shaking me vigorously and shouting, "Yeoman, Yeoman, wake up! Traffic's fallen and I think he's dead!"

Clearly startled and extremely worried, I rapidly jumped into my trousers and ran outside and headed to the Bde Ops wagon. Amazingly and thankfully, Traffic (Ronny) seemed to have been reincarnated and although clearly in some pain, his death seemed far from imminent. As a field ambulance arrived to take him to hospital, I had established that he had slipped on the vehicle steps and fallen badly, injuring his back. It was quite comical seeing Ronny being taken away on the stretcher, whilst a panicking Nick Leviseur ran alongside him trying to ram a £20 note in his pocket to make sure he had some cash with him!

Having made the earlier point about bad TA officers, I think it is only right that I should balance that story up. Maj Nick Leviseur was a barrister by trade and part of the Inns of Court & City Yeomanry Sig Squadron based in Gray's Inn, in the City of London. Nick, rumoured to be a cousin of Her Majesty the Queen, was a real character. A man of means, posh, and clearly very well-educated, he was, as they say, "as mad as a box of frogs". However, he was also highly committed, always helpful, and very considerate of the soldiers. Left alone, he could be relied upon to take some unique approaches to communications planning, but letting him drive anywhere was a very risky exercise, as he may get lost for hours on end.

The difference between Nick and the other TA officer I described, is that he was a real gentleman, accepted that he was a part-time officer and had no desire or need to be pretentious; he was the real deal – a proper toff. A mark of his kindness, not to mention wealth, was evident when, on completion of a two-week exercise, he invited every soldier in the HQ for a drink during R&R and picked up a rather substantial tab, paying the bill with his Coutts bank card.

My final memory of Nick was when my commissioning dinner was held. He strolled up to my wife and asked her, "Who do you belong to?" Sue was amazed by this rather sexist comment (which was made with absolutely no malice, it was just Nick's way), but luckily, he managed to avoid a clipped ear. We often chuckle about that memory.

An Older Soldier's Challenge

I always made a point of maintaining a high standard of fitness. Let's face it, not many employers provide time for training during work hours, pay you to undertake that training, and provide all the facilities for free!

Each year, one of the Bde units, 2 Sig Regt in York, would organise a competition that was open to units across the services. It was known as 'Race the Sun'. I took part every year, representing the Bde HQ. My event of choice was the forced march, which was eight miles in full combat gear, carrying 45 lb and a weapon. The event finished with a fearsome assault course, but I loved that type of test. It was quite unusual to see a WO1 as part of a team, mainly because the units tended to choose the younger guys.

One particular year, I was paired with a Cpl from the Royal Marines who was a good 10 years my junior. In typical Marine banter, he informed me that he would wait for me at the start of the assault course, as the rules stated that the pairs had to undertake that part together. "Don't worry, boss, I'll wait for you," he said cockily as we set off on the run.

I passed him at about five miles and had to wait around ten minutes for him to join me at the start of the assault course, so I was feeling happy with myself. But, as only soldiers can, my bubble was burst as I heaved my body over the top of a cargo net at 5m, and I heard two young soldiers at the bottom of the obstacle say, "Look at that old bastard! He looks knackered!" I think they realised I had heard them because they were nowhere to be seen when I finished. In truth, I had a bloody good laugh at what they had said; they were spot on!

Formby Village

Formby was a lovely village to live in and we enjoyed our time there as a family very much. To be fair, I also love the city of Liverpool, but the short trip home to Formby each evening was a welcome opportunity to relax and shake off the stresses of the working day.

We often popped into the city on Saturday mornings and getting stopped outside the St John's indoor market by some bloke wearing a massive overcoat asking if you wanted to buy a shirt always made me laugh. I found Scousers to be friendly, funny and loyal friends, but they did have some very dodgy areas of the city, and some real bad boys, so you had to be sensible as to where you went.

Formby was quite upmarket, something I quickly found out when I first arrived from Germany. As it has a Liverpool postcode, I just assumed it was classed as part of the city, so when a lad in West Derby asked where I lived and I said Formby, he made it clear that I was mistaken.

"Dat's not Liverpool, la," he shouted out, "dat's posh, dar is!" The village did have some nice pubs and a few good restaurants, with Don Luigi's Italian being our particular favourite.

One evening, Sue and I had gone there for a quiet meal and were quite surprised when Kenny Dalglish, his wife Marina, and daughter Kelly, walked in and sat down next to us. He lived in the village, as did a lot of professional football players, but we hadn't seen him before. As Kenny is one of my all-time heroes, Sue told me to stop staring and ask for his autograph. I couldn't bring myself to do that because I didn't feel it was right when he was out with his family.

After an hour or so, I headed off to the toilet and as I walked in, there was Kenny washing his hands.

"Awright?" he asked, in his gruff Glaswegian accent.

"Aye, good, thanks," I replied.

"You're a Jock, where are you from?" he asked.

"Aberdeen's my home city," I said, and he launched into a story about his visits there while he was playing for Celtic. I couldn't help but recite my story about my father-in-law being a footballer who had played against him early in his career.

"What was his name?" Kenny asked and when I replied "Jim Fraser," he laughed out loud, rolled up his trouser leg and said, "I'm just checking the scars he left on me! How is the old bugger?"

When I told him Jim had died a few years ago, he was genuinely upset to hear it and he insisted on introducing himself to Sue, which he duly did. It was a great honour to meet one of my biggest heroes and even better to see what an unassuming, charming guy he was.

I mentioned that a lot of famous players lived in the village, on Victoria Road, a row of very prestigious houses. My other encounter with one of these icons occurred one day when I was out running on a very wet and windy Sunday afternoon. I was running from the Red Squirrel Reserve down Victoria Road, with the rain driving into my face, and was crossing a large driveway when a Jaguar swung off the road, nearly knocking me off my feet.

As you can imagine, I wasn't best pleased with the plonker driving the car, but when the car braked, and a huge bloke stepped out, I thought better of saying anything. I couldn't see him clearly because of the rain, but as I wiped my eyes I recognised him as Alan Shearer, the ex-Blackburn Rovers and England legend. He was a lot bigger than he appeared on TV!

"You OK?" he asked. "I was a bit quick there."

Nice of him to accept he was in the wrong I thought as I answered, "Yes, no problem, Alan," and ran off.

The time came for Brigadier Mike to retire and my third Bde Comd duly arrived. I hadn't met this guy but his reputation as a difficult character proceeded him. I had long since been selected for a commission, but my pride demanded that I never allowed myself to become complacent and wanted to ensure I did a good job for the new Brigadier. I never changed any aspect of how I delivered my role, but the new boss was a very self-aware person who didn't really like it if he wasn't the centre of attention.

I worked hard to ensure that I didn't cross him, as I had no doubt that he was the type of character who would take pleasure from derailing a career. I will always believe that he was little more than a bully who simply didn't like it if you weren't one of "his". Having served with a range of outstanding Brigadiers who were liked and in certain cases revered, I had no intention of giving him that opportunity. Professionally, of course, I was hurt by his attitude but remained buoyed up by the fact that the other two Brigadiers and other key characters, including the COS, trusted me implicitly.

I managed to avoid any direct conflict with him apart from one instance in the gym. He had joined us for a PT session which ended with a game of indoor football. As was his way, he was running around kicking everybody and he eventually caught me with a rather painful stamp on my ankle. Stupidly, I made the quick but harsh decision to repay the tackle in kind, and shoulder-charged him. He hit the wall at a fair pace and immediately lost his temper, but I think he quickly regretted his outburst which was at best childish. The rule in the army is 'if you can't take it, don't give it', and I had simply provided a short, sharp reminder of that.

In truth, the Brigadier didn't dwell on the incident, but I never really felt comfortable with him. It seemed to me that the appropriate course of action was to get my head down and work my socks off until I was commissioned and posted. I had sweated blood on this tour and enjoyed the respect and support of some great people. There was no way I was going to let them or my family down.

Tfc Officer & Yeoman of Signals Refresher Course 1995.
Rear rank (from left): Me, Granville Yeomans,
Martin Fielding.
Front rank (from left); Tommy Baldwin, Jack Cowan,
Alf Thomas, John Tyreman.

Tfc Offr & YofS Refresher Course Certificate 1995.

My Commissioning Course, 1996.
Rear rank (from left): Noddy Baugh, me, Guy Richards.
Front rank (from left): Dave Stewart, Steve Toms,
Dougie Wright, Mark Wright-Jones.

POSTING 11
3 (UK) Armd Div HQ & Sig Regt
(Bulford Camp, Wiltshire)

Achieving My Professional Ambition –
Commissioned

Whilst I was immensely proud to have been selected for commissioning in the Corps, I was also extremely frustrated to be subjected to a significant delay between selection and actual promotion. This was the story of my life really, proving that I was worthy of the next rank and successful selection, but being held back due to my age; I was always hampered by the "too young" tag. Surely, if you are good enough to be selected, then it should simply be a case of finding the right job and being promoted into it?

All of that said, I was having a fantastic time in 11 Sig Bde where I was probably the most powerful WO1 of any "flavour" in the Corps. Let me swiftly say I am not as conceited as to believe this was all down to me. I had the best Bde Comd I could ask for, a COS that trusted me completely and mentored me at every opportunity, and the absolute need to step up to offset the lack of any true ability within the HQ TA staff officers who were dire, to put things mildly. I absolutely loved it.

The wait also became much easier to bear once my posting to 3rd Armoured Division Headquarters & Signal Regiment had been confirmed. The CO was a real star and I held him in the highest regard on every front. If I couldn't learn from him, I couldn't learn from anybody. Lt Col Graham Leach had been an instructor when I attended my Yeoman's course and made a genuine impression on me, to the point where I had secretly decided that I would do everything possible to work for him in the future.

I learned so much from my time in 11 Sig Bde, where any doubts I had about the commitment and quality of TA soldiers were quickly removed. There are good and bad in all walks of life, I know, but some of these guys and girls really went above and beyond what was asked of them.

My only concern regarding the TA was focused on the staff officers or "Watch keepers", as we often referred to them. They were inevitably from an era where the TA was just a gentleman's club and attracted people who wanted to wear the rank just to feel superior to others; well, they weren't! On the plus side, I had some excellent regular colleagues who had been hand-picked to get the Bde up and running as a major player within UK Defence and in doing so, changing the role of the TA for ever.

My commissioning dinner, or "Dining In", to the officers' mess was a very special moment for me and my family, who did and put up with so much to help me achieve my career goal. Lots of friends were able to attend from around the Corps, such as Lt Col Andy Forster from whom I had learned so much and with whom I had gone to war; Major Chris Wakerley, my mentor and guide; and Ronny Allan, my lifetime friend and inspiration. Donning my brand new mess dress with a Captain's pips on my shoulder meant a great deal to me. My life, to that point, had all been about this moment, and to be mixing with people that I held in the very highest regard made the effort worthwhile. Andy Forster and Chris Wakerley had shown such faith in me; it felt as though this was my opportunity to repay that trust and the start of the next chapter in my life. Sue looked beautiful in her dress and the five-course dinner was incredible. It was certainly a night that Sue and I will never forget.

Eventually, my posting date arrived, and we were allocated a married quarter, 1 Kiwi Road, Bulford Camp. We travelled down to Bulford a week before my start date to sign for our house, a process referred to as a "March In", get settled and get some preparation done for Day 1. We were absolutely

Officers' married quarters (MQ) in Bulford

delighted with our quarter, which was a beautiful, detached house with a large garden, right next to the woods on the slopes of Kiwi Hill. I knew the area well from my time in 249 Sig Sqn, which had been based about a mile down the road in the centre of camp, as well as the very many miles I had run with that squadron all over the local area; it felt good to be back. This, of course, was my second tour with 3rd Armoured Division Headquarters & Signal Regiment, albeit it was quite different as a Captain than it had been as a Corporal and we were in the UK, as opposed to Germany.

Monday came and I got dressed in my uniform and set off for work, which was a very enjoyable 10-minute stroll from my house. As I approached the side gate, the sentry threw up a salute and bade me, "Good morning, Sir," as he checked my ID card. I had waited all my career for that moment, and it felt very good!

As I arrived at my office inside the secure Ops area in Regimental HQ, I was met by the Ops Officer, Major Roy Freeman, whose hair made him look as if he had a finger in a power socket. Roy was a nice guy, newly promoted and shortly to move on to his next role.

My predecessor, Major Dave Gilchrist, was waiting for me in his – soon to be my – office. The first thing I noticed was that there was no computer on his desk; it was still early days on the computer front, but everyone else appeared to have one. I had last seen Dave when I was a boy soldier at Harrogate, when he was a SSgt (YofS). He had been a real pain in the proverbial in those days, but the relationship between Apprentices and Instructors was necessarily distant, so I was more aware of the big age gap between us. Dave was a seasoned Traffic Officer, whilst I was a brand new one and cut from very different cloth. My generation had been brought up in the operations environment, whilst Dave was an old school Crypto Custodian that wrote up his element of the Communication Electronic Instruction (CEI) prior to deployments and had little input anywhere else.

As we were discussing the role, Dave mentioned the security aspects which included acting as ITSO/Unit Security Officer. "So where is your computer?" I asked and he pointed under the desk. No, it wasn't broken or awaiting replacement; he informed me that he was too old for computers and didn't like them anyway, so he had never set it up!

I was completely amazed by this and asked him how he could fulfil his role of ITSO if he wasn't IT literate. "The Regimental Yeoman keeps them all on the right track with that," he said.

I immediately knew it was in good hands as the Regimental Yeoman was WO1 (YofS) Sam McElreavey, who was the best in the Corps in my opinion. What Dave had meant to say is that he found IT difficult and simply pushed it all on to Sam. Given his quality, Sam just sucked it up and amongst, the multitude of other ops-related activities he led, just got on with it. I had no axe to grind with Dave, but I knew at the end of Day 1 that our planned five-day handover was already over, as we had covered everything I needed from him, less the handover of the Div crypto account. What I needed was to spend time with Roy Freeman and Sam to get a full and detailed handle on my role.

We threw a leaving party for Dave at a local pub at the end of the week where we presented him with a gift and wished him all the best for the future. We hadn't fallen out in any way, just accepted the fact that we were from different eras with different ideas; we shook hands warmly on his departure and I genuinely wished him well.

On my second day, I had my arrival interview with the CO, Lt Col Graham Leach. During our discussion, Graham asked how my handover was going and I informed him that we were largely finished, hoping he wouldn't be annoyed that I couldn't string it out a bit.

"I thought it would be short and sweet," he said. "Dave is not interested in Ops and is pretty much your complete opposite, but I want you to deliver the role your way." That was music to my ears, and I knew this was going to be a great tour, working for somebody that trusted and respected me, and from whom I would get total support, not to mention a great education on how to be an Officer.

I was an Ops-oriented individual and had followed my heart on that path since first qualifying as a Yeoman. I was completely comfortable that my overarching appointment included the role of Divisional Crypto Custodian, but at the same time it was a very traditional task that simply wasn't particularly taxing. Add that to the fact that I had Sam as my deputy and an excellent crypto team, led by SSgt Keith Stewart whom I had known for years, and it was a straightforward BAU task.

I did have to travel the length and breadth of England every year conducting an inspection on Div unit crypto accounts, but that wasn't particularly hard either, given I was able to blag a helicopter flight to the furthest flung unit locations. Being honest, I was able to do this because of the inherent fear of anything crypto at unit level, which I milked at every opportunity. I had to chuckle some months later when the GOC, Major General Cedric Delves, commented that I'd had more flights than he did in a year! Oh well, ultimately, it was his crypto.

The rest of the first week passed quite quickly as I met my new colleagues, settled into mess life and consumed endless briefing sessions; it was clear to me that I was now part of a great team with some real characters. In some ways, it was a bit surreal to be sitting in the mess with guys like Major Mick Beasant who, like Dave Gilchrist, had been an instructor during my training in Harrogate. Mick was a lovely bloke with lots of great stories and very sage advice. He had also been one of the most respected instructors at the AAC, so I had no hesitation in seeking his input on any subject.

The young officers were also a great bunch which ensured that mess life was never boring and frequently punctuated by superb parties. Roy Freeman, the Ops Offr, moved to a post in Div HQ meaning he could remain in the same house just down the road from me and, given we had become good friends, that was very helpful in my settling-in period. His replacement, Captain Jonathan Sutton, was an outstanding guy who was relaxed but professional in everything he did; he became my partner in crime and a lifelong friendship was born. I will always be grateful to Jonathan for his understanding and support as I got involved in every aspect of Ops life; he knew it was what I did and how I brought real benefit to the role, and he never once got precious about anything.

Together with Sam and his eventual replacement, WO1 (YofS) Bob Nixon, we were an awesome team. In addition,

Captains Tony Sarginson and Nigel Cullen filled the key technical role of TOT during my tour and were both excellent members of the Ops team.

As in any Divisional Signal Regiment, the environment was manically busy. It was the time of rotation of units through the Metal Factory in Banja Luka, Bosnia and Herzegovina, so called because the building has been a metal factory in a former life. It was where Signal Regiments would be based and act as Force HQ for the region, whilst we were almost permanently on exercise when we were back in the UK.

I was also constantly sending squadrons to the South Atlantic to fill the role of Joint Communications Unit Falkland Islands (JCUFI) and servicing a seemingly endless stream of requests for resources to backfill gaps in other deploying units.

The pressure on our soldiers was very intense and it was a real eye-opener to see young soldiers, Cpls and L/Cpls, wearing two or three rows of campaign medals having deployed on so many different operations. However, these tours weren't all exciting and glamorous. Whilst the first tour in a place like the Metal Factory is not too bad, despite being largely static for most folk, subsequent tours could be tedious beyond belief, which didn't help our retention figures.

Fun in the Falkland Islands

I did a lot of visiting during my tour, flying down to the Falklands on three separate occasions to check all was well with whichever of our squadrons had been deployed down there.

On the first of these trips, I had been allocated a Land Rover and driver whilst I was there, so I was able to get out and about on the island, visiting various sites. One of my favourite locations was the radio rebroadcast detachment at Campito Mountain. From the top of the mountain, the view over San Carlos Bay on the west coast of East Falkland was breathtaking. This was the infamous "Bomb Alley", where the Argies had attacked and sunk HMS *Antelope* and HMS *Ardent*, both Type 21 frigates, and HMS *Coventry*, a Type 42 destroyer. The troop-carrying LSLs – *Sir Lancelot*, *Sir Galahad*, and *Sir Bedivere* – all of whom I had sailed in, were also attacked there as they unloaded British personnel at the start of the campaign. It was occasionally possible to see the Antelope's mast sticking above the water which was a very poignant sight indeed.

Having overnighted at Campito, I took the opportunity to walk down to the beach and along to the site of the field hospital. It was simply amazing to consider how many lives had been saved in what was little more than a disused farm outbuilding. The building had paintings on the inside walls that had been done by patients; these were extremely touching and took my breath away. It was quite sad to think the Argentinian casualties brought here had been terrified but given their propaganda machine was telling them that the British actually ate their enemy wounded, it was hardly surprising!

The reality, I am very proud to say, is that they were treated the same as our own injured and every effort made to save their lives and keep them safe. The walk along the beach was an experience, with literally thousands of penguins waddling around. It was hilarious to watch them as aircraft passed overhead as they naturally follow the flight of the aircraft, to the point that they actually topple over. They are very funny little creatures and not at all fazed by the presence of humans amongst them.

We travelled to most of the key sites, including Goose Green, Wireless Ridge, Two Sisters, and Mount Longdon, to name a few well-known places. Goose Green was particularly sad for me as this was the battle in which my friend Lt Jim Barry had been shot and killed whilst taking the Argentinian surrender. Bizarrely, the exact position where Lt Col "H" Jones had fallen, fatally shot during the battle, had been outlined in white paint. Very close was a small brass plaque which had a box alongside it containing a tin of Brasso and a cloth. It is deemed respectful to clean the plaque during a visit, which I duly did. Lt Col Jones, of course, was awarded a posthumous Victoria Cross (VC) for a solo charge against an enemy position during the battle.

Whilst visiting Port Stanley, the island's capital, I had the privilege of placing some flowers at the war memorial there, in memory of Jim Barry and my great pal, Cpl Rab Burns. There were a few more names of personnel from my Corps on the memorial, which made it feel even more special to acknowledge the loss of these heroes. Whilst there, we visited the famous Upland Goose pub; it didn't do draught beer, of course, only cans (and often past their best-before date), but it was a way to toast my friends, and I doubt that Jim or Rab would have minded.

I have travelled to the Falklands several times, but I can't mention them without telling a little story that always tickles me. Stilton cheese is a firm favourite in the army, served at most, if not all, mess functions. Tours on the islands used to be six months but more recently have been reduced to four, but that's a long time for ardent Stilton lovers. To get over this, Stilton became almost a currency for those posted there, and it could win you some serious favours if you arrived in possession of a full round. There is little better than cutting out the centre of a Stilton round, filling it with good quality port, replacing the plug and letting it soak for a few days. The taste is absolutely heaven; for any cheese lover that hasn't tried it, please do give it a try.

The last of my visits to the Falklands was with Graham's replacement, Lt Col Neil Couch. The two COs were like chalk and cheese. On the day of departure, I drove us to Brize Norton for our flight and fairly quickly realised during registration that I seemed to be getting a lot of attention, even more than the CO, from our "Crab Air" colleagues. Crab Air was a term of endearment we used for our RAF friends, who were assigned to this type of transportation duties, acting like civil aircrew, taking care of their passengers.

"They must recognise me from previous trips," I thought and then forgot about it as we went through the various pre-flight processes. Boarding the VC10 for departure is a sobering undertaking; although strictly speaking the VC10's are civil aircraft in service with the RAF, they are suitably stripped down, with anything remotely related to comfort being removed, so there were no video players embedded in the headrests, no bar, just a basic offering of tea/coffee/ soft drinks and snack packs. When facing an 18-hour trip with one refuelling stop at Ascension Island, it's a daunting prospect.

However, on this specific trip the constant mollycoddling by RAF staff towards me just carried on. My cup was always

Port Stanley, Falkland Islands –
heroes remembered

first to be refilled, my snacks delivered first, and so forth. My CO seemed to always be served after me; what on earth was going on?

As we arrived into Ascension, I found out. I was approached by the RAF Loadmaster who suggested I might like to lead the troops off the plane and head towards the rest area at the side of the runway; that was just too much for the CO.

"Hang on, Captain Greig is my Ops Officer, and I am a Lt Col commanding the Regiment. Why is he getting such preferential treatment?" he asked.

"Oh dear," said the Loadie with a wry smile on his face, "Captain Greig's documentation has been completed as Group Capt Greig, which is equivalent to full Colonel, one rank above you, Sir."

I nearly wet myself trying not to laugh my head off! Neil, on the other hand, was extremely irritated and seemed to blame me for some reason! As you may imagine, I wasn't first off or indeed, first back on, I just followed my CO. I'll never forget his face when the Loadie connected the dots for him.

There weren't many benefits of visiting the Falklands, other than to see how the lads were getting on and being able to visit the war memorial in the capital, Port Stanley, where I could spend a few quiet moments thinking of the friends and colleagues I had lost during the war. Those that have been to the Falklands will remember how bleak a place it can be, but for some reason, every time I went to Stanley the sun made an appearance. Maybe it was Rab or Jim having a word with the Boss, who knows…

As I am sure most would anticipate, my journey back to the UK was rather less "comfortable" than the outward journey but then again, the crew didn't think I was one of their own this time, so I wasn't given the senior officer treatment.

Taking Care of our Own

The "Iron Division", as 3rd Division is known, has a tremendous war record and each year we had the immense privilege of hosting a reunion of World War II veterans. It was always a really great day, bringing together many brave men and women to whom our nation owes a huge debt of gratitude. The Regiment put on all sorts of activities, including equipment displays, sporting events, food stalls and fairground-type stands, with evening events in the various messes. It was very humbling to spend time with the veterans, some of whom were wearing more medals than most of us had ever seen, listening to their stories and learning how they had spent six years at war. Many of our young soldiers had experienced operational deployments and even war, but none of us had spent anywhere near that length of time in a single conflict; the respect for the veterans was incredible.

On our first Veterans Day in 1996, Sue and I were wandering around the stalls whilst Mark was enjoying some of the sporting stuff, when we heard a bit of a commotion a few yards away on the "dunking" stand. We made our way over to find that the CO at the time, Lt Col Graham Leach, had been accidentally injured when the RSM had jokingly pulled the lever to dunk Graham in the water. To the RSM's absolute horror, Graham got a finger caught in the mechanism, the tip of which was severed! Whilst we weren't there at the time of the incident, rumour had it that the adjutant, Major David Kinnaird, had immediately jumped into the water tank and recovered the digit, shouting, "I've got it, Colonel!" as he resurfaced. Knowing David, that didn't surprise me in the least.

Everybody just stood around until the ambulance arrived and took the CO off to hospital; I think the RSM felt that he had probably just reduced his chance of commissioning significantly. The CO never attached any blame and just accepted it as a very unfortunate accident. Col Graham spent a few days in hospital before returning to work with a heavily bandaged hand and at his first major meeting, his 2IC, Major Adam Ewell, demonstrated that military humour was alive and well, by opening a box of chocolate fingers to accompany tea and coffee at the break!

Mess life in Bulford was very enjoyable and I have many great memories from my time there. The young officers were a good crowd, whilst the married guys and girls, or "pads" as they were referred to, always supported the mess very well. It could have been very different, given our mess catered for the Div HQ staff as well as the Regiment, but the mix worked well and a lot of that was down to the CO of the Sig Regiment.

Our functions were always well planned and a lot of fun. I will always remember the antics of some of the young officers, particularly towards the latter stages of the events when they realised that they couldn't actually control their body movements anymore. I have witnessed most attempts to demonstrate sobriety in the presence of the CO, with a range of disastrous outcomes; falling asleep as the CO

3 Armd Div HQ & Sig Regt - Officers' Mess 1997.
A superb group of Officers.

is talking to them, sliding off the seat onto the ground asleep, using the CO's first name as if he was one of their mates, and even being sick into their pints whilst trying to continue to talk! For the sake of those still serving, who may be relatively senior at this stage, I will not name any of the transgressors!

One of the funniest young officer tricks I witnessed was conducted on one of my oldest friends, Nigel Cullen. Nigel, like me, was a LE (Late Entry) officer and was my sidekick in the Ops team. He had an incredibly bushy moustache and prominent set of eyebrows, both of which were quite dark. If Nigel ever made the mistake of falling asleep at the end of a function, the youngsters always took the opportunity to remove one eyebrow and half of his tache which, I must admit, was extremely funny. To give Nigel his due, he took it well and just got on with life the next day, having removed the rest of the moustache and thinned the remaining eyebrow down to try and disguise the absence of the other one. I have never told Nigel this, but I was delighted that I served with him; he was technically outstanding and always gave it everything he had.

3 Div was a very busy tour which suited me perfectly and indeed, I was so settled there that I would happily have extended my time with the Regiment. As time passed, I was asked whether I might consider staying in Bulford taking up a staff role in the Div HQ if it was offered. I was delighted by the implied offer and immediately said yes. I had been selected to attend the JCSC (Junior Command & Staff Course) anyway, so for me to have the incentive of a role in Bulford following the course was hugely exciting. I had never hidden my view that once commissioned, there should be a clear route and opportunity for LE Officers to

choose this path and on successful navigation, convert to a different type of commission that allowed direct competition with our Regular counterparts. I got on very well with the Div COS, Col Hamish Rollo, who seemed to be leading the charge to retain my services in Bulford, as part of his staff; his direction to me was simply to get JCSC out of the way and the new role would happen.

*Junior Command &
Staff Course.
To be selected to attend was
a huge honour for me.*

*Royal Military Academy
Sandhurst (RMAS).
An awesome experience.*

Staff Officer Training –
JCSC (RMAS, Camberley)

Sandhurst – What an Honour

LE Officers weren't commonly selected to undertake the JCSC at Sandhurst, but I was delighted to be allocated a place on Course 44. Whilst I was immensely proud to be a LE Officer, I accepted my commission in the hope that I might be allowed to do the same jobs as my Reg C counterparts (Sandhurst graduates), particularly if I undertook the key courses and achieved suitable results. To some in my era, that might sound a bit naïve, but I wasn't kidding myself that I would, or indeed could, be promoted beyond Lt Col. The army simply weren't ready for that at that time, and I knew they wouldn't change the rules for me. However, I also knew my capabilities and they were very well documented, so I did hope to compete on a level playing field to a point; this course would provide me with the staff qualification that I hoped would help me achieve this aim.

The course had around 150 students from every cap badge; unsurprisingly, the vast majority were young regular Captains with only five, including myself, from the LE community. It took about 15 minutes before the other four LE Officers had made it clear that they were there to finish the course and nothing else. I knew the score, but it still sickened me. In my world, you attend a course to do the best you can or have the decency to pass the vacancy to somebody else. I wasn't hugely surprised by their stance; there was a Gunner, a Tankie and two Infanteers who had been told to attend and their promotion would be secured. My worry was that I would be classed alongside them and therefore not taken seriously, which wouldn't have worked for me.

As the course got underway, it soon became very clear that this would be an exceptionally tough challenge. The LE officers would see and experience just how hard the Regular Officers had to work on their promotion exams. It quickly became common practice to work a full day, following which we would join a syndicate or partner to do homework related projects. Truthfully, it gave me a whole new level of respect for these young guys and girls, and I was absolutely loving what we were doing and the fact that I was able to do more than just hold my own. There were some incredibly bright individuals, and it was interesting to consider where they might be in a few years' time. I would image a significant number of my course mates went on to command at regimental level and several still further into General Staff appointments. I take my hat off to them and hope they all got their just rewards.

I found the course to be quite intense, but I had prepared for that as I appreciated how fundamentally important this qualification was to these youngsters and their future careers. Indeed, that helped me to focus in order to try and bring my experience to bear to help them. As things moved forward, I was increasingly proud of the fact that my colleagues would often ask for my opinion and seemed to genuinely find it helpful when proffered. We spent an awful lot of time traipsing over wide, open spaces during the tactical phases, appraising the various options for attack, defence, and movement. It struck me as so very different from my previous military training experiences as a soldier, but in fairness it was set at a very different level.

At the end of the first term, we were individually debriefed by our relevant SO1 Senior Instructors. In my case, I was delighted when I received recommendations to support future employment as an Ops Offr and/or Adjutant, which were traditionally appointments filled by Regular Officers' only. When I was given the opportunity to speak, I told the SO1 how pleased I was with this, but also how surprised I was, considering I was an LE Officer.

He looked at me and said, "You're not an LE Officer, surely?"

"I am, Sir," I replied, to which he countered, "Well, you have done very well but I will need to revise that part of the report." To me, I was just pleased to be doing OK and felt that I must at least be a credible student. I was also very happy to have been mistaken for somebody in their late twenties and left the office feeling very smug!

I managed to travel back to Bulford on a couple of weekends for a bit of a break, but the course continued to be very demanding and hard work, with lots of late nights. I was amazed at the sheer quality of some of the students and their ability to maintain their standards, exam after exam; it wasn't hard to identify those who were truly special and for whom a form of greatness awaited.

As the course came to an end, I felt that I had achieved my aim and that hopefully, that would be sufficient to help secure a role in the Div HQ and an extended period of service in Bulford.

By this stage, Mark was attending a boarding school near Reigate in Surrey, the Royal Alexandra and Albert School, which he enjoyed, and Sue and I were happy with our life in Bulford; everything was shaping up nicely.

Return to 3 Armd Div HQ & Sig Regt (Bulford, Wiltshire)

Shattered Dream

On my return to work, the CO seemed very happy with what I had achieved and was bullish about my posting to Div HQ as the SO2 Comms. Personally, I was completely cock-a-hoop as the promotion had not previously been mentioned and it was a dream staff job for me. One of the great things about the army and, being honest, all three services, is their ability to laugh at themselves and one another. It's very unusual for such banter to get out of hand and is a very important bit of humour that underpins morale. This flows across most, if not all, areas of competition, and certainly between the various trades and in later stages of service, between those that remain in-trade and those that take up a regimental duties (RD) role.

The latter follow a path through SSM/RQMS to RSM, and if selected for commissioning, fill roles as a QM or Families Officer. This focuses the banter between commissioned Yeomen or Foremen who have remained in-trade and their RD counterparts, but I would like to think that there is a common bond and never had any real issues with any of my RD colleagues throughout my career. That isn't to say I didn't meet some real jealousy along the way. As an ex-A/T RSM, my turnout, drill and military skills were very well honed and this did occasionally seem to upset some RD folk; strangely, it was usually the rather low-quality ones. Perhaps they felt threatened, which simply doesn't make sense.

Throughout my career, I made a lot of very close friends and although we were a very transient population, I have retained the vast majority to this day. Many people made a mark on my life that will never fade, even some that I didn't even know for that long. One of these guys was Major John Hornby, who was sadly quite ill when I first met him. He was doing a special projects role within the Regiment whilst undergoing treatment for cancer, but his character was such that he was always looking to help others. If there was a charity event going on, John was either running it or just embedded within it; he never stopped thinking about other people. John was a commissioned RD man, I can't remember if he had been an RSM, or whether he had filled a different appointment as a WO1. Either way, he would have delivered his role with humanity, empathy, and decency, as he was that kind of guy.

I will always remember John's kindness when I was going through a stressful time, thinking whether it was time for me to leave the army to find out what I could achieve in Civvy Street. I was still completely army barmy, but I knew that would never change. What I was striving to decide on was whether I should take an offer that had been made to join a telecoms company, or stay on to achieve my career goal of reaching Lt Col.

One day, John was passing my office when he decided to pop in for a chat. I still don't know how he knew I had this conundrum eating away at me, but he said some very powerful things in his attempt to help.

"You and the last CO were a hell of a combination," he said, "and I think you have a lot to offer either in or out of uniform, but there is only so much you can achieve if you stay in because of the 'glass ceiling' LE Officers face." I knew that he was right and that he had nothing but my best interests at heart; that was John's way.

Even though I had done well on JCSC, I knew the army would not be in a hurry to promote a LE Officer beyond Lt Col, irrelevant of how well they had done. I knew it would happen eventually, but not in the time frame available to me. At that point, my mind accepted that I should start paying attention to opportunities on the outside, or face the rest of my military career knowing exactly where my progress was capped.

I decided to focus on my next role in Corsham and got stuck into the preparation for handover, having learned that my successor had been nominated. My replacement was to be Captain (Tfc) Al Paterson, a great friend and rival from our time in Bradley Squadron at the AAC in Harrogate. I say rival because Al had come from a military family and his dad, Adam, had been an R Signals WO1 which meant that Al had spent most of his life within the service environment as an "army brat", as they were known.

Inevitably, Al's knowledge of everything army/R Signals was infinitely superior to mine whilst in Harrogate and a competition developed between us as to would reach the highest rank. I would point out, however, that there was never any animosity between us and, it bonded us as pals.

I had never served with Al since Harrogate, so it was good to see him and to handover a job that I absolutely loved to a long-standing mate. He was a big, tall man, but very gentle and easy-going in how he dealt with people. That said, only a fool would take the chance of upsetting Al as I imagine the consequences could have involved a lot of pain. We enjoyed a very good handover and as I had done for every handover I had ever undertaken, I provided an enormous folder with absolutely every aspect of the job recorded within it, for which Al was extremely grateful.

The beauty of a handover/takeover is that you immediately know when it is complete, as the other guy gives off certain signals and you know it's time to let him crack on. I shook Al's hand and wished him every success, knowing he would give it everything he had.

All packed, my family and I headed off for DCSA in Corsham.

Sadly, John Hornby never made the recovery we all hoped he would, and he passed away some 18 months later, by which time I had moved on to my next job. He was a remarkable human being, and I will never forget the advice he gave me. Thankfully, I was able to attend his funeral and say a little prayer, together with a very genuine thank you.

POSTING 12
HQ DCSA
(Corsham, Wiltshire)

The Beginning of the End

Corsham is a relatively short hop from Bulford Camp, but it still meant packing absolutely everything and completing yet another full move, which we had hoped to avoid by remaining in Bulford, had I got the SO2 Comms job in the Div HQ. However, that's the life we had chosen, so we just clicked into the right mindset and got on with it; having moved so many times over the years, we were actually very good at it.

We had been allocated a quarter in Park Avenue, which certainly sounded the part, but nothing could have prepared us for what we found on arrival. As you would expect, we had done some previous visits prior to our move and knew that it was a significantly smaller house than the one we had so enjoyed in Bulford.

What we weren't prepared for was the totally unacceptable condition of the property on the inside. It was dirty, dingy and had a large array of problems associated with it, including patches of damp on the walls that were very off-putting. At this stage, to be allocated the worst accommodation of our married life was hard to accept. I am a natural pragmatist and was very aware of the pressure on the system at the time; however, when you know that you are going to be working long hours in a very busy role with lots of trips away, the very least you need is to know your family is in a safe, clean, and liveable environment. If they had asked us to stay in Bulford whilst the house was fumigated and repaired, that would have easily resolved the matter, but it hadn't even occurred to them.

I took over from Captain Tom Hall as the SO3 Ops/ Commitments, working within a small tri-service team in the Ops & Plans Department. Tom had prepared and conducted a good handover and to be honest, we had a Royal Marines WO2 (YofS), Al Keir, who knew the job inside out, which made things even easier.

After the five-day handover, Tom and I shook hands and off he went. The job was certainly busy but exceptionally mundane; with a good Yeoman in the team, there was no need for a Traffic Officer, and to be brutally honest, even less for a staff-trained one.

A large part of the job was about explaining to commanders at various levels that you couldn't squeeze 10 MB down a 512 KB SATCOM pipe, no matter how important they were! I suppose it's more appropriate for senior officers to berate a captain than a WO, albeit Al Keir was more than capable of putting them clearly in the picture.

Luckily, Major Alf Thomas, with whom I had served during the Gulf War, was also on the team, filling a Grade 2 staff post, a critical role that was central to the successful operational delivery of mission critical communications. Alf was both a friend and an outstanding Traffic Officer, so I was pleased to be working alongside him again; in fact, if it hadn't been for Alf's support, I would probably have left earlier than I eventually did.

The rest of the team was a mixture of RAF and Navy SO2s (equivalent to an army major) and our direct boss was Lt Col Gareth Smith, an R Signals officer whom I had met previously. Gareth was a real gentleman, a good officer, and an excellent communicator. He knew that the role wasn't giving me what I needed and desperately tried to help, but his hands were tied as to the options open to him. However, I will always be grateful for his efforts.

As life went on, I became increasingly frustrated that PB11 had seen fit to send me to DCSA at a stage of my career where I needed to be challenged and stretched much more. They had sent me to a non-staff post, which made somewhat of a mockery of my recent attendance and qualification at JDSC. In fairness, this was something that Gareth Smith took upon himself to rectify and he achieved that.

Talking with Sue each evening, we agreed that it might be the right time to consider my future options. If I were to leave at 40, it would provide sufficient time to build and enjoy a lengthy second career, which had to be part of my decision-making cycle; after all, I was leaving something that would be in my heart forever.

Just as I was finalising my plan, Alf sat me down to tell me he was unwell and would need to take some time out for

Me with Mum in Corsham, 1999

a major medical procedure. As always, Alf had developed a plan and he wanted me to take over his role as SO2 Comms Plans, knowing that I had the experience and staff qualification to do so. I was delighted to take the role on, and Alf successfully staffed the change to facilitate it. Now that I had a real staff role, I began to settle into the task at hand.

The Balkans

The responsibility for the provision of the strategic communication planning and support for the UK contingent of SFOR (Stabilisation Force) in Bosnia and Herzegovina, and elsewhere around the world on other operational deployments, was a very high-profile task. However, it was also a huge frustration in many ways as our hands were tied, given the relatively poor availability of genuine strategic capability within our control. I have already highlighted the constant in-fighting between senior staff seeking to stuff huge amounts of data down a very narrow satellite pipe (512 KB); professionally, as a communicator, it felt that we simply didn't have the tools for the job. That's probably why the role in Corsham wasn't initially recognised as a "weapons" post requiring a staff qualified officer.

I was, therefore, extremely happy when I was tasked to get involved in a project to enhance the communications infrastructure in the Balkans. Working with a couple of huge British companies and a range of other participants from various military establishments, the task was to design and deliver two satellite solutions, one being intertheatre from the Balkans back to UK, with the other being intratheatre connecting some key in-country locations. This was a real step forward from my perspective and an opportunity to apply some of my knowledge and experience to a truly critical requirement.

One of our first tasks was to deploy a team from the UK on a series of recce visits as part of the information gathering exercise, so about a month later, we assembled in Brize Norton for our flight to Split in Croatia. I had never been to Split previously but I was aware of its reputation as a very pretty city on the Adriatic coast; it certainly was a beautiful location, but somewhat spoilt by many of its buildings showing clear signs of the war.

We didn't stay long in Croatia before we collected our vehicles and set off on a long trek across the border into

313

Bosnia and on to the HQ site for MNDSW (Multinational Division South-West) in Banja Luka. At that time, the HQ was being provided by 2nd Signal Regiment, normally based in York.

I knew a lot of the guys from the Regiment, and we spent a few days with them giving and receiving numerous briefings. As mentioned, the HQ building in Banja Luka was known as the "Metal Factory". Surrounded by a huge number of shipping containers, used as accommodation blocks for the personnel, it was quite a drab, boring place, but it was dry and relatively comfortable. I could only imagine what it would be like on a second or subsequent tour of duty; pretty mind-numbing, I would have thought.

Once all the initial briefings had been completed, it was time for us to set off on a bit of a magical mystery tour around Bosnia. The route took in all the usual places, including Mrkonjić Grad, Vitez, Gornji Vakuf, Skopje and Šipovo, to name a few. We undertook lots of technical discussion, planning, site measurement, satellite visibility testing and the sorts of things that the civilian commercial personnel had to complete, so we stayed a day or two at most sites. Life was hard for the personnel in the outposts, so we tried not to get in their way, and it was fascinating to see them go about their daily business. Hopefully, the implementation of these two projects would have a marked impact on those that followed on future operational tours.

At the end of our recce period, we headed back to Split where we spent a couple of days before our flight home in a requisitioned hotel by the sea. It would have been a great holiday hotel for the family, had it not had significant war damage, but I guess it probably recovered in the following post-conflict years and once again became a magnet for tourists from all over the world. That is part of the satisfaction that soldiers take from their long stints on peacekeeping/ peace enforcement operations such as this.

Head v Heart – The Final Battle

Whilst I really enjoyed being part of the ongoing work to deliver these services into the Baltic theatre of operations, getting back into the mainstay humdrum of DCSA was not providing the stretch that I thrived on. It also got me thinking of my remaining 16 years of service and frankly, just going through the motions was not my way. I had never genuinely considered leaving the army, albeit I made a pact with Susan that the day she stopped enjoying the lifestyle, we would leave. Army barmy or not, my marriage would always be my priority; too many of my friends had suffered the pain of divorce and I didn't want us to suffer the same fate.

However, I was also struggling to come to terms with the way I had been treated towards the end of my tour in Bulford and found the "Staff" job in Corsham very unfulfilling. The latter point was magnified by the fact that it wasn't even a staff earning post initially, which made me consider how much career planning had been applied in deciding my posting beyond 3 Div; the inevitable deduction was not a lot.

It didn't help my frame of mind when the COS from HQ 3 Div, Col Hamish Rollo, called and asked me why I had chosen not to stay in Bulford! Safe to say he wasn't at all pleased when I told him that the decision wasn't mine and that I was deeply disappointed to have missed out on my dream job. Apparently, my posting officer in PB11 had felt that I was too young for promotion, despite three straight "Outstanding" grade reports, successful attendance at JCSC and a direct request from GOC that I be posted to his HQ. I knew and liked the posting officer in question and suspected this wasn't a factually accurate position. I also know that if ever Col Rollo had found out the truth, he would have been livid.

I do know exactly what transpired but I don't want to share the details as that would undermine everything I believe in and paint the wrong picture. I was disappointed but never bitter; I had a new job and just wanted to get on with it.

Unfortunately, "just getting on" with a job that doesn't present a genuine challenge or provide the type of rewards that you are accustomed to, is rarely a recipe for success. In my case, the lack of career planning and job satisfaction combined with the housing situation, drove me to consider whether a further 15 years of service would simply deliver more of the same, a thought that started to haunt me. Here I was, a product of the best training environment in the world, prepared, committed, and ready to deliver everything I had, only to realise that the system wasn't ready to accept that. It wanted me to be a LE Officer, nothing more, and whilst I had always known that to be the case, this was the first time that I had to completely accept that fact and the restrictions that it would place upon me for the rest of my military service if I chose to remain.

On balance, that seemed extremely unfair and whilst I was confident that it would change in the future, I knew that would come after my full-service retirement date.

I took a telephone call a few days later from an ex-colleague who meant a great deal to me. He had recently retired and taken a role as Ops Director with a multinational telecoms company. When he dropped in a question as to whether I knew anybody looking for a role in Civvy Street, that sealed my decision. Funnily enough, I told him, I did know somebody... me!

Whilst I make the decision sound very easy, that was certainly not the case, but I had done my due diligence and knew that in this instance, my love for the army simply wasn't enough. I needed to determine whether I could take everything I had learned during this fantastic adventure, moulded with the superb training and mentoring I had received from some of the finest people the British Army had ever produced, and maximise my contribution. I had to accept that this would never be an option if I remained in the army. On the other hand, the opportunity being offered was heaven-sent; I knew had to take it.

Following my resignation, there was a round of discussions with the great and good, with offers to pick my own posting, be promoted to acting rank and several other late attempts to change my mind. Whilst I was grateful, those who knew me understood my reasoning and that the agonising decision I had taken would not be reversed; blackmail is not a virtue and not something I would ever wish to be associated with. I had always said the only one that truly knows when the time is right to leave, is the individual themselves; it was my time.

As I walked through the gates and out of Basil Hill Barracks on a bright winter day, a tear ran down my cheek. I had walked through a gate like those 27 years before, a shy, lost young soul with hope in his heart and a desire to show his worth.

Now, here I was stepping away from a world that meant everything to me, a product of the finest training regime in the world. It hurt, a lot. I knew that I was born to be a soldier and I had shown that I was bloody good at it, being the youngest in every rank I achieved. But that, more than anything, had convinced me that I would be betraying everything I had learned if I accepted the "glass ceiling" that existed in the army at that point.

It wasn't by chance that I had been given responsibility way beyond my rank, or that I had enjoyed the trust, respect and support of some of the finest officers in the R Signals and beyond. As I strode on, my face lit up and my heart started to pump very hard; I had this. I was a highly experienced leader and manager, a successful team builder, a committed 'people' person, and very confident in my own ability.

I now had the opportunity and privilege to showcase what the British Army had taught me, to "be the best", and to prove that I could rise to the many very different challenges that industry would throw at me. Much as my heart was aching to be leaving a life I truly loved and that had given me so much, I almost started to run towards my second career. I had so much to do, so much to learn, and such unshakeable belief that I could do it. "Squaddie to Civvy" – they say that life can take you full circle!

I couldn't wait to demonstrate what I had learned on that journey. Let's do it!

REMEMBRANCE POEM

They say old soldiers never die, they just fade away, and that makes me smile, but sometimes it can be hard to watch the years go by when remembering friends that never had the opportunity to grow old. That's why remembrance is so special to me. I think of them often and through poetry, I am able to express my thanks for knowing them and the shared love of our Corps. I want to share my poem for Remembrance Day 2021.

Remembrance 2021

I thank the Lord for my service every single day,
for the friends I still have, and those I lost along the way.
Where Warriors fell, we brought them home
and laid them down to rest,
for these were heroes who died for us,
who deserved the very best.

I remember each and every one as if they were still here.
That's because they were my mates
and I will always hold them dear.
As the years roll past and we grow old,
they will stay forever young.
We will always see them as they were;
healthy, fit and strong.

As they gather in Valhalla,
we know they will wait for us there,
to help us make our journey
and to offer us their prayer.

We are a band of brothers
who don't always get things right,
but we always care for each other
and keep our friendships tight.

Their loss lives with us now,
and it will last for evermore,
until we too have had our time
and we step through Valhalla's door.
Our lives have been all the better for our time
with these brave men.
They gave their lives for us
until we meet again.

Remembering them is easy because they gave their all,
to keep us safe and let us live, forever standing tall.
For our Queen and country, their great sacrifice was made.
Young men who would never grow old,
because with their lives they paid.

Rest in Peace, lads. God bless you all.

Certa Cito

Read More

Imust admit to some serious concerns regarding the army's pre-release resettlement scheme. Here I was, a LE Officer from a Technical Corps, with 27 years of military service, 15 individual, merit-based promotions as a soldier and officer, yet I was being advised to ensure my driving licence was up to date, with my track vehicle qualification included!

If I had been leaving the service other than by choice, having already secured a job that immediately doubled my salary, I would have been both mortified and terrified. The very machine that had trained and developed me to be the *best I could be*, had absolutely no idea, or interest, in assisting me on the next leg of my career journey.

I was saddened beyond belief. I had given absolutely everything I had to the army and will be forever grateful for the opportunities that it provided to me, but if attaining a role as an HGV driver was what they expected me to settle for, then they didn't deserve to retain my services.

I was hugely excited to take my skills into industry, to seek, meet and overcome the challenges I hoped my second career would demand. I like people and knew I had the management and leadership knowledge and experience to deliver a level of care, support and mentoring that few would have been accustomed to, never mind expect.

The army instils personal strength, resilience, and a will to win that is rarely seen in civilian life. When combined with core values that demand mutual support and respect, and encourage open, honest and transparent working, something special happens. In the years that lay ahead, my **aim** was to demonstrate how successful these beliefs and factors could be in building great teams, growing businesses and most importantly, helping others to achieve their dreams.

Twenty-two years and some superb roles later, I think I have achieved what I set out to do, but I will let you guys decide for yourselves. My next book, ***Unlocking the huMAN Code***, is under production and will be released in the winter of 2023. I believe it will provide a unique insight into how a professional soldier can bring a lifetime of focused leadership, mentoring and training to bear on the lives of civilians in industry, helping them to *"be the best"*. It's a wonderful adventure and I hope you will join me on the journey.

#untappedpotential #huMAN #howdidthesquaddiedo

ACKNOWLEDGEMENTS

To my parents: My mother was a slightly built woman who possessed the heart of a lioness; she brought up a family of four whilst my father was regularly absent, working every hour God sent to earn enough to take the best possible care of his family. It was my mother that prepared me for military life, teaching me things that genuinely gave me a head start as a recruit; how to properly iron clothes, repair tears and holes, polish shoes, and so much more. I put these seemingly innocuous skills to good use, which made settling into training much easier and far less painful.

The loss of my father broke her as a person, but she was always there for me, no matter where I was in the world, ready to listen and to provide sound guidance where needed. To me, she was simply incredible; I only wish I could have helped her more during the tough times in her life, as she did for me.

I remember seeing a short poem as a child which has stuck with me forever:

You only have one mother; faithful, kind, and true,
No other friend in all the world will be so true to you.

I have never forgotten that verse because it's absolutely true. Thank you, Mam, I love you and miss you every day.

My father was my hero in every way; sadly, he was away a lot during my childhood, providing for me and my siblings. I managed to see him briefly as he lay in his hospital bed and I will never forget his smile when I turned up in my uniform, as a boy RSM, wearing my ceremonial sword,

Sam Browne, and forage cap. That was the last time I saw him; he died before my Graduation Parade, but I felt his presence on that special day, and I think he would have been proud of me. Not a day has gone by where I haven't thought of him over the last 45 years.

For life-affirming change: The Army Apprentice College completely changed my life, teaching me self-respect, personal discipline, the power of teamwork, the true meaning of leadership, and to always put people first. I have embraced these lessons and principles throughout my personal and working life, and will try to continue to do so for the rest of my days. Integrity is something that the army demands, and which sits at the heart of its teachings; when you embrace it and live your life with it, good things happen.

My debt of gratitude can never be repaid, nor my love for my Corps be undermined in any way; I am a soldier and I thank God for that.

To my military mentors: I owe everything in my professional life to the incredible leaders and mentors that I had the privilege and pleasure to serve alongside during my career in the Royal Corps of Signals.

I want to formally register my undying gratitude to the following ex-colleagues, each of whom I count as a friend for life:

Sgt (latterly Major) (Retd) Ron Hails (Late R Signals)

Lt Col (Retd) Danny Fisher (Late R Signals)

Lt Col (Retd) Andy Forster (Late R Signals)

Lt Col (Retd) Chris Wakerley MBE (Late R Signals)

Col (Retd) Graham Leach (Late R Signals)

Brig (Retd) Bill Backhouse (Late R Signals)

Maj Gen (Retd) John Stokoe, CB, CBE (Late R Signals)

Lt Gen (Retd) Sir John Kiszely, KCB, MC, DL (Late Scots Guards)

Each one of these outstanding officers allowed me to be myself, encouraged and mentored me, and supported me to be the best I could be. It was an absolute honour to serve under and alongside them, some of them twice. I thank each of them for believing in me.

For the love of my family: Lastly, but most importantly of all, I want to thank my immediate family.

My wife Sue is the love of my life, without whom I simply couldn't function; she is and always has been the centre of my world. I remember my SSM, Steve Marshall, telling me that choosing the right girl to marry would make or break my career; well, I definitely found the right girl.

My son Mark is, and always will be, the apple of my eye. If I could have nipped up to Heaven and asked God for a son, I would have chosen Mark; he's my best mate and I am very proud of him and the man he has become.

ABOUT THE AUTHOR

George Greig is a Highland Scot, born and raised in rural Aberdeenshire. A hard-working but restless scholar, he left school at 15 and took up an apprenticeship as a stonemason, but quickly realised that his dreams outstripped his hastily chosen career. Joining the army at the age of 16, George attended the Army Apprentice College in Harrogate, North Yorkshire, a decision that changed his life.

Graduating as a Radio Telegraphist in the Royal Signals, he spent the next 24 years in what he describes as "army barmy" mode, totally focused on securing each promotion at the earliest opportunity.

As a professional communicator, George started his industry career in telecommunications, but the 9/11 attacks impacted that sector significantly, whilst IT took centre stage.

Having taken up his first management role as a 16-year-old A/T Lance Corporal, George is currently CEO of his own IT solutions and services business, some 47 years later.

George has a deep love of words and has also written children's books and poetry. He is an experienced public speaker who is committed to "giving something back" to society, and to following his dream of becoming a prolific writer. He currently lives in Wiltshire with his wife Susan and their son Mark.

GEORGE GREIG

Author | Speaker | Entrepreneur

www.georgegreig.com

THE BEAUTY OF BEING BRITISH
Understanding the Doric Dialect

*"If yer cumin te Aibeirdeenshire
ye'll need to ken foo te spik"*

Doric, the popular name for mid-northern or north-eastern Scots, refers to the Scots language as spoken in the north-east of Scotland.

There is an extensive body of literature, mostly poetry, ballads, and songs. In some forms of literature, it is found as the language of conversation, while the work as a whole is in Lallans, Scots or British English. A number of 20th and 21st century poets have written poetry in the Doric dialect.

The Scots Doric dialect is perhaps one of the fastest spoken words in Scotland. It is often described as poetic and rhythmic with a soft gentle flow and a pronounced roll of the 'r'. It dates back centuries and has its roots in farming, so though it is a soft dialect, it can have some rude phrases! It can be quite comical at times; just look up *"Fit fit fits fit fit?"* or *"What foot fits what foot"* to translate that phrase to English!

I have always loved the United Kingdom and am immensely proud of our diverse culture and amazing range of dialects.

For a country of its size, it is possible to take 50 mile steps in any direction and find the dialect to be quite different, sometimes completely so.

As a people, we should value and protect our culture, for once lost it will be gone forever and that would be a tragedy. As we welcome people from all corners of the globe, we must learn to share our customs and our language. I am sure it will fascinate and delight them; furthermore, it will help us to retain something that is hugely important to these islands.

We are British and the very diversity we take for granted has allowed us to build and grow one of the most culturally rich countries in the world. Let's ensure that we work together to keep our various dialects and indeed, our national languages alive.

Doric Word	English Translation
Aabody	Everybody
Aathing	Everything
Aaf	Off
Affa	Awfully
Aifter	After
Aneth	Underneath or below
Anither	Another
Atween	Between
Aye	Yes
Aye-aye min	Hello
Bairn	A baby or young child
Baith	Both
Banter	Gossip/chat/tease
Bawbee	Halfpenny
Ben	Down or through
Bide	Stay
Biodag	Dagger or dirk
Birl	Spin
Birling	Drinking match
Bitcallant	Lad
Bitty	A little piece
Black affrontit	Embarrassed
Blether	Talk rubbish
Blootered	Drunk
Bosie	Cuddle or hug
Brae	Road (usually steep)
Brakk	Break
Braw	Good or great

Doric Word	English Translation
Brawly	Well
Brikks	Trousers
Burn	Stream
Cantrips	Magic spells or incantations
Caul	Cold
Clachneart	Putting stone
Claes	Clothes
Claik	Gossip
Clamjamfry	Company or mob
Clarsach	Harp
Clarty	Dirty
Coorse	Coarse
Craiter	Creature
Deray	Uproar
Dhe	God
Died	Dead
Dinna	Don't
Dirdum	Tumult
Dirled	Vibrated
Div	Do
Doited	Foolish
Doon	Down
Doon aboot the mou	Depressed
Douche	Kind or gentle
Dreich	Wet and windy
Drookit	Drenched or soaking
Eese	Use

Doric Word	English Translation
E'morn	Tomorrow
Eneuch	Enough
Fa's?	Who?
Fan?	When?
Far ye gyan?	Where are you going?
Fash	Trouble
Feart	Afraid
Fecht	Fight
Fechtin	Fighting
Feel	Daft or stupid
Ficher	Fumble or interfere
Fin?	When?
Fit?	How?
Fitbaa	Football
Fit like, min?	How are you, man?
Fit wye?	Why?
Fleg	Fright
Flit	To remove
Foostie	Stale or rancid
Gad	Horrible or yuk
Gallasus	Braces
Gangrel	Tramp or vagrant
Ganzie	Sweater or jumper
Gash	Grim or dismal
Gaun	Going
Gawaaah	Get away
Gey	Quite

Doric Word	English Translation
Ging	Go
Gipe	Stupid
Girnin	Complaining
Girss	Grass
Glaikit	Vacant
Glesses	Spectacles
Glower	Scowl
Glunching	Frowning
Gowkit	Mad
Grapt	Wept
Greetin	Crying
Gyan	Going
Gymmies	Plimsolls
Hale	Whole
Heid	Head
Hich	High
Hirpling	Limping
Ingins	Onions
Jist	Just
Ken	Know
Loanings	Bypath
Loon	Boy
Lugs	Ears
Maist	Most
Mare	More
Mear	A mare
Messages	Shopping

Doric Word	English Translation
Min	Man
Mony	Many
Moulds	Graves
Muckit	Mucky or dirty
Nae	No
Neen	None
Neep	Turnip
Nivver	Never
Puckle	A few
Quine	Girl
Richt	Right
Riped	Searched
Riving	Raging
Routh	Abundance
Sair	Sore
Scowp	Run
Scutter	Delay
Silver	Silver coin
Sotter	Mess
Spik	Speak
Spikin	Speaking
Spleeterin	Spilling everywhere
Spotter	Mess
Steen	Stone
Stocious	Drunk
Stot	To bounce
Stotter	Beautiful

Doric Word	English Translation
Swicking	Cheating
Telt	Told
Toom	Empty
Tossue	Ruffle
Trachled	Exhausted
Trig	Active
Tumshie	An idiot
Twaa	Two
Waabit	Tired
Wanchancy	Wicked
Wifie	Woman
Wintit?	Wouldn't it?
Yersel	Yourself

Don't You Love a Dialect?

My pride in being British is very strong you know,
I love hearing different accents everywhere I go.
In the far north of Scotland, their speech is very clear,
most folk don't realise, they speak Queen's English here.

If you come down the country just a little bit,
you'll hit the Doric speakers and you'll get none of it.
Travel a bit further south and then you will hit Dundee.
Stay there just a little while and you'll understand a bit,
wait and see.

When you come down to Glasgow
with Edinburgh off to the east,
you'll be OK in Edinburgh,
but the Glaswegian accent's a beast.
Don't worry too much though,
there's plenty more to go.
The next stop would be the Toon,
now that'll be some show.

In Yorkshire there will be a challenge,
as every Riding has its way.
What you might hear in Harrogate,
in Sheffield holds no sway.
It gets more challenging when you head out to the west,
Mancs have a slow, steady drone,
Scouse is more cryptic than the rest.

The Brummie twang will fox you
when you arrive there too.
They say things like "am ye" and "y'am"
and that will be strange to you.

Across to the west you might hit Stoke,
they'll have something to say.
There aren't too many miles between them
but they talk in a different way.

When you get down to the southern belt
then it gets really great.
In London they have cockneys,
who make up their own slang at a rate.
Whilst in Bristol they are West Country
and everything's gurt lush,
if you come from the Home Counties,
then that's just verbal mush.

I mustn't forget Wales, of course,
in the north they sound like a Scouse,
In the valleys it's simply not the same,
it's a very different house,
They all speak some Wenglish,
but few do speak Welsh,
They are just as confused with it
as everybody else.

If you nip across the water,
then the real problems will start,
The Irish lilt is soft, a lovely twang,
but in North you'll simply lose heart,
So that's my tour of the British Isles,
our language is complex, not easy,
Foreign folk find it tough,
they think we're all the same,
but that's a little cheesy.

George Greig, 2021

CPSIA information can be obtained
at www.ICGtesting.com
Printed in the USA
BVHW031815220722
642797BV00012B/154

9 781913 770440